D0656532

Law and Order: Arguments for Socialism

Also by Ian Taylor

The New Criminology: for a Social Theory of
Deviance (*with Paul Walton and Jock Young*)

Critical Criminology (*co-editor and contributor
with Paul Walton and Jock Young*)

Politics and Deviance (*co-edited with Laurie Taylor*)

Deviance and Control in Europe (*co-edited with
Herman Bianchi and Mario Simondi*)

Law and Order
Arguments for Socialism

Ian Taylor

Senior Lecturer in Criminology, Centre for Criminological and Socio-Legal Studies, University of Sheffield

© Ian Roger Taylor 1981

All rights reserved. No part of this publication may be reproduced or transmitted, in any form or by any means, without permission.

First published 1981 by
THE MACMILLAN PRESS LTD
London and Basingstoke
Companies and representatives throughout the world

ISBN   0–333–21442–0 (hard cover)
ISBN   0–333–21444–7 (paper cover)

Typeset in Great Britain by
STYLESET LIMITED
Salisbury · Wiltshire

Reproduced from copy supplied
Printed and bound in Great Britain
by Billing and Sons Limited
Guildford, London, Oxford, Worcester

The paperback edition of this book is sold subject to the condition that it shall not, by way of trade or otherwise, be lent, resold, hired out, or otherwise circulated without the publisher's prior consent in any form of binding or cover other than that in which it is published and without a similar condition including this condition being imposed on the subsequent purchaser.

To Jean and Anna

Contents

Introduction   ix

1   The Reality of Right-Wing Criminology   1

Criminologists of the Right   5
The basis for 'dangerousness'   9
Progressive education and the working class   12
A mistaken realism   17
Retributive and remoralising measures: juvenile
justice since 1979   24
The attack on social democracy   29

2   The Failure of the New Jerusalem: Post-War
    'Social Democracy' and the Social Order   36

Social democracy in 1945   36
Social democracy and social order   43
Social democracy and the enforcement of law   62
The elaboration of treatment   71
Social democracy and social control in the later
post-war period   74

3   The Reconstruction of Socialist Social Policy   86

Socialism and the professionals   91
Socialism and the authoritarian state   96
Socialism and reform   101
Socialism and an alternative social strategy   105
(a) The family   105
(b) Youth   114

4   Reconstructing Socialist Criminology   123

The prison movement: rehabilitation, abolition,
justice   125
The police critics: accountability and popular
demands for policing   146
The legal critics: taking the people to the law   164
The women's movement and law enforcement   180
Democratisation and social reconstruction   204
Right-wing criminology: class rhetoric and
social disorder   207

Bibliography   224

Introduction

Prior to the summer of 1981 the concerns of this book — with the political preconditions of social order — might have appeared a little abstract or hypothetical. But the events of July 1981 have made these concerns immediate and tangible. For many people living in Britain's urban centres they have often been a matter of frightening personal experience.

The riots of 1980 in Brixton and Bristol — which had been authoritatively explained as resulting from peculiarly local conditions — were now followed by a series of major disturbances in Southall, Toxteth, Brixton (on several separate occasions), Moss Side, and elsewhere. Massive amounts of property damage and looting occurred and large numbers of police and the public were injured. On 13 July 1981 the Merseyside police became the first force in mainland Britain to make use of rubber bullets and the notorious CS gas on civilians, and, in the same week, the government announced that army camps would be used to house those who received prison sentences as a result of the riots. The government also announced its intention to legislate for a new Riot Act and generally proclaimed its support for more aggressive police responses in any future situation where there was 'a threat to public order'. As in Ireland, and as over the question of soccer violence at home, the social violence of the inner-city under-class was to meet with the force of intensified penal discipline.

But the riots in English cities were clearly rather more alarming, for the popular press, than even the troubles in Ireland or the 'aggro' of the soccer grounds. The rioters had been seen to be white *and* black, and adult as well as youthful. They were normal residents of the English inner city,

which was now obviously in an abnormally depressed and dis-
traught condition. They were not untypical of the readership
of the English popular press itself. So *The Daily Star*, which
had urged its readers to vote for the Tories in 1979, now
responded to Margaret Thatcher's moral denunciations of the
riots with the angry headline 'Work, not Talk, is the Answer'
(*The Daily Star*, 7 July 1981). Nearly all editorial writers in
the popular press supported some reversal of the government's
policy of cutting public expenditure, especially in so far as
these policies affected the inner city. Margaret Thatcher spoke
of the riots as her most difficult ten days in office, and
although community leaders in Toxteth and Manchester
deplored the government's complete failure to understand
the resentments which fuelled the attacks of property and
police, it seemed as if the events of the summer were going
to force some mitigation of the unremitting monetarism of
the Thatcher government. A fundamental assumption in
British society — that the underclass will acquiesce in the
housing, the work and the social facilities it is offered, as well
as in the place it is assigned in the class structure — was
obviously at risk.

Whether or not a reversal in government policy does occur,
the riots unambiguously achieved one other object. They
decisively undermined the claim of the radical-right leadership of the Conservative Party to be offering a politics of
social order. From the moment of achieving power within
the Tory Party in 1975, this radical-right leadership has
carried out a campaign against liberal and progressive politics
generally, insisting that the educational, welfare and crime
policies of both Labour and liberal Tory governments were
the cause of a breakdown in social order. Throughout 1978,
and during the election campaign of 1979, the Tory leadership,
with the implicit or explicit support of senior members of
the judiciary and the police, proclaimed that the victory of
the new Conservative Party would result in a restoration of
a real sense of order in social life. This renewed orderliness
in social life would emerge, it was asserted, out of a combina-
tion of both morality and discipline. The freeing of the
market from excessive interference by the state would

encourage individuals to take on a new responsibility for themselves and their families. Social discipline would therefore emerge out of individual self-discipline. In the meantime the reversal of years of permissive policies in schools and in the criminal justice system would ensure that the acceptable limits of social behaviour were clearly visible and effectively enforced by the deterrent presence of the police and the correctional effects of the detention centre and the prison. So state law would be revised to ensure, via coercion, that the normal activities of self-interested individuals, the pursuit of possessive individualism, would be carried out in an orderly and legitimate manner.

Two years into the Thatcher government the fallacies in the political assumptions of the radical right are plain to see. The freeing of the market forces has resulted in a widespread sense of hopelessness and anger among large sections of the population, who are now experiencing a level of unemployment and poverty far beyond their previous expectations. The social relations that have resulted, so far from being those of a disciplined individualism, have taken the form of collective insubordination in the inner city, militant self-defence by the beleaguered black communities (against police harassment and racist organisations alike), and, most ominously of all, the collective violence engaged in by skinheads and other poor whites against their Asian or West Indian neighbours.

Each of these developments has a lengthy history, going back at least until the 1960s, but it was not until the late 1970s, and the moment of Thatcher's election victory in 1979, that the desperation of a divided and dislocated underclass spilled over into violence on the streets. In the course of the election campaign itself, on 23 April 1979, the Asian population attempted in their thousands to prevent the holding of a meeting of the National Front in the centre of their community by a massive peaceful sit-down: they were rewarded for their efforts with 347 arrests and a violent attack by the Special Patrol Group of the Metropolitan Police. The significance of the events in Southall on 3 July 1981 (a massive attack on the *Hambrough Tavern*) is clear: the exclusively Asian Southall youth movement acted independently both of the police and their more moderate elders in order to remove a racist presence (a skinhead band that attracts fascist support) from their community.

Throughout 1979 and 1980 popular organisations in Bristol, Manchester, Liverpool and other major cities had forced the liberal press, and some television programmes, to pay critical attention to police practices, especially in the inner city and in areas of South London. Particular anger was directed at the use by police of ancient legal statutes to arrest young blacks, in particular on suspicion, and at the inflexible enforcement of the criminal law on drugs and alcohol in raids on West Indian social clubs and parties. Few of these complaints, however, found a place in the popular press, which continued to advocate uncritical support for the 'British bobby'. In 1980 and 1981 popular frustrations at the indifference of the media and officialdom, and the continuing harassment by the police, gave rise to the riots which occurred in Bristol, Brixton and Moss Side. And once again, in the course of the Scarman Inquiry into the Brixton riot, and during Mr Heseltine's three-week investigation into the background to the troubles in Liverpool, leaders of the black community insisted that the central topic in these enquiries must be the question of police harassment and police racism. What was at issue was the question of racism within the law-enforcement apparatus itself as well as within the broader society.

This was not, even now, a favourite topic for the popular press; the riots were primarily to be interpreted as the effect of the overwhelming deprivation in inner-city areas. The looting that occurred in some of the riots enabled the press to present events as examples of individualism at work but in an indisciplined fashion. According to *The Sun*, people were 'shopping without money'.

This interest in consumer goods was hardly surprising. It had been in the name of such individual consumerism that the major transformation of Britain's urban centres had occurred throughout the post-war period. But this prioritisation of the interests of *some* possessive individuals over the social communities in which most individuals lived had massively prejudiced the possibility of social order in these areas (and also in the privatised council estates to which many were removed). Housing policies have continued to pursue the goal of providing *individual* privacy and possession, without reference to the communal traditions which sustained these neighbourhoods; and employment and social policy has continued to work to the advantage of the already employed individual wage-earner, to the detriment of women, blacks and young people in the underclass, who were thereby excluded from the consumer economy. It is no surprise that the symbols of individual consumerism (like videocassette machines) were the most highly prized targets of the looters. But the individualism that was present in these events was an *effect* of years of living in a mass-media-dominated capitalist society, rather than being the cause of the riots at such. The riots were primarily significant for the way in which they expressed the desperation of the 'marginal' populations in British class society, in a highly patterned and collective fashion. The anger of black youth was directed at symbols of white racism (like the *Hambrough Tavern* in Southall) or police racism (the police headquarters attacked in Moss Side and police cars burnt in Brixton), while the anger of the poor whites involved in the Toxteth riots was also directed at the police and, in particular, at the constant harassment that appears to be endemic in that police force's contacts with its local community. If only the possessive individualism so beloved of the Right (and the popular media) had been involved in the riots of 1981, the damage caused to property and to persons would have been much more random than it actually was. Thefts and looting would have occurred from all available sources, and the police would have been avoided rather than confronted in the streets.

The market forces have been active enough, throughout the post-war period, in ensuring the advance of possessive individualism throughout society, and it has surely been this advance (rather than the advance of social welfare, for example) which has disrupted and dislocated the communities in inner-city urban areas. It is also this individual consumerism that has resulted in the extension of a narcissistic individualism in the middle class, which often prevents the members of that class from realising that they are members of a human collectivity, encouraging instead an individual competitiveness that obstructs the growth of friendships and trust in social relationships. It is difficult to see the contribution such individualism makes to a social order that operates in the universal interest. But it is on the basis of a further extension of free-market economics and possessive individualism that Margaret Thatcher in 1979, and Ronald Reagan in 1980, predicted the restoration of order in their troubled late-capitalist societies. Indeed, in the United States, as some American observers of the British riots have now anxiously realised, the Republican commitment to 'supply-side economics' has been accompanied by a popular-academic literature which announces that this version of monetarism has '*no* social cost'. That literature is looking transparently empty in the aftermath of the British riots of 1981.

Margaret Thatcher and the New Right are, however, to be thanked for reminding the Left of the importance of 'law and order'. For the campaigns waged during the late 1970s by the new Tory leadership did help to re-establish the importance of fundamental political debate, and, in particular, the ancient debate about the preconditions of workable and human social order. As I have already indicated, the prospect offered by the Right was one in which orderliness in social life would be restored and then maintained by freeing individuals from their dependency on the state and by ensuring that the appropriate boundaries of social behaviour were enforced by legal coercion. This fundamentalist vision was never really spelt out in philosophical or behavioural detail. Instead, it was articulated in and through ideological attacks on the failure of liberal attitudes and welfare provisions, amongst other things in 'the war against crime'. The attack on social democracy and liberalism was effective for a variety of reasons, but it is not at all clear that fundamentalist Conservative philosophy was a key factor in itself in the popular electoral support given to Margaret Thatcher. The attack was effective primarily because of the *real* limitations that existed in the bureaucratic form of the British welfare state and also because post-war social democracy *had* failed to provide a sense of social order. The anxieties experienced by working people and the elderly living in dilapidated and isolated housing developments *are* real, and these *are* the areas in which there is greater risk of vandalism and street crime generally than others. Large numbers of traditional Labour voters reported that they changed their vote to Mrs Thatcher in 1979 on the basis of the attacks she had made on Labour's record on crime; and there is little doubt that, until the summer of 1981, the law and order issue *was* working overwhelmingly, in on-going and ideological debates, to the advantage of the Right.

Many of the Left have thought this inevitable. A former Under-Secretary of State in one of the post-war Labour governments came to a talk I once gave on socialist criminology to a fringe meeting at the Labour Party conference. After the paper he came over and observed, sympathetically but straightforwardly, that 'law and order will *always* be their issue, I'm afraid'.

Hence this book. The argument, simply put, is that law and order need not always work as an issue for the Right. As the desperate economic policies of the Right wreak economic and social havoc in Britain, and threaten to have a similar effect in the near future in the United States, one can expect to see *large increases* in crimes of violence and crimes against property in both countries. The Right's rhetoric on the way to build and maintain a social order will become increasingly contradictory. Economic policies that are constructed primarily in the interest of capital *by definition* carry a social cost for labour. In periods of deep crisis in capitalist economies, of the kind now encountered at the end of the post-war boom, the costs are heavier than at other times, and they are borne most by those who are least able to defend themselves from the effects of the public expenditure cuts or redundancy. They are borne primarily by women, blacks and the ever-increasing number of unemployed. Crimes of violence and also crimes against property may have a variety of immediately presenting 'causes', but they are always in the end an expression of the desperation produced in individuals and in particular social groups by economic and social inequality. So — although it will appear as a dogmatism — we can assert that the essential significance of a very high rate of interpersonal and property violence in a society is that it expresses the lack of socialism in the personal and social

relations of that society. And we can define the absent
socialism here, quite conventionally, as a political and social
formation which guarantees equality of life-chances and
mutual regard between people, irrespective of race, age and
sex. It is the obverse, therefore, of the conditions that exist
in an unreformed class society like Britain today.

It is clear that an assertion as bald as this will do nothing
to persuade criminologists or indeed people in general of the
merits of socialism as a form of crime prevention or as a
guarantor of social order. The murky managerial politics of
the post-war Labour governments have clearly failed to
produce a satisfying form of life and a genuine sense of order
in Britain, but these governments often claimed to be engaged
in building something called 'socialism'. So the arguments
presented here do depend on a reconstruction of the dominant form of politics in the Labour Party, of the kind that is
currently being attempted by Tony Benn. This task of
reconstruction should not depend on any one individual,
however, and neither should it automatically follow any given
line, 'Bennite' or otherwise. The particular form of the reconstruction of socialist politics should be the responsibility of
individuals and groups who, by virtue of their gender, race,
age, training or life experience, can bring a detailed knowledge
to bear on particular areas of policy. In this book I try to
bring my own experience (as a male, white criminologist
with some experience of Labour Party, left sectarian and
prison movement politics) to bear on the question of reconstructing socialist criminal politics. I also try to contribute to
the thinking that is going on currently into the character of
an alternative social strategy for the Left.

I want to make three self-critical observations about the
book.

First, I realise that I will be attacked by some orthodox
Marxists and by others on the Left for the sins of idealism
and reformism. This is a hazard for any socialist who tries to
think about the creation of 'transitional' programmes. It was
obviously a problem occupying Bob Deacon in an article on
transitional social policy which appeared as I sent this book
to the publishers. He puts the point straightforwardly:

Socialists who know their marxist philosophy have always

been keen to point out that there can be no blueprint for the socialist society — no *a priori* resolution of issues that can then simply be acted upon. The freedom of the working class is the act of the working class. When . . . Lenin . . . talked of the form of socialist society, he was, after all, basing his ideas amongst other things on what the workers of Paris in 1871 actually did when they took power, albeit briefly. The problem of letting the question rest there is . . . [that it leaves] socialists with no positive alternative conception of the Welfare State to replace the tattered and discredited reality we still defend. This leaves the way open for ideologies and visions of the Right to fill the gap.

> (Deacon, 1981, p. 46)

Entering the struggle over state policy is important because of the massive extension that has occurred in state activity in the twentieth century. The point is put clearly by the London—Edinburgh Weekend Return Group in *In and Against the State*:

Take an average working woman with children. In the mid-19th century her sole contact with the State would have been the Poor Law Guardians and the police. Today such a woman has dealings with the education authority over her children's schooling; with the doctor and the hospital over her own and her family's health; with the Town Hall Directorate of Finance over rates; the Housing Department over rent. Besides, she will be visited by the social worker, the probation officer and possibly the juvenile department of the police over the kids' street life; Inland Revenue over her earnings; the Unemployment Benefit Office or Social Security if unemployed. She may well approach an Industrial Tribunal over her unequal pay, or a Rent Tribunal over her unfair rent.

(London—Edinburgh Weekend Return Group, 1979, p. 5)

Morever:

Relations between men and women and their children are relevant to state institutions, they appear to matter to the

authorities. Men are designated 'head of household' and
have certain rights and duties. Women, as housewives and
mothers, are expected to carry out, to a certain standard
of proficiency, many jobs that the state also has a hand in,
such as training children and nursing the old and the sick.
(London—Edinburgh Weekend Return Group, 1979, p. 5)

So the state is no longer merely the 'nightwatchman' of capitalist society. It is an integral and central institution, crucially
influencing and/or coercing the form in which everyday life
is lived.

It is also a massive employer of labour. In Britain, as the
London—Edinburgh Weekend Return Group (1979, p. 5)
observed, 'about a third of all people in jobs today are employees of the state—whether as cleaners of buildings or roads,
caretakers, clerks, cooks, social workers, architects, teachers,
directors or administrators'. So the question of state power
and state policy is a living issue for those who are employed
by the state as well as all those who are affected by the directions of that policy. It should be self-evident that this everyday experience of the state is a key factor in the 'class struggle'
in the late twentieth century.

The particular focus of this book, on state law and on the
criminal justice system, is itself of increasing importance in
capitalist societies like Britain and the United States, where
the exercise of state power has recently become much more
coercive and aggressive, but where the continued existence
of formally democratic institutions gives space in which to
make alternative demands upon the state. We have the chance
to formulate demands requiring the state to act as guardian
of human rights and social needs rather than acting merely
as a manager of unequal class societies. It is in occupying this
space, and trying to create such demands, that we are clearly
in danger of 'reformism'. The struggle for particular reforms
may take over from the larger struggle for the transformation
of capitalist social relations, or else the reform may be itself
transformed into a positive support for the existing social
form. These are difficult problems, which I will not address
here.[1] But in noting the danger of reformism, I hope I have
also underlined the importance of creating a set of demands

for alternative and socialist arrangements in every area in which the state imposes itself on the citizens of our unequal class society.

The second point of criticism I want to make is to admit to the incompleteness of the historical accounts provided in this book. My primary interest here – in the reconstruction of the conventional social democratic position on crime – required that I spent some time in excavating the post-war origins and later development of that version of 'social democracy'. In Chapter 2 I am able to spell out some distinctions between the notion of social democracy that was constructed within and by the Labour Party (a form of *class politics*) and the social democratic state form that was supported by the liberal Conservative governments of the 1950s. I am also able to distinguish the long-standing commitments of the Labour Party and Labour movement to social democracy from the vague rhetorical flourishes of the 'Social Democratic' signatories and supporters of the Limehouse declaration of 1981.

But I do not give the attention I should to the *detailed* history of Labour's involvement in the development of the welfare state and criminal and social policy in the period after 1951. This is paradoxical because *Law and Order: Arguments for Socialism* began life, in 1976, as the attempt to examine the play of conservative and social democratic ideology on crime throughout the post-war period. But that manuscript, originally mistitled 'Crime at the End of the Welfare State', just grew and grew, and now contains some detailed analysis of social democratic and conservative approaches to capital punishment, the youth problem in the 1950s and 1960s, the criminality of women, crimes against women, pornography, organised and white-collar crime, the criminality of the powerful, and the questions of the police, the courts, the prisons and juvenile institutions. The manuscript is now too long to be published in an affordable volume. So instead it remains in Sheffield University Library (Taylor, 1981). The current book draws on material in that manuscript but it does so very selectively, according to the overall, mainly political, purposes that inform this particular intervention into 'criminology'. It also concentrates on the period of greatest potential for social democratic politics and policies in their original form — the Labour government of 1945—51 — as the moment in which the reformist achievements were considerable, while the limitations of reconstruction were already becoming apparent.

The third problem with the book is that it is already out of date. This is probably also inevitable in a book which tries to deal with contemporary political and social developments in an analytical way. But the riots of 1981 have undoubtedly opened a qualitatively different era in British politics and in the sphere of the law and the criminal justice system in particular. They resulted in the first use of CS gas on the British mainland, and in a form of aggressive riot policing, which I did not discuss in the text when it was written.[2] I have had to consider whether the events of the summer required me to rewrite and 'update' a manuscript which was already ready to put into print, but I have decided against this course of action for two reasons. First, to do this would further delay publication of a set of arguments which I think are vital to the present political moment. And, second, the issues raised by the riot (like the threat to inaugurate special riot courts, the use of army camps for detention, the imposition of curfews by the courts, the control of police actions in situations they define as riots, etc.) are crucial for socialists working in the area, but, in my view, they add to (and in no way contradict) the argument for democratisation of the control of the police that is one of the major points in this book. I am well aware that many of the riots of July 1981 appeared to be directed at forcing police out of certain areas of cities, and, in nearly all cases, at putting an end to police harassment. But in my judgement the call for the withdrawal of the police from these areas did not amount to the demand for a once-and-for-all withdrawal of the police. Rather, the riots were the insistent, desperate and in some cases violent expression of demands that black and white inner-city dwellers, youth organisations and others have been making, in a much more moderate and acceptable way, for years, for a different kind and quality of policing. In particular, as I tried to argue in this book in advance of the riots, the demands from black communities are for policing that is adequate to defend their people and their homes from the murderous violence of the

British Movement and the National Front, while the demands
of women are a more concerned and effective defence of
women from sexual harassment and danger, especially at night.
So the arguments advanced on the question of the police in
this book have not been substantially altered by the events of
the summer of 1981. But they *have* been made more urgent,
in the same way that the use of riot courts to administer quick
discipline to rioters, and the untroubled expansion of the
prison population, have underlined the discussion of law and
of prison presented here. Events may yet occur in the period
before publication of this book which will alter even further
the detail of our discussions here, but the key point — to
offer a socialist framework for the developing struggles over
criminal politics — will remain unchanged. So the book offered
here is the manuscript which was completed in May 1981.

Law and Order: Arguments for Socialism has been five
years in preparation and there are many people I could and
should thank for help and support of one kind or another.
I want to single out Ruth Jamieson, who gave up time, the
most precious commodity there is, and also contributed enormously with ideas and suggestions. Mike Fitzgerald and Carol
Smart also gave me a massive amount of help, and Patrick
Devlin was an inspiration without knowing it. Alan Clarke,
Stuart Hall, John Pratt and Jock Young have also been supportive and influential in this work; they will probably each
see the influence of some of their own work in here. My
thanks go, too, to John Winckler and Keith Povey of the
Macmillan Press for substantial editorial help.

I also want to apologise for 'borrowing' the title of Tony
Benn's recent book of essays as a part of the title for this
book. The compromises of the post-war Labour governments,
and the ideological attacks that have been mounted on
'socialism' by the Right, do mean that the argument for
socialism has once again to be made, and that the essential
character of socialism (as the defence of the interests of all)
to be reasserted. Tony Benn has clearly realised the necessity
of this reconstruction and rearticulation of socialism. In the
same mood this book is offered as a first move in the possible
reconstruction of socialist criminal politics.

The typing of the manuscript for this book had to be done

at great speed in the middle of other demands. As usual, Vera Marsh worked like a Trojan, and Shirley Peacock really helped out, too. I thank them both.

Sheffield   Ian Taylor
July 1981

Notes to the Introduction

1. I discuss the relationship between campaigns for justice and rights and the struggle for socialism as such in a forthcoming book of essays, written with Jock Young (see Taylor and Young, 1982).
2. The use of what the Merseyside Police chose to call 'positive policing' was accompanied, on 29 July 1981, by the death of 22-year-old David Moore, disabled in one leg, who was caught by a police landrover during the clearing of a 'riot' in Toxteth.

1

The Reality of Right-Wing Criminology

Writing in 1973, the American 'futurologist', Alvin Toffler, observed that

> Not so many years ago, the National Commission on the Causes and Prevention of Violence prophesied that, unless corrective action was taken quickly, the US ghettoes would become 'places of terror, perhaps entirely uncontrolled during the night-time hours'. It went on to predict that schools, playgrounds, apartment houses, libraries and other structures would need day-time police, and that armed guards would have to 'ride shot-gun' on our means of transportation, our buses and our trains. Anyone who lives in a major US city, or who has been frisked on the way into a jet, knows that we have already fulfilled many of their nightmarish predictions.
>
> (Toffler, 1973, p. 13)

Until very recently, British observers would have thought of this kind of breakdown in urban life as being intrinsically American, and they would have distrusted any attempt to speak of any such breakdown in the British environment. 'It couldn't happen here', in a country that was traditionally non-violent and crime-free, especially when compared to the street corner of American ghettoes, viewed every evening on television police shows like *Kojak* or *Starsky and Hutch*. British commentators would also have thought that accounts like that provided by James Q. Wilson, Oscar Newman and others, in which street crime was depicted as *the* cause of the collapse of any 'sense of community' in American cities, were simply inapplicable to a stable and solid British social order.

Times have changed. There *is* now a widespread belief in British cities that crime in general is on the increase, and that it is becoming more violent and predatory. Eighty-eight per cent of a quota sample of adults questioned in 1979 thought there was more violence and lawlessness than there was ten years ago, 62 per cent thought there would be more ten years in the future, and 22 per cent thought it fairly or very likely that there would be a serious breakdown in law and order within the next ten years (*New Society*, 29 November 1979).[1]

During 1978 and 1979, there were more and more assaults reported on bus drivers, conductors and other public service workers throughout the country. Bus drivers in Glasgow refused to operate bus routes going to certain football grounds. Two-way radios and alarms were installed on buses in nearly all major cities to enable bus drivers to call for help when attacked. Fifteen bus drivers in South Shields, County Durham were in the meantime taking karate classes twice a week for self-defence (*Now!*, 57, Report on 'Violent Britain', 10–16 October 1980). In London, some 1,300 people were attacked on London Transport during 1979, 293 of whom were staff (*The Guardian*, 29 March 1980) and in April of the following year, the managing director of the London Underground announced that the rail network might be closed at 10 o'clock every evening as a result of the violent attacks committed on Underground staff (*The Times*, 10 April 1981).

These particular incidents of violence were often the product of continuing and increasingly pathological rivalries between young working-class supporters of football clubs. It is the fear of violent youth involved in this kind of 'aggro' that now causes shopkeepers and publicans with businesses near football grounds to shut down as a matter of routine on match days and to board up their front windows, even in the knowledge that this will involve a significant loss of income. Rail and bus stations en route to and from football stadia have to be heavily policed in the attempt to protect members of the public from attack and harassment. But none of this prevents pitch invasions or the outbreak of violence on the terraces, including the attacks mounted by members of the fascist British Movement in the West Ham crowd on visiting Tottenham Hotspur supporters (on the grounds that they were Jewish) during a League Cup game on 2 December 1980, or the constant invasions of the pitch that characterised major and minor games at the end of the 1980—1 football season.

There have also been an increasing number of reports in the last ten years of violence in schools,[2] in hospitals, on the streets and in public space generally.[3] There is no question that the reports were sometimes exaggerated and sensationalised, as were similar reports sometimes in the past, but there are grounds for believing that the frequency and the injuries resulting from incidents involving interpersonal violence are greater now than in the earlier post-war years or, indeed, in the inter-war period. The anxieties expressed in the survey reported in *New Society* appear to be confirmed: amongst transport workers and significant sections of working-class people the threat of violence has now become an urgent and significant problem. Certainly the magistracy, the police, headteachers, members of the National Association of Schoolmasters (plus the Union of Women Teachers), the National Viewers and Listeners Association and the National Union of Licensed Victuallers are in no doubt that the situation is getting worse, since each of these bodies has been involved in the last ten years in major offensives against the 'liberalism' and the 'permissiveness' of official responses to delinquency.[4]

The attacks that were mounted by these bodies on particular items of legislation, such as the Children and Young Persons Act of 1969, or on particular methods of progressive and/or permissive education and social work treatment, were taken up and generalised by the leadership of the Conservative Party during 1977 and 1978. Mrs Thatcher observed at the Conservatives' annual conference in 1977 that

> People ask me whether I am going to make crime an issue at the next election. The answer is no. It is the people of Britain who are going to make it an issue.[5]

A leak to *The Guardian* revealed that Tory strategy in any general election held in 1978 would definitely have included 'an attack on Labour's record on crime' (21 October 1978).

In the by-election in Liverpool held just prior to the fall of the Callaghan government, Conservative spokesmen, including Mr Whitelaw, the future Home Secretary, alluded continually to people being frightened to leave their flats and houses after dark[6] and a regular refrain was that there was now 'a crime every 12 seconds' in England and Wales.[7]

On the day of the no-confidence motion in the House of Commons which brought down the Callaghan government, 28 March 1979, it was already apparent that the Conservative Party's own demand for law and order was more generalised in intent than the specific campaigns waged earlier by the various interest groups. Mrs Thatcher observed that

> A trade union leader had advised his members to carry on picketing because they would act in such numbers that the authorities would need to use football stadiums as detention centres. That is the rule of the mob and not of the law, and ought to be condemned by every institution and minister in the land. The demand in the country will be for two things: less tax and more law and order.
>
> (quoted in *The Daily Telegraph*, 29 March 1979)

The election campaign itself entirely followed this projected programme, as Conservative spokesmen, aided by representatives of the police and judiciary, pressed home the argument for the restoration of law and order through increases in police powers and salary, increases in the use of detention centres and prison, and a curtailing of the permissive interventions of social workers. For the first time in any post-war election, the question of crime and law and order emerged quite clearly as an important issue between the parties — with what appears to have been significant effect. A survey by Market and Opinion Research International put law and order as the fourth most important issue after inflation, industrial relations and strikes, and unemployment,[8] and an Independent Television News research survey, reported on election night after the closure of the polls, indicated that 23 per cent of voters had switched their electoral allegiance to the Tories on law and order, compared to 26 per cent who had switched on prices, 22 per cent on trade unions and 13 per cent on taxation. Given the extent to which Margaret Thatcher had cut into traditional Labour constituencies during the election,[9] the articulation of 'law and order' by the right-wing leadership of the Tory Party had clearly had significant *popular* effects.

Criminologists of the Right

The 'shift to the right' in the posture of the Conservative leadership, in the mass media and in many popular quarters, has been paralleled by a rightward movement on the part of conventionally liberal academics. Along with senior officials in social services departments, these liberal academics have increasingly been drawn towards analyses of crime and also towards new penal policies that have been constructed by influential spokesmen for the Right. One of the key sources for these revisions of liberalism in academic criminology is the work of the American right-wing liberal, James Q. Wilson, who has attempted to participate directly in the reconstruction of criminology in this country. In a piece he wrote in a collection of right-wing essays on Britain published in 1977, Wilson claimed that

> if you were to ask a taxi driver, hotel clerk or newsvendor in London, they would explain the increase in violent crime, especially robbery, by the presence of West Indians.
> (James Q. Wilson, 1977, p. 69)[10].

Wilson then proceeded (on flimsy evidence) to reproduce for Britain the kind of analysis of crime developed by the radical right for the USA. This kind of analysis flows out of a nostalgic reference to the past, and in particular to some unspecified historical period some time before the 1980s. The reference is to the orderliness of the small American town and/or to the suburb. The orderliness of these small towns and neighbourhoods is then said to have had other empirical characteristics of trustworthiness and lack of social conflict. Some time in the 1960s, however, the orderliness of these communities was disturbed by the entry of the black population, a process that resulted from internal migration within America (from south to north) and from invasion of upwardly mobile blacks from inner-city zones into 'respectable' neighbourhoods. This migration had the effect of pushing many of the educated, white, middle class (whom Wilson calls the 'community leaders') out of the surburban areas and the previously respectable inner-city neighbourhoods, and in some cases out of the metropolitan areas. So the inner-city neighbourhood, in particular, lost homegeneity (it became racially mixed) and therefore it also lost a sense of community. This weakening of the sense of community, and the quality and authority of community leaders, has led to an increase in 'predatory crime' on the street, which has further weakened the sense of community in inner-city neighbourhoods.

No conventional criminologist in Britain has yet broken with the liberal consensus which prevents open discussion of the impact of immigration on working-class neighbourhoods. In the forcing of most immigrants into the overcrowded and declining inner cities, immigration *has* of course added to the problems of already overburdened working-class populations. It has been left to the National Front and the British Movement to make an explicit connection between race and crime, but entirely from a white racist perspective.[11]

The British right-wing writer on social policy, Patricia Morgan, has avoided these connections and concentrated her attack instead on what she calls the 'consensus psychology' encouraged by social workers, by official social policy, and by intellectuals from the liberal centre through to the Marxist left. This 'consensus psychology' is taken up not

> with how children come to understand and adjust to complex social requirements. It has rather been concerned with what the innate 'needs' of the child are, which the adult world can provide for. The adult looks to the child and is guided by the child's behaviour, rather than acts as his

initiator and instructor into the rule-governed tasks and arrangements of his culture ... [for Morgan, this] short-circuit[s] the cumbersome process of choosing, defending, transmitting and maintaining social rules.

(Morgan, 1978, p. 51)

The failure of liberal and permissive parents to take responsibility for the teaching of proper social rules is the cause of

the spread of what could be called a delinquent syndrome, a conglomeration of behaviour, speech, appearance and attitudes, a frightening ugliness and hostility which pervades human interaction, a flaunting of contempt for other human beings, a delight in crudity, cruelty and violence, a desire to challenge and to humiliate, and never, but never, to please.

(Morgan, 1978, p. 13)

Parents are primarily responsible for this, but they have been aided and abetted by liberal and social democratic social policies at the level of government which have been oriented to a child's (expressed or repressed) needs rather than to the task of reproducing established, dominant morality. It is obvious that this teaching of key cultural values can also be disrupted, for right-wing writers, by the introduction of migrant groups of different cultural backgrounds into unitary, orderly British culture, and by a variety of other challenges to the authority of established, dominant *morality*.

The casual theories of crime advanced by Wilson and Morgan have significant differences. But they have two major features in common.

On the one hand, they bemoan the passing of an allegedly unitary dominant culture. This culture may have been imposed by coercion (as surely the culture of the American pioneers *was* imposed on the Indian, the black slave population and, indeed, on later attempts to form socialist and trade union organisations). Or it may have been imposed by benevolence and paternalism (as the traditional aristocratic rulers of Britain have preferred). But whether coercive or benevolent, this cultural domination is seen by Wilson and Morgan to be the source of a social stability that is now missing in American and British society. The loss of traditional culture's domination over society is then explained as arising, not out of any inadequacies or contradictions in the culture itself, but by reference to undesirable changes that have occurred in the structure of the population mix in particular localities (the migrations of blacks) or by reference to undesirable changes occurring in the moral education of children in families and schools (the advent of progessive education and consensus psychology). By clear implication, the true corrective to the social disorder experienced by the citizenry is the *re-imposition* of traditional culture. What neither Wilson nor Morgan can grasp is that traditional 'culture', in all its various manifestations, is experiencing its own contraditions. The norms and values of traditional class society (in the United States or Britain) may be the topic of nostalgic novels and television series, but they are of little direct applicability to youth groups in those societies struggling to find work in a declining labour market or, indeed, to other groups caught between contemporary moral codes emphasising traditional respectability and individual self-expression.

Wilson and Morgan do not have much sense of the 'real history' of traditional culture. Traditional culture may have been effective and appropriate in producing a sense of order in small-town America in the early twentieth century, but it was certainly ineffective in preventing American cities from becoming, in the same period, places of gang warfare and violent industrial conflict. Similarly, it may possibly have produced some sense of social cohesion amongst the gentry in late eighteenth-century England, but it did so in part by being supported by a notorious 'Bloody Code' of laws which imposed capital punishment on artisans and peasants found guilty of stealing deer, grain and other foodstuffs, and for a massive number of other offences. Traditional culture was in this instance a class rhetoric, supported by laws which enforced the existing division of property 'by terror'. In the nineteenth century, the traditional cultural forms were given a much more consensual and indeed contractual form, but they were still transparently used by the Victorian bourgeoisie to legitimate crushing social inequalities and the use of penal discipline to correct and control the 'dangerous classes'. So Wilson's and Morgan's nostalgia for a consensual and unitary culture is blind to the frequently violent and divisive history of this culture, and it is also silent on the actual working of culture and education in reproducing unequal and unjust social relations.

The other common feature of Wilson's and Morgan's academic writings on crime and delinquency is their full recognition of the existence of social disorder in both Britain and the United States. This is also a feature of the popular journalism in which both writers routinely engage, self-evidently because they both see the need to *popularise* their criminologies. This concern for 'realism' and 'populism' in New Right criminology makes it a much more powerful form of criminology, especially journalistically, than liberalism, because it takes the anxieties and fears of working people seriously and indeed proclaims that these anxieties and fears *are* real. In contrast, there *has* been a marked tendency in recent years for liberal criminologists, and especially those who work entirely within universities or colleges, to want to deny or to qualify popular fears, especially about crime, by pointing to the statistical 'facts' about crime or by stressing that many of the popular anxieties are the result of 'moral panics' resulting from the over-sensitive reactions of the media to particular events. This kind of liberal criminology has been extremely weak in recent years, as working people have increasingly come to experience real, material, social and personal problems deriving from the long crisis of the British economy and the unstable character of social order in America.

The basis for 'dangerousness'

Right-wing accounts are more advanced than existing liberal accounts in having provided a *new penology* for crime control. That is, unlike liberals, the New Right writers do *not* believe in the utility of continuing with *more* of the same kinds of welfare, treatment or rehabilitation, as a solution to an increasingly disorderly set of social relations. This new penology operates under a variety of rubrics, but one of its defining elements is a concentration on the control of 'dangerousness'. This 'renaissance of dangerousness', as Tony Bottoms has called it, is not always expressed in the philosophical terms that more fundamentalist radical right writers like van den Haag would prefer: that is, it is not always a reference to the existence of evil.[12] More frequently, in fact, dangerousness is expressed in terms of the traditions of reformist criminology: dangerous people are *sick*. For the Scottish Council on Crime, reporting in 1975, there are 'violence-prone offender(s) . . . [for whom] continued detention is required . . . until it is safe for them to be released, to protect the country from such offenders' (p. 39, quoted in Bottoms, 1977, p. 71). For the Committee on Mentally Abnormal Offenders (the Butler Committee), reporting in the same year, for England and Wales there are offenders 'who are dangerous, who present a history of mental disorder which cannot be dealt with under the Mental Health Act, and for whom the life sentence is not appropriate' (p. 76, quoted in Bottoms, 1977). A period of indeterminate detention, periodically overseen presumably by psychiatrists and other 'expert' definers of normality and health, is proposed for these offenders.

A new penal apparatus has arisen to allow the segregation and incapacitation of individuals who are deemed, for various reasons, to be dangerous to the public or disruptive of the 'good order' of conventional prisons and hospitals; and these new penal institutions are justified by a new, realist penology that speaks of the existence of dangerous (evil or sick) individuals.

The need for such a penology was widely supported throughout the 1970s by workers in mental hospitals calling for the extension of secure psychiatric facilities, as well as by senior and junior social workers who argued for the expansion of secure accommodation in the community home system, on the grounds that youngsters were becoming more 'unruly', and needed to be contained before they could be 'reached' in a therapeutic relationship. It was also supported by the law enforcement apparatus on the grounds that containment could prevent the more disturbed repeat offenders from wreaking damage on society. The 'renaissance of dangerousness' was accepted as a fact, in other words, by liberal professionals as well as by law enforcement personnel. Indeed, the structures of prisons, juvenile institutions and hospitals in the 1970s were increasingly modified to include within them a 'warehousing' or containment provision for the minority of dangerous offenders and patients — in control and special units in prison, in 'secure accommodation' in the juvenile justice system, and in secure units in psychiatric hospitals.

But even more important than the support given the concept of dangerousness and its connected penology of containment by liberal professionals was the general resonance of this for working-class people in general, and for those in the inner city in particular. Official recognition of 'danger' and the need for its removal and control *appeared to answer particular, real problems of the class*.

We can put this in starker terms. The successful marketing of racialist themes, of notions of disorder and dangerousness, and of the need for coercive segregation of individual predators all have a *real* material basis in recent working-class experience of urban living. The pattern of urban segregation of the classes established in the middle to late nineteenth century has been subjected recently to a second major transformation. The first of these transformations, in the 1920s, involved the massive expansion of suburbia, and the broader separation of the respectable sections of the middle and working class, the latter being left behind in the inner city where they acted as guardians of respectability. In the United States, this post-war transformation had the additional feature of involving massive migrations of new populations into the large cities, in particular the migration of Italians, Eastern Europeans and southern blacks into northern metropolitan cities. In the United States, in other words, early twentieth-century population growth ensured that the creation of suburbia was paralleled by the creation of the infamous 'zone of transition', the site of a struggle over housing amongst migrant groups and also the site of 'social disorganisation' and predatory crime. In Britain, the emergence of this zone was postponed until the second major transformation in the urban living conditions of working people. The rehousing of large sections of the class in the aftermath of the Second World War in new towns and on large council house estates, occasioned by social democratic demands for new homes and by the decline of traditionally localised craft industries, resulted in a widely experienced dislocation of old class communities (with all of their neighbourhood institutions) and a real decline in the benefits of urban life for the class. This decline was most keenly experienced by working people left behind in the inner city (whilst other members of the class moved outwards into the new suburban estates), but it was also experienced by people who were rehoused into 'dump estates' or into the high-rise flats so beloved of social democratic planners in the late 1950s and early 1960s. It was into these two urban spaces – the inner city and, latterly, the high-rise flat – that a black proletariat recruited by British capital in the 1960s as a solution to labour shortages was introduced, or managed by struggle to introduce itself. The relation of the class to 'its' city was already disrupted, inexplicably and lamentably so far as the class was concerned, when cultural strangers from the West Indies and from Asia came to take up residence in the declining and changing local neighbourhood.

Progressive education and the working class

Just as neighbourhood social life had been one of the compensations of being subordinated in class society, so also did education have specific functions for working people. It could indeed be a means of escaping one's class position, albeit at the cost of having to accept the authoritarian domination and often alien values of teachers in traditional schools. Given the deferential traditions with which large sections of the British working class were inculcated, grammar school education was in fact quite widely accepted as an opportunity for working-class children to grasp and to advance themselves. It was evidence of the paternalism of 'authority', and of authority's willingness to make its own 'high culture' and civilised values available to those lower-class individuals who were worthy enough to appreciate and internalise them. However, the 'liberalisation' of education that occurred in Britain and in many other Western societies in the later post-war period has tended to undermine the claims of traditional class authority and to advance the claims of other notions of educational value and purpose. But these other 'progressive' notions of education have often been attacked (as in the case of the William Tyndale School in 1976) *by working-class parents themselves*, who feel that progressive methods of education do not equip their offspring sufficiently for the competitive existence of class society.

Progressive education in schools has tried to replace the traditional teaching subjects of earlier 'academic' schools (Latin, history, civics, etc.) with a variety of subjects which progressive staff think are either socially relevant or useful for occupational training. This reform has the apparently progressive concern of trying to make education 'useful' to the immediate experience or the intended careers of the mass of pupils. But, as Christopher Lasch has argued, what it has actually accomplished, particularly in the United States but also increasingly in Britain, is the separation of education processes from the process of learning a culture. That is to say that education in schools has become much more concerned with responding to the expressed needs and the everyday experience of pupils rather than with the process of imparting knowledge about world literature, history, politics or economics. But in the attempt to act as a carrier of skills and a provider of experience, progressive education has come a poor third to children's own practical exploration of culture and also, of course, to television, which has its own particular set of entertainment and educational programmes for children and adolescents. Writing about the permissive education and the television culture of the United States, Christopher Lasch observes that

> In the space of two or three generations, enormous stretches of the 'Judaeo-Christian tradition', so often invoked by educators but so seldom taught in any form, have passed into oblivion. The effective loss of cultural tradition on such a scale makes talk of a new Dark Ages far from frivolous. Yet this loss coincides with an information glut,

with the recovery of the past by specialists, and with an
unprecedented explosion of knowledge — none of which
. . . impinges on everyday experience or shapes popular
culture.

(Lasch, 1979, pp. 260–1)

These contradictions may not have emerged so clearly in
Britain as they have in North America (where pupil and student
illiteracy and a certain cultural insensibility are thought by
Lasch to be common outside of elite educational institutions).
But there is no doubt that some of the 'progressive' education
in British schools does disappoint and fail to involve its
students, precisely because it is, literally, mundane (or worldly)
in its orientation to the tasks of education. It is not only that
the successful learning of skills or the insightful excavation of
neighbourhood or family experience does not guarantee a
child or young person employment and economic security: it
is also that they do not provide children or young people
with an explanation of the complex, impersonal, repressive,
anxiety-provoking and alienated culture in which they live. It
does not provide the means for making sense of the world as
it is.

Supporters of traditional education will conclude from the
disorder that is current in some schools that the solution,
following writers like Patricia Morgan, is to reinstate traditional
culture at the centre of the curriculum. In the same way,
parents, especially in the working class, may also bemoan the
loss of the certainty of traditional relations between teachers
and pupils, parents and children, and authorities and subjects,
and attribute this in part to the undermining of proper moral
training by progressive educationalists and liberal school-
teachers. Jeremy Seabrook has vividly caught the bathos of
this loss of parental influence:

As [parents'] role decreases, the bewilderment of the
parents grows. 'He only sleeps here'; 'I'm the ever-open
purse'; 'It's the kids he mixes with'; 'I don't know where
they get it from'; 'He's never heard things like that in this
house'; 'I've tried to teach him right from wrong'. There
has been a progressive relaxation of a grasp they never

really had, and they cannot imagine where the values which their own child seems to embody, actually come from. Poverty, for them, has meant control and self-denial; . . . but [their children's] appetites are kindled at the expense of their abilities; and the sense of destiny turns out to be a future of underemployment, idleness and lack of function.

(Seabrook, 1978, p. 101)

The 'debate' between traditional and progressive forms of education is really besides the point in current circumstances. Any attempt to reimpose traditional forms of education can only work in schools which draw their pupils from particular and restrictive class backgrounds (like private schools — currently in the process of expansion once again). It can have no real purchase across the contradictory and fractured class structure as a whole, especially in conditions of rapid decline in the size of the juvenile labour market. Figures for unemployment amongst school leavers are now not published separately by the Central Statistical Office, but a very considerable proportion of the 2,304,100 unemployed people registered in Britain in February 1981 (9.5 per cent of the working population, as compared to the 2.6 per cent who were unemployed in 1974) were young people who had recently left school. The proportions would have been much higher had it not been for the number of young people in the artificial jobs created by the government-sponsored Youth Opportunities Programme and the Work Experience on Employers' Premises projects.

But the prospect of medium- and long-term worklessness is not the only 'structural' development to threaten the legitimacy of dominant culture. The 'lucky' young people on the appropriately named WEEP projects are being paid £19.50 a week plus £4.00 a week travel — paid out by attendance rather than as a wage — which even employers see to be exploitation of youth by the state (*The Leveller*, 51, 6—20 March 1981). Young people in full employment are once again (as in the 1950s) being used, often in lieu of workers made redundant, on unskilled jobs involving little training and few prospects for advancement, at extremely low rates, of pay. The experience is of one of tedious and repetitive exploitation by the employer, distinguishable from workless- ness primarily by the hours to be worked for the salary received. It is a way of living and working that the dominant culture of traditional education has always disdained and rejected.

The attitude of the dominant culture to more socially advantaged middle-class children is also uneasy. Young people are being urged by the government, and by other 'realists', to train in areas like business studies, science and technology, in which there are prospects of employment. But the culture which is dominant in British schools is *not* a commercial cul- ture, but a culture of liberal education born of the long history of aristocratic rule. From the late nineteenth century onwards, the advance of commercial and technical subjects into British education has been successfully held in check by proponents of liberal education in public schools and grammar schools. It is a liberal education which fails to provide the particular skills and the particular qualifications required by a free mar- ket economy.

Thus calls for the reimposition of traditional culture as a solution to social disorder are incoherent in failing to recog- nise the changed relation of both working-class and middle- class children to the larger capitalist economy. Support for progressive education makes little direct sense of the econo- mic realities facing children from the different classes (and is really only sensible as a way of training children for the 'leisure' of worklessness). The only kind of educational re- form which makes sense of the economic realities would be one which celebrates the virtues of (and gives children the skills for) a competitive and individualistic, entrepreneurial life: the contradiction is that such an educational culture is hardly a recipe for the restoration of social order and com- munity. It is a recipe only for the self-centred acquisitiveness of the petty bourgeois.

None of these options makes sense as the basis of a socialist critique of the educational crisis. An analysis with these pur- poses would indeed recognise, with Patricia Morgan and other right-wing critics of progressivism, that teaching has 'a pivotal role in cultural transmission'. But the culture to be transmitted would not be the *class culture* that was formed in the moment of aristocratic hegemony in late eighteenth-century Britain, nor would it be the more middle-class version of the same culture that was institutionalised in the Victorian period. It would have to be a culture deriving directly from the best of humanist and radical traditions in philosophy, literature and political economy, providing (as those traditions did) a *critical* understanding of the inequalities of industrial capitalist society and a standpoint from which to glimpse an alternative.

Short of any such socialist alternative being articulated in a popular fashion, however, there is no question that the demands put by the New Right for a return to traditional authoritative methods, both in the school and in the home, will have considerable popular appeal. Such demands will appear to make sense of the dislocations in the relationship of teachers and pupils and of parents and offspring. They will also quieten anxieties about the rapid changes that are occurring in the structure of capitalist societies generally, in what is clearly a fundamental process of *transition*, by appearing to re-institute *familiar* educational processes and institutions. In particular, it may appear to offer very dislocated working-class populations the possibility of the restoration of the 'traditional' integrity of class relations, where social mobility was minimal but where it was at least understood to derive from talent and from merit.

A mistaken realism

When we insist, as we have been doing, that the arguments advanced by the New Right on questions of law and order, on education and youthful behaviour, etc., relate to 'reality' and that this constitutes their popular appeal, we do not mean that the realities described in the rhetoric of the Right are *equivalent* to the lived reality of working-class people at large. Working-class neighbourhoods as a whole are not places of random or routine, everyday violence or predatoriness. In fact, residents of even the roughest working-class housing estates, with very high official rates of crime, complain and

demur when the suggestion is made that they live in essentially criminal areas.[13]

The inner city and 'downtown core' of the average British
city may be unpleasant, litter-ridden and generally unsettling
and ugly, especially at night, but there is no firm evidence to
suggest that these areas are dangerous in the sense that the
downtown areas of Manhattan, Detroit and Philadelphia quite
certainly are. Violent offences constituted a total of 95,000
in 1979 (only 3.7 per cent of the 2,376,700 offences known
to the police). This was certainly a significant increase over
ten years earlier, when there were 37,000 offences so recorded.
Britain none the less remains a much less violent society
overall than the United States and also than other European
societies. In 1975, for example, there were 1,645 murders
and non-negligent manslaughters in New York City, 818 in
Chicago, 633 in Detroit, 554 in Los Angeles and 434 in Philadelphia, with an overall total of 18,642 murders known to
the police in the United States as a whole. In 1979 there was
a total of 629 murders in the whole of England and Wales.
Comparative homicide rates are difficult to obtain and by no
means reliable because of different legal definitions, but in
1965 the United Nations Demographic Yearbook, attempting
to standardise these definitions, calculated Britain's homicide
rate at 0.6 per 100,000 population, much lower than the rates
for Finland (2.2), Germany (1.2), Italy (1.1), Austria (1.0)
and France, Denmark and Sweden (all at 0.8) (Winslow, 1970,
p. 202). There is no evidence to suggest that the relationships
between these rates has changed in any startling fashion over
the last fifteen years, although it is clear that the rate of
increase for offences involving violence has increased in all
these societies much more quickly than has homicide.

The interpersonal violence occurring in Britain is localised
both geographically and socially. That is to say, offences like
assaults, woundings and even rapes and other sexual attacks
do tend to occur either in the more decrepit and depressed of
working-class housing areas or alternatively in areas adjoining
them. In particular, there is a tendency for offences of violence (along with offences of vandalism and hooliganism) to
be associated with the poorer estates on which local councils
have housed their problem tenants, or with the high-rise flats

which are now recognised to be monumental failures of the planners' imagination, breeding isolation and other nervous conditions amongst their residents (see Baldwin, Bottoms and Walker 1976, ch. 6).

The violence that does occur is therefore concentrated among populations who (in the housing planners' own terms) have been 'dumped' into the most rapidly deteriorating and unpleasant housing stock. It tends also to be most frequent in the early and late evenings, resulting either from the 'play' (or 'aggro') of adolescents attempting to manufacture excitement or from the playing out of aggressions and frustrations at the end of an evening in a pub, a local discotheque or working men's club. It is a violence which may also find expression at the weekend, in the context of domestic squabbles or violence, or from fights spilling over from the weekend's football games in the locality. So the violence is more common at some times than at others: it is patterned and to some extent predictable, and certainly local residents can and do take action to avoid being involved in the worst incidents.

There are some exceptions to this predictability, and certainly both the popular press and Conservative spokesmen have given a great deal of prominence in recent years to, for example, cases of attacks on old people in their own homes. Women have also been attacked in their own homes and in daylight in open urban space, although sexual attacks as such still seem to be most common and predictable at night and in particular urban territories, like parks or dark side streets, especially in the vicinity of hospitals, universities and colleges. A definite exception to the previously predictable character of 'mundane' violence is the rapidly increasing number of attacks on blacks by white racist youths, aided and encouraged by the British Movement and the National Front. In the winter of 1979—80, several Asians were gratuitously murdered by white racists in the East End of London, either on the streets or in their own homes, and an untold number of other assaults, woundings and harassments have been visited on black individuals and families in widely different parts of the country. Some 3,827 racial attacks were reported to the police in 1979, compared with 2,630 in 1975 (*Hansard*, 31 December 1980), though both results were clearly a gross underestimate of the overall total. It is now well known that black people are reluctant to report such events to the police. The success of the British Movement in recruiting skinhead youths has now prompted the National Front to shift away from its quest for electoral respectability, announcing its intention to engage in the politics of 'destabilisation'. This change in policy may not be unconnected with the spate of harassments of well-known socialists living in South London and with the bombing of a left-wing bookshop in Birmingham early in 1981. These are serious and frightening developments, and they should act as a corrective to any impression of complacency that may have been created by the preceding remarks. It certainly is no intention of this book to argue for an acceptance of existing crime rates or for a popular accommodation to the facts of violence. I entirely concur with the criticism of liberalism made by Leon Brittan QC, the first of the present government's Ministers of the State at the Home Office, when he told the 1979 annual general meeting of the National Association for the Care and Resettlement of Offenders, that

> One primary danger facing those dealing with the crime problem, whatever function they may fulfil, is that the more common the phenomenon becomes, the more it may be seen as intractable and as the normal pattern of life ... That is a temptation which we must absolutely resist.
>
> (Brittan, 1979)

But I do not accept the idea that the phenomena of crime and violence are present *throughout* society (being an effect of the random distribution of evil) or that the violence is unpatterned. Crimes of violence in particular are behaviours occurring primarily within the rough working class and victimising members of the same class, usually those who are imprisoned in impersonal, cheap and architecturally oppressive housing developments. The victims are therefore usually in roughly the same (deprived) position within the social structure as their aggressors, as also, for example, are the young working-class males who routinely act violently against each other at football games, in discotheques and dances, usually as a result of fights over women or over the defence of the name of a football club or a particular urban neighbourhood.

The very names of punk rock groups and the titles and lyrics of their songs proclaim the essential significance of the violence of the times.[14] This is clearly a generation of youth which sees itself to be rejected (as the names of the various new wave and punk bands, like the *Epsilons*, the *Damned*, the *Cockney Rejects*, proclaim). It is not only that there are no jobs, and that therefore a 'culture of worklessness' has arisen. It is also that, even if there were jobs, they would be mean, unrewarding and depersonalising little jobs on production lines, in supermarkets, or similar. However regular or generous the salary received, the young person would still be asked to live in dreary and impersonal housing whilst subordinating himself or herself psychically to the discipline of the working week and to a medium- and possibly long-term future of rejection in meaningless and demeaning work.

Punk culture identifies what Conservative rhetorics on law and order attempt to displace or to silence. It highlights the way in which British society has increasingly appeared to accommodate to the *rejection* of a significant proportion of its population, a significant proportion of its youth. Again, it is not simply that there has been a net loss of employment possibilities for youth, beginning around 1968.[15] It is also that heavy ideological work has been done throughout the 1970s, by accredited or self-appointed spokesmen for authority, to put an end to the earlier 'revolution of rising expectations' of the 1950s and 1960s. Rough working-class youths in particular no longer nurture any serious expectation of being allowed to escape from the mean and repressive neighbourhoods of their parents, from work routines or from worklessness, or from the overweaning oppressions of inequality and hierarchy which still dominate the oldest unreformed class society in the world. Working-class adults, after years of respectable conformity and productive labour, may still believe in the possibility of some eventual reward, but the general population of working-class youth, in its embrace of nihilistic and interpersonal violence and other illegitimate, anti-social activity, is clearly acting out *its* disbelief.

All of this affirms, as we signalled earlier in the critique of James Q. Wilson and Patricia Morgan, that there exists what has been called a 'crisis of social reproduction'. This crisis is primarily a crisis in the inability of the capitalist mode of production to generate anything like a sufficiently large number of employment opportunities for youth (this arising out of the impact of the new technology in reducing labour requirements of capitalists and also out of the renewed, classical tendency of the capitalist system to encounter major crises of profitability at the end of periods of boom). But it is also a cultural crisis in the sense that there is a widespread withdrawal of legitimacy from 'the system', and a withdrawal which (though Patricia Morgan cannot see it) has a rational basis in the way the system rejects its youth. Teachers, especially in rough schools, speak of unteachable and unmanageable pupils who have no motivation to learn, while teachers in higher education encounter a rather cynical and instrumental, fundamentally uncommitted, cohort of students, who proclaim only their disenchantment with the system. Children of rough working-class families living in tower blocks or in other 'dump' environments may spend their time looking for 'aggro', playing Space Invader computer games in amusement arcades, or simply doing nothing (see Corrigan, 1979), while other young people may spend equivalent amounts of time in discotheques or in fashion shops, engaging in a youthful version of what Christopher Lasch called the 'narcissistic' celebration of the self (Lasch, 1979, ch. 2).

The violence, like the achievement of a glamorous self, is therefore an activity that tends to be pursued for explicable reasons at particular locations in the social structure. But violence, unlike narcissism, is destructive of others, of the physical and interpersonal environment, and eventually of the young person himself or herself. This last factor may indeed be a part of the essential rationale of violence for a cohort of youth that sees itself to be 'damned'. It is brutal, explosive 'rejection of the rejection' that a class society like Britain has routinely and unremittingly visited on its most deprived and also most socially dislocated populations.

Now the reality of crime and violence which Conservatives and New Right ideologues identify, when they propagandise for law and order, does not look like this reality at all. The rhetoric of the Right is almost always silent on the *specific social context* of any crime. Instead, serious crimes are explained as examples of the behaviours of individuals, whose essentially evil intentions or desires have been inadequately deterred by law. In more reformist accounts, Conservatives will sometimes recognise the existence of badly, or undersocialised, individuals who are essentially in need of care and attention at the hands of social workers. In the work of Patricia Morgan, *both* behaviours and moral considerations are involved together, since for her 'acceptance of responsibility for long-term welfare of the child' is or should be equivalent to the 'acceptance of responsibility for care *and* education'. So there are deterrent *and* educative features of the role of parents and the state in the prevention of delinquency.

But both these Conservative accounts attempt to reverse the causal logic that would be offered in almost any social explanation of our contemporary disorder. That is, they attempt to explain the dislocation that is occurring in the social relations of the broader society in terms of the dislocated character of individual personalities and consciences. Morgan argues that

> delinquency has now ceased to be merely a symptom of urban breakdown in *this* country (if it ever was) and has become a major contributor to it.
> (Morgan, 1978, p. 12, emphasis in original)

So right-wing criminology quite consciously attempts to displace crime and delinquency from their origins in the social formation itself, and in so doing asserts that the disorder in social relations is unrelated to the accelerating crisis of social reproduction in capitalist society. The 'nihilism' of youth is disconnected from the collapse in the juvenile labour market, from the unremitting rejection of lower class youth by authority, of the black community and black youth by white society, or from any fundamental inadequacies in the social relations of inequality and division that are required by the capital—labour relationship. Right-wing criminology's essential project is indeed to disconnect the facts of social disorder from the (developing) disorderliness of social relations, by remaining silent on the specific social context of crime and by speaking ideologically about crime as individual moral defect. Speaking about the riots by the black community in Brixton in April 1981, Margaret Thatcher insisted that 'Nothing, but nothing, justified what happened' (ITN News, 13 April 1981). She ruled out any further provision of financial aid for the area, on the grounds that 'Money cannot buy either trust or racial harmony. We have to try to go about it in a different way.'

Trust is here an *act of will* which can be expressed, like crime itself, at any point in the social structure of a racially and socially polarised society, even across the divide between poor blacks and the police, between residents of the inner city and their landlords, and generally between a deprived and workless population and the state. A failure by any individual to recognise that these social divisions are quite secondary to the proper and moral conduct of one's life (and the social contract struck between free individuals) may indeed lead the individual who is so misled into crime. But the key precipitating factor will be moral defect — individual wrongfulness — and not the wider disorderliness of a social system that divides human beings against each other.

This is not the only displacement which right-wing criminology, in both its academic and more directly political forms, attempts. It also increasingly offers out, as we indicated earlier, a penal policy that claims to be able to bring about a new sense of order in society. This penology is organised in part around the control of dangerous individuals, the 'hard core' delinquents and criminals — a project which does relate to popular anxieties — but it is also articulated around the remoralisation of the population at risk.

Retributive and remoralising measures: juvenile justice since 1979

The three major initiatives taken by the Thatcher government in the field of juvenile justice since 1979 have been concerned with the fundamental revision of the liberal Children and

Young Persons Act of ten years earlier. Though never fully legislated in its original form,[16] the passage of this Act had marked the victory of what Patricia Morgan called 'consensus psychology' in the juvenile court, by insisting on the primacy of the needs of the child in courtroom proceedings over the findings of guilt and by interpreting delinquency as a 'presenting symptom' of some deeper maladjustment in a child's personality, requiring the expert intervention of social workers. Under the care proceedings instituted in this Act, local authority social services departments were to be given full discretion over the kinds of disposition appropriate to children who were deemed in court to be in need of care and attention outside their families.

The revisions that have been made or proposed to the 1969 Act by the Thatcher government are the result of a continued campaign of criticism of the Act waged by the Magistrates Association, the police, and by representatives of local authorities (especially in Conservative areas) throughout the 1970s.

At the Conservative Party conference in October 1979, Mr Whitelaw informed a delighted audience that the government was to introduce new experimental regimes at two existing detention centres for young offenders (New Hall, near Wakefield, and Send in Surrey). Life would be lived 'at a brisk tempo', and young offenders would learn that criminal behaviour would not be tolerated. When these centres were opened, in April 1980, it was clear that the government intended, if possible, to investigate the possibility of running detention centre sentences that were much shorter in length than the existing sentences of three months and six months, thereby enabling a much larger number of young offenders to be given the beneficial experience of the 'short, sharp shock'. In March 1981, the Minister of State at the Home Office, Patrick Mayhew, announced the extension of the experimental regimes to two other existing detention centres and also revealed that a number of borstal places were to be converted to the new regime. These announcements were a profound defeat for the original liberal architects of the 1969 Act, for whom the Act was a first move in the eventual abolition of the essentially militaristic and uncaring detention centre institution. In the meantime, in its White Paper on

Young Offenders released in October 1980, the government indicated that the length of detention centre regimes was indeed to be reduced to a minimum of three weeks and a maximum of four months. This White Paper also proposed the creation of a new sentence of 'youth custody' for young adult offenders (those aged 17—21) to be served primarily in senior detention centres, borstals and prisons. This will be a determinate sentence imposed by the magistracy as they think appropriate, given 'the circumstances of the particular offence and the young adult offender'. The courts will in this way have powers restored to them which they lost in 1961, at the high point of post-war optimism about the possibilities of rehabilitative work with offenders by social workers. The 1980 White Paper also proposed that in dealing with the younger offender under 17 who is already in the care of the local authority social worker and who reoffends, the courts should have the power to require the child's removal from home 'so that this can be seen by the public and by the offender to be a direct result of the offence and the court appearance'.

So troublesome young adults and youths are once again to be subjected to the punishment of being locked up in institutions and thereby expelled from the community (irrespective of the diagnosis preferred by any social worker). It is an expulsion which will find favour, as we have said, not only in the Tory Party conference but also in working-class communities in appearing to rid the community of troublesome elements (and thereby removing anxiety over the orderliness of life). It may also, of course, satisfy the retributive feelings that are always general in a divided class society.

But even the expulsion of the 'hard core' into institutions is thought in the conservatism of the New Right to have an essentially moral dimension.

In the *Young Offenders* White Paper, the government insists that training and education must be provided for young offenders, for they 'may be at a turning point which decides whether they will become recidivists or *responsible citizens*' (para 12, my emphasis).

Shocking young offenders into the responsibilities of citizenship through short detention centre sentences or

lengthier sentences of 'youth custody' is the coercive and
deterrent method that is to be preferred with young offenders
who are thought to be already heavily committed to delinquency (the 'deep end' offenders). But for other young people
at the 'shallow end' of social control — youngsters who may,
for example, have been cautioned by the police for acts of
petty vandalism — the Thatcher government has given its
support (to some observers rather surprisingly) to the Intermediate Treatment (IT) programmes which were initiated by
the otherwise mistaken Act of 1969. Intermediate treatment
was a very vague but expansive concept in the minds of the senior child care professionals who were responsible for the Act:
it was treatment intermediate between the social casework
focused on a young offender in his or her own family situation and the imposition of a care order removing the child
from home for a lengthy period. Under the Act, an intermediate treatment order can be imposed for a period of up
to 90 days, and a young person can be required to participate, under the supervision of a social worker, in the particular IT projects available in a particular locality. These projects
vary enormously across the country, ranging from work with
other disadvantaged groups in a local area to outward bound
style courses in rugged countryside. In the minds of the
liberal professionals who constructed them, IT was justified,
variously, as a way of bringing youngsters into touch with
nature, as character-building, as a demonstration of the kinds
of care that are possible between groups, and indeed quite
often as a way of providing holidays for children who might
never have them otherwise.

Almost immediately after the general election, the Social
Services Secretary, Mr Patrick Jenkin, spoke to a major
national conference of over 800 social service department
directors, and announced the Thatcher government's intentions on the financing of intermediate treatment in the
following terms, indicating that it was the government's
view that

> local authority child care services share a major responsibility
> with the police, probation and prison services for coping
> with delinquent young people on remand or found guilty

by the courts. To this extent, the Government are prepared
to regard child care services as an integral part of the
national pattern of law and order services, and to have the
priority which that attaches to it.

(Patrick Jenkin, 9 July 1979)

In case this should be mistaken, Mr Jenkin went on to underline the fact that IT should be

something positive, preventative and purposive. It is intended to lead to a better result. It is most emphatically not
just a way of passing the time. Nor must treatment be
confused with treats.

(Patrick Jenkin, 9 July 1979)

In order to ensure that this particular conception of IT should
prevail over any more liberal or permissive formulation, the
Young Offenders White Paper of 1980 proposed that magistrates should have the power of specifying a particular programme of activities for individual young offenders and that
social workers working on IT would therefore be merely
executives of the court's discretion. The purpose of the 'IT
order', as it may officially be called, will be to remoralise
individuals by providing them with tests of character and
with the experience of what individual effort can achieve.

The attempt to remoralise individuals in the working class
is quite clearly thought of by the Right as a constituent
element in a larger project of social reconstruction, rather
than being simply a retributive response to troublesome or
violent delinquents. This larger project — of constructing a
'social market economy', dominated largely by pioneering
entrepreneurs (the true creators of wealth) — is to be supported and underlined by social policies which give priority
to the personal benefits that can be achieved through individual effort and which de-emphasise the benefits of collective
solutions to social problems generally, and of 'dependency on
the state', whether this takes the form of being a client of a
social worker or a claimant at the welfare office. It is a fundamentally utopian project of a right-wing government which
appears to believe that the contradictions of an old class

society can be resolved via a return to nineteenth-century principles. It is also, of course, an ideological project which legitimates a massive attack on social welfare, on state dependency, and indeed on social democracy itself.

The attack on social democracy

Partly because of the support that they have given to the expansion of state welfare expenditure, liberals and social democrats are now heavily under attack from the Right. But this attack is not essentially a cynical use of ideology, mounted in order to mask overall reductions in expenditure by the state (leaving monies available which can then be appropriated by capital). State expenditures have not been massively reduced by the Thatcher government, at least up until April 1981. But they *have* been significantly redirected. The state is no longer intent, in the formulation of Lord Beveridge, on providing 'security from the cradle to the grave'. Instead it is concerned to provide the legal and institutional framework within which, it is hoped, entrepreneurial individuals can initiate a new wave of capital accumulation and of industrial and commercial productivity, without having to bear the costs in taxation, to support the ever increasing costs of social welfare. A constant outlay of state expenditure on police and prisons and on social discipline generally will be required in order to maintain social peace and the conditions for production, but the costs of individual socialisation, care and attention, and even health, will increasingly have to be met by individuals and families themselves.[17]

In this utopian project of desperate ruling-class politicians, one of the prime targets of the government is the fabric of the welfare state itself and its ideological support in social democratic politics. The social reconstruction initiated by the Labour Government of 1945—51, which was subsequently institutionalised as the form of the post-war consensus (a partnership of the state and civil society underwriting a 'corporate' mixed economy), has itself become a target. So we have witnessed a massive ideological offensive from this government (beginning in its years in opposition) on nearly every traditional wisdom of the post-war consensus: social workers, applauded in the 1950s and early 1960s for their professionalism and altruism, have been shamelessly pilloried in the 1970s for their unprofessional permissiveness and naivety, while the welfare state itself has been spoken of as if it were mainly an instrument that is abused by 'scroungers'.

In 1977–8, as we indicated earlier, the offensive extended into the question of crime control, with the Conservative Political Centre releasing an increasing number of broadsheets on the question of crime and the rule of law. In the 1979 election, the use of right-wing criminology became quite explicit as Margaret Thatcher made all the required connec- tions, for a popular as well as for an authoritative audience, in her speech in Birmingham on 19 April. Beginning by remembering the presence of moderate Labour Ministers on picket lines outside Grunwick's in 1977, Mrs Thatcher pro- claimed that

> Labour Ministers do not seem to understand their own responsibilities in the unending task of upholding the law in a free society . . . Do they not understand that when Ministers go on the picket line and when Labour back- benchers attack the police for trying to do their difficult job, that gives the green light for lawless methods right throughout industry?

> Do they not dimly perceive that their silence when con- fronted with flying and violent pickets carried a louder and more deadly message to every lawbreaker than any speech? . . . In their muddled but different ways the vandals on the picket lines and the muggers in our streets have got the same confused message — 'We want our demands met or else' and 'Get out of our way, give us your handbag or else'.

Thatcher went on to recall a 'chilling' debate at the Labour Party annual conference of 1978 at which, she said, there were attacks on the police, the judiciary and the rule of law itself:

> The path Labour delegates were charting on that occasion

was the path to social disintegration and decay, the path to a pitiless society in which ruthless might rules and the weak go to the wall.

Across that path we will place a barrier of steel. There will be no passing that way once a Conservative Government is again in office.

By the time of the 1979 election, then, some rather novel connections were being made by the leading politicians of the Right. The rule of law had emerged as a major defence of 'the weak' against 'ruthless might', which was identified as the Labour and trade union movement (especially when on a picket) and their allies (the muggers and vandals). The plight of the weak, in this 'analysis', was disconnected entirely from patterns of ownership of wealth in Britain and internationally, and also unrelated to the pitiless pursuit of anti-working-class policies by both Conservative and Labour governments in the 1960s and 1970s. It was connected instead to the 'demoralising political activities' of organised labour and, by implication, to the inability of social democratic politics to understand the centrality of law to the universal interest.

It was and is an absurd diagnosis, based on a nineteenth-century theory of the origins of wealth residing in the individual 'freedom' of the capitalist, and oriented towards what for the Right was a utopian project — the construction of social order or community out of a mass of private households. But it was at least a radical break from the crushing monotony and failures of post-war consensus politics in Britain. It appeared to offer something other than the meanness of post-war social democratic social policy and the impersonal bureaucracy of the professionals who operated it. It seemed to recognise the failure of the New Jerusalem.

Notes to Chapter 1

1. Findings from opinion surveys have obviously to be treated with some caution. The survey reported in *New Society* was silent, for example, on the fact that 'lawlessness' (if defined as crimes known to the police) had actually declined during both 1978 and 1979,

albeit only by 2.9 and 0.8 per cent respectively. Public opinion would be more correct in its perception of increasing lawlessness if it was referring to offences involving 'violence against the person'. These increased from 37,800 in 1969 to 95,000 in 1979, an increase of 154 per cent.

2. The National Association of Schoolmasters has been at the forefront in campaigns to alert the public to violence in schools. In 1971, the NAS issued a report on violence in schools, identifying the presence of a 'disruptive minority' whom teachers had not previously been prepared to identify because of 'likely parental response and pressure from administrators' ('Violence in our Schools: the Grim Reality', *The Sunday Times*, 21 November 1971). At their annual conference in 1975, the NAS passed a motion actually refusing to teach 'the violent pupil'.

3. Patricia Morgan provides a selection of these incidents in *Delinquent Fantasies*, as does the special inquiry on 'Violent Britain' in *Now!* magazine. These glossaries of violence emanate from explicitly right-wing sources: but they are nearly all taken from national and local press reports.

4. The National Union of Licensed Victuallers, for example, was involved in the establishment in 1979 of a campaign to 'ban the thug' from public houses, and also created a sub-committee of its own association on law and order, demanding the restoration of corporal punishment.

5. This particular formulaton of a populist argument was repeated by Margaret Thatcher during her speech in Birmingham on 19 April:

> some people feel that law and order should not be an election issue. But it is not the politicians who have made it so. It is the electorate. It is the millions of people who are deeply frightened and anxious about what is going on in our streets and cities.

6. William Whitelaw, speech at Edge Hill by-election, 27 March 1979.
7. The 'crime every 12 seconds' formulation was originally advanced in the Conservative Research Department's *Politics Today*, No. 7 on 'Protecting the Citizen' (17 April 1978). The figure was derived from the total number of indictable offences known to the police in 1977 (3,636,500).
8. It is some indication of the effectiveness of the ideological work done during the election period that law and order should have been mentioned by 33 per cent of voters as an important issue. Two months earlier, in February 1979, only 14 per cent had accorded law and order this importance.

9. The Tory Party achieved a popular vote in 1979 (of 13,697,753) that was almost as high as their highest ever post-war total in 1959 (13,749,830). Even more significantly, the Tories were successful, as Margaret Thatcher had predicted they would be, in obtaining the votes of significant proportions of the working-class electorate and the young. Some 37 per cent of skilled and semi-skilled workers voted for the Tories in 1979 against only 28 per cent in November 1974, and 41 per cent of the 18–24 year old age group voted Tory, compared with only 24 per cent in 1974 (Kellner, 1979).

10. Wilson's casual recital of the racism of London taxi-drivers, hotel porters and news-vendors speaks volumes for Wilson's curiosity as a tourist, and yet says very little about his understanding of the relationship between popular attitudes and historical and structural analysis. We should add that Wilson attempts to rescue his reputation as a social scientist by commenting that 'race . . . may explain some of the increase in violent crime . . . [but] . . . it cannot explain much of the increase in crime generally' (J. Q. Wilson, 1977, p. 71).

11. The response of liberals to the immigration of the past twenty years *has* been fundamentally contradictory. On the one hand, liberals have continued to urge governments to adopt policies which will positively advantage the working-class areas of cities into which immigrants have been forced to move, especially in order to improve the quality of housing, opportunities for employment and leisure and the possibilities of community life as a whole. This pressure has constantly encountered the problem of resentment from other working-class areas at the special attention being given to 'the ghettos'. In the face of current right-wing reactions against black minorities and their alleged involvement in street crime, liberals are left in the contradictory position of demanding *more* resources for these same areas (further exacerbating resentment in other areas), or alternatively they may try to deny that street crime or other forms of interpersonal harassment are a feature of the inner-city areas. The only way in which these contradictions could have been avoided would be for liberals to move towards a politics emphasising positive discrimination in favour of deprived working-class areas as a whole, irrespective of their racial mix.

12. This belief in the existence of evil is a common feature of nearly all the various forms of right-wing criminology that are currently on offer. Patricia Morgan's attack on 'consensus psychology' in *Delinquent Fantasies* is mounted in a chapter entitled 'See No Evil', while the ideological offensive mounted by the police and the magistracy on the Children and Young Persons Act of 1969 was often accompanied by assertions that the Act failed to recognise

that 'there are deprived children and there are depraved children'
(Leslie Male, Chairman, Police Federation, speech to annual
conference, 19 May 1976).

13. Reporting on a study of a pre-war council estate in Sheffield which
has a *very* high official crime rate, Baldwin, Bottoms and Walker
observed that whilst the

> residents were fully aware of the estate's adverse reputation
> . . . they themselves did not believe that offender rates for the
> estate were higher than for the city as a whole, nor that crimin-
> ality had been increasing recently . . . Hardly any spontaneously
> mentioned crime as a social problem for the area [and] very
> many of the respondents believed (erroneously) that the 'crimi-
> nal element' was to be found elsewhere than in their own im-
> mediate vicinity.
>
> (Baldwin, Bottoms and Walker, 1976, p. 182)

14. I am aware that punk and new wave have significance over and
above their 'economic' origins. Punk rock is not merely the music
of the dole queue, but also expresses a rejection of commercialisa-
tion of music and pleasure as well as being (in particular in the
clothing and hair styles it adopts) a continuous satire on bourgeois
normality. For a good analysis of the contradictions in punk, see
Hardy and Laing (1977).

15. 1968 was the first year in the post-war period in which the supply
of young people from schools exceeded the demand for youth
from employers; and in the following three years, it became clear
that the shortfall was an aspect of a long-term trend rather than the
peak of a particularly unfortunate trade cycle. According to the
Youth Employment Council, there was a job loss of about 25 per
cent for boys and 27 per cent for girls during the period 1966 to
1971.

16. Soon after the election victory in 1970 the Conservative government announced that it would never bring section 5 of the 1969
Act, which was to restrict the use of criminal proceedings with 14
to 17 year olds, into force. Also they would also raise the age at
which 'care proceedings' would be compulsory to 12 (rather than
14). The consequence of these two decisions was that the care pro-
eedings which were intended to be at the very centre of the Act's
operation were left optional. The practice since 1969 has been for
care proceedings to be used extremely rarely in cases involving any
kind of offence.

17. We are referring here to the closure or curtailment of local authority
    nurseries and playschools and to the cuts in support for local
    authority childminders, as well as to the massive increases in
    National Health Service prescription charges and in the costs of
    National Health spectacles and dental treatment. In the conceptions
    of the welfare state that were operative until recently throughout
    the post-war period, these charges were always to be borne by the
    state. They have very rapidly been shifted from the state to the
    population as a whole.

2
The Failure of the New Jerusalem: Post-War 'Social Democracy' and the Social Order

It seems a shame. I thought I would see socialism in my lifetime. It looked like it, even in 1945. We've got to start all over again. I shan't be here to do it; but there will be those who will.

Mr Llewellyn, retired miner, interviewed by Jeremy Seabrook (1978, p. 270)

Social democracy in 1945

It is difficult now to understand the degree of anticipation and commitment which was excited by the advent of the Labour government of 1945.

In part our lack of comprehension arises out of a failure of our own historical imagination. Most of us have no direct experience of the social and economic conditions that preceded the war, which were the human effects of the free market economy that pre-dated the Keynesian remedies later to be applied. Nor do most of us have any personal experience of the conditions of community and togetherness (a suspension of the otherwise unending social divisions of a class society) which obtained in many parts of Britain throughout the Second World War, and which were taken by many working people and some middle-class people too as an embryonic demonstration of the benefits to be expected in the planned economy of the post-war period, oriented to social needs rather than to private profit (see Addison, 1975). But we shall see later that there was indeed such a vision, and that this vision was able to mobilise not only working people and organised labour but also the vast majority of the academics and professionals of the time. The commitment was to the building of a reconstructed 'social democracy'.

The key element in this social democracy was a commitment to a vastly expanded role for the state in the management of the market economy (via nationalisation and the use of government intervention to help plan investment, supply and demand). But the state's economic role in managing the market (articulated in part around the attempt to smooth the cycles of boom and slump and to avoid a return to the days of the depression) was linked closely to its role in the provision of social justice and the construction of a caring community.

The *political* concern of social democracy was to mount an attack on the unequal and individualistic form of so-called 'liberal democracy' (especially on parliament and the civil service). There was to be an attack on the 'citadels of privilege' in order to broaden the basis of political and administrative decision-making and to attack the monopoly of power exercised over existing institutions of the state by narrow, largely upper-class sections of the population. The working class was to be much more fully represented. So the function of the interventions in the economy was to enable the government to organise production and distribution, in part, around the provision of particular social needs. According to social democrats of the 1940s, capitalism could be organised in its productive capacities in order to supply an abundance of resources, which a reorganised system of distribution could then direct to people and to communities in particular need. Earlier, unreformed capitalism was indicted for its inability to meet social needs and for being responsive only to the 'needs' of the market. It therefore did not care for the real, just needs of the community as a whole.

We shall want to show later that the intensity of pre-war commitment to Labour's project of social reconstruction was largely a product of the immediate experience of the war, and in particular the way in which the war had for the first time brought members of previously isolated social classes into close contact with each other in a common struggle. The war had suggested the possibility of forms of social order other than the uncaring and socially divisive class society of the inter-war period. This 'war radicalism' was celebrated in the novels of J. B. Priestley, and in the weekly photographic magazine, the *Picture Post*, both of which were taken up with the new found purpose of the British people, struggling against adversity and a common enemy (see Cultural History Group, 1976; Hall, 1972). The insistent refrain was that these people should never again suffer the ignominy of being treated, economically, politically or socially, as they had been in the pre-war period. But the broad parameters of Labour's project in 1945 and also some of the particular detail (for example, the commitment to the provision of a universal state system of social security and national insurance) were born of the long-term insecurities experienced by working people in a capitalist economy. Many of these commitments were formulated in the nineteenth century, in the early years of capitalism, and were now thought at last to be capable of realisation. The utopian logic of Labour's reformism in 1945 consisted in the belief that the various measures of social reconstruction, taken together, would amount to a *revolutionary* transformation of the long experienced inequalities and injustices of an unreformed capitalism and class society.

It *is* difficult now to credit the intensity of this belief, or to understand the real importance of the social democratic reconstruction that was initiated by the Attlee government, without this sense of the pre-history to 1945.

Understanding of this form of social democracy is also made difficult by the way in which the political commitments of 1940s social democrats were very quickly accepted within the Conservative Party after its heavy election defeat in 1945, following a successful internal struggle by the Right Progressives against the traditional Tories. In the late 1940s and 1950s, the Conservative leadership, under the influence of

R. A. Butler, Iain MacLeod and others, moved closer to the policies of the Labour Party under Clement Attlee and then under Hugh Gaitskell than at any previous moment. The result was the form of consensus politics known colloquially as 'Butskellism'.

In Butskellism, a commitment to state planning and intervention, to the financing of social welfare and to political and economic reform, made Conservatism appear as a mild form of Labourism, distinguishable only by the concern of Conservatives to protect the traditional institutions of legal authority (the courts, the police and the law itself) and the liberty of the individual from the encroachments of the increasingly powerful welfare state (see Gamble, 1974, ch. 3). In other words, the dominance of social democracy as popular politics in the 1940s had very quickly forced a transformation in the political thinking of the traditional party of the English ruling class: to an extent that is now the subject of regret on the part of the groups that seized the leadership of the Conservative Party in 1974. By 1951, the year of the Festival of Britain and also of the third post-war election, the Conservative leadership had succeeded in extinguishing the then popular view of their party as a party of privilege, by moving onto the terrain of 'consensus politics', giving support to the expansion of the welfare state and to the expansion of state expenditure on some social needs.

Social democracy was also increasingly taken as a description of the goal and rationale of an increasing number of liberal professionals employed by the state. The project of social reconstruction articulated through the state involved the deployment of large numbers of planners, researchers and executives to work on the development of state housing and of industry, a considerable increase in the numbers of health service professionals, social workers and teachers, and a variety of other professionals employed to work for the state. These professionals were officially seen then, as to some extent they still are, as *servicing agents*, giving support to the larger task of social reconstruction in specific areas in a non-political and neutral fashion. But in the various areas of their work, the professionals did gain enormous areas of power and discretion for themselves. Architects and town planners did not

merely service the larger housing policies of the post-war
governments: they designed the new towns, the new council
estates and, latterly, the new high-rise flats which were
intended to provide new leisure space and new homes for the
working class. The officials employed by the housing departments exercised considerable discretion over the allocation of
the new housing stock. The increasing number of child care
workers employed by local authority children's departments
won a considerable reputation professionally for the support
they provided for broken and troubled families, but they also
exercised very considerable discretionary power over parents
and children, especially over decisions about the adequacy of
the parents' (or parent's) childrearing and the question as to
whether a child could be kept at home. Most obviously of all,
the introduction of Lord Beveridge's plans for universal social
security placed large sections of the population (for example
the unemployed, the disabled and pensioners) in a position of
great dependency on state officials, especially in respect of
the calculation of needs and entitlements to particular forms
of state benefit. From its earliest days, the welfare state proper
was characterised by the problem of thousands of entitlements
going unclaimed, officially because of the popular fear of the
stigma of state dependency, but also because of the loss of
dignity involved for individuals in having to submit to official
exercise of discretion. In some areas, like child care, the sense
of powerlessness of the client was exacerbated by the great
social distance of the (usually working-class) client from the
(almost exclusively middle-class) professional. What was rarely
voiced at the time, but was quite clearly important, was that
this discretionary power was exercised on behalf of the state,
by whom the professional was employed. In no direct or
meaningful sense was the state professional *accountable* in
any recognisably democratic sense to his or her client, or to
the client's family or community, for decisions taken in a
particular case. The consequence of this professionalisation
of the reconstructed social democratic state was that the
conception of *social need* at the heart of social democracy
was actually put into application concretely by professionals
and not by the class itself or even on its direct behalf. In the
hands of the social worker, economic and material needs were

often recognised as being inextricably or essentially psychological, whilst in the hands of the housing department officials,
the cry for help of a severely disadvantaged family was identifiable as evidence of social inadequacy.

So the 'social democracy' anticipated with such widespread
popular enthusiasm in 1945 was qualified and confused in a
very short time by the advent of a 'social democratic' Conservatism (Butskellism) on the one hand, and by the growth
of an essentially middle-class and unaccountable liberal professionalism, employed by the state, on the other. These two
forms of 'social democracy' have of course continued to be
confused with the original social democratic aspirations of
1945, which were concerned to underwrite the development
of the state as an instrument of economic planning by a
democratisation of the state, in order to end the monopoly
of decision-making power of the established ruling class.

In this book, therefore, our use of the term 'social democracy' is beset with problems. It is made no simpler by the
launching in January 1981 of the Council for Social Democracy, later transformed into the Social Democratic Party. The
SDP's announced commitments are to the 'values, principles
and policies of social democracy', which is amplified only to
mean the desire 'to create an open, classless and more equal
society, one which rejects ugly prejudices based upon sex,
race or religion' ('Limehouse Declaration', 25 January 1981).

Like the social democratic commitment of Butskellism,
the social democracy of the SDP is mainly identifiable by its
lack of commitment to social democracy as a specifically
working-class politics. Indeed, its most clearly proclaimed
commitment is its opposition to the 'extremism' involved in
any attempt to restore class politics to the centre of the
Labour Party's programme.[1]

So the meaning of 'social democracy' is tarnished and
confused. But I still want to retain the term in this account
where possible because of the importance of its stress on
social provision and democracy, taken together, as a form of
socialist politics. In 1945, as we have said, these twin demands
were a very popular and necessary form of politics constructed
by and for a largely working-class Labour movement, albeit
with considerable support of sections of the middle class.

They were a recognition of a broad social need (and not simply of unmet individual needs): the general need to prevent a return to the anarchy and inequality of a free market economy and also to initiate a genuine and thoroughgoing democratisation of British political institutions.

For reasons explored by Ralph Miliband and others, the social democratic politics of the Labour Party were inadequate to this task (see Miliband, 1961; Nairn, 1964). Keynesian economics proved to be capable of mitigating the worst effects of capitalist economic cycles (there was no immediate return to the deep slump of the early 1930s); but there was no *fundamental* liberation from social inequality or from the routine of the working week spent in depressing factory and office buildings, working for capital. The presence of a significant majority of Labour MPs in the parliament of 1945–51 and the use of Fabian intellectuals as advisers in the formulation of policy did not convey any real sense to the class that it had won power for itself. In the face of the concerted opposition of organised private industry (later to be examined by Arnold Rogow) and in the context of the significant resistance from the civil service, 'parliamentary socialism' could not conjure the promised 'social democracy' (see Rogow, 1955; Crossman, 1972).

To record this failure of parliamentary socialism is, however, to signal the continuing importance of the programme it failed to achieve. The demands for social justice (in the distribution of economic resources and rewards) and the demand for a caring community are still unmet in Britain, which remains one of the most class-bound and uncompassionate of the older industrial societies. The Scandinavian social democracies, by contrast, have succeeded in putting an end to the worst features of class inequality and privilege and also have been significantly more generous in the provision of state support and facilities for the mentally ill, the disabled, the elderly, and unemployed claimants than has Britain. Overcrowded and ancient mental hospitals like Rampton, homes for the elderly reconstructed out of nineteenth-century workhouses, and decrepit hospitals servicing working-class areas, are monuments to the limitations placed on the welfare state in post-war Britain, and they have few parallels in Scandinavia

or Northern Europe generally. And we shall see later that
even the prisons are now being described officially as a 'disgrace to civilised society'.

So the social democratic commitments of 1945 remain as
unfulfilled demands. They did not then, and would not now,
constitute a thoroughgoing socialist politics in themselves:
they could never resolve the fundamental contradiction
between the drive to profit that is essential to the capitalist
mode of production and the popular demand for an economics of social need. Nor could they resolve the contradiction
between the need for capital to ensure its ultimate domination
over institutions of state power and the popular demand for
democratisation of the local and national state. But they were
a politics that could have advanced, and still could advance,
the cause of the more fundamental transformation to socialism, by giving voice to popular demands for social justice and
for real democratic involvement in, and control of, state social
provision.

Social democracy and social order

In the law and order campaigns mounted by the Right during
the 1970s, the ultimate source of the allegedly rapid decline
in the social order in Britain was the advance of 'socialism'.
In particular, as we saw in Chapter 1, socialism was indicted
for its indifference towards the 'rule of law' and also for its
mistaken assumptions as to the real character of 'human
nature'.[2] Speaking on BBC Television's *Campaign Report* on
20 April 1979, Mr David Howell, appearing as 'a Conservative
spokesman on Home Affairs' made the connections in the
following way:

> We are saying that if you have a background, a philosophy,
> let's say, which on the whole . . . treats private effort and
> private property with some contempt and does not place
> the upholding of the rule of law absolutely as the highest
> priority, then this creates an atmosphere in which you get
> vandalism, disrespect for the law and the vast increase in
> the crimes which we have seen. And that worries us very
> much indeed and worries many millions of people.

We can see now that the 'socialism' being identified by the spokesman for the Right throughout the 1970s was a hybrid of the various forms of 'social democracy' which were elaborated during the earlier period of consensus. The targets of the attack (from politicians, police and judiciary) centred on the permissive child-centredness of the professional social worker, but also special attention was given to the subversive attitude to law of the trade unions and 'the left'. They also extended to include the socially reformist priorities of Labour governments and even of earlier conservative governments as well.

The essential argument of the Right, as we saw in Chapter 1, was that the key to the creation and maintenance of social order was never to dilute the majesty (if not the terror) of the law, and never to subvert or to 'relativise' the claims of 'morality'.[3] By implication, therefore, social democracy in all its forms was seen to be 'lawless' and 'amoral', if not by intention then by default.

The 'social democracy' that was dominant in the Labour government of 1945—51, and which still had echoes in Labour circles later in the post-war period, is unrecognisable in these right-wing attacks. So far from being lawless and amoral, social democracy had a very clear commitment to the creation of social order and to the defence and extension of the upright morality of the nuclear family, dominated by the respectable working man. It is true that the project of social reconstruction did not centre around the supremacy of law as an instrument of social order. Instead it depended on the success of the social democratic project of reconstruction itself (in creating a sense of social justice in a caring community). The key to the creation of social order here was the ability of a Labour government to conjure the conditions for a successful reconstruction of traditional class society.

Thus social democratic conceptions (or theories) of the sources of disorder in society were (and to some extent still are) altogether different from the theories advanced by the Right. The consensus of the later post-war period served often to suppress these vital differences from public view.

The sources of social disorder for social democrats were twofold. In particular, of course, crimes against property were understood by social democrats to be a product of the ongoing inequalities endemic in unreformed capitalist societies. They were produced by the poverty that was experienced by the low-paid and, especially, by the unemployed. In this respect, crime could be combatted at the level of the economic policy of government. But crimes against property were also produced by the tendency of an unreformed and profit-orientated capitalism to place an unchecked and overwhelming emphasis on the ownership of material possessions as the key to worldly success. In the study group report, *Crime: A Challenge to Us All*, produced by the Labour Party in 1964, these earlier social democratic arguments were repeated with considerable force. Conservative politics were seen as encouraging what R. H. Tawney had described as an 'acquisitive society', stressing individual material advancement, and 'weakening the moral fibre of individuals'. In 1964, as in 1945, 'socialists [would] substitute the ideal of mutual service and work towards a society in which everyone has a chance to play a full and responsible life' (Labour Party, 1964, p. 5). So capitalism, unless subject to control by the state, had a general tendency to release *demoralising* forces into society and individuals. *Unreformed* capitalism was the obstacle to an orderly ('responsible') and productive life of 'mutual service and work'.

The general tendencies of capitalism were amplified, especially so far as 1940s social democrats were concerned, by the specific effects of the war. In an essay written in 1947, the social democratic emigré criminologist, Hermann Mannheim, summarised the arguments about the effects of the war as follows:

it would be altogether wrong to regard the rise in crime as something extraordinary or particularly alarming. It is nothing but the natural result of six years of total war with all its inevitable moral, psychological and economic repercussions, and there is consequently nothing original in the many official and unofficial attempts to explain the present situation. The general cheapening of all values, loosening of family ties, weakened respect for the law, human life and property, especially property of the State and of big firms, scarcity of all consumer goods, the black market,

and the resulting rise in prices, rationing and the well-justified austerity policy of the Government, easy accessibility of many bomb-damaged houses, and lack of trained police officers and, finally, the activities of deserters are, usually, maybe rightly, put forward. It was Mr. Chuter Ede, the Home Secretary, who said 'No one would have a thought of stealing a second hand shirt in 1939; today the sight of a shirt on a clothes line has become a temptation.'
(Mannheim, 1947, reprinted in Mannheim, 1955, p. 110)

The increases in crime being referred to here were a reference to the general rise in the number of indictable offences known to the police throughout the wartime period (see Table 2.1) and also to the increase between 1939 and 1943 in the number of offences that had occurred against the Defence Regulations (which governed a variety of matters thought relevant to the proper pursuit of the war, from the control of industrial and building operations to the protection of financial markets). Offences against the Defence Regulations increased from 59,911 in 1939 to 186,429 in 1943, before declining slightly in the last two years of the war.

There was no sign, in the immediate aftermath of the war, of any reversal in the trend of rising crime. But social democrats insisted that the problems were temporary, being a product of certain obvious features of wartime conditions and also being open to the ameliorative effects of the programme of social reconstruction that had just been initiated in 1945.

These obvious features included, in particular, a collapse or substantial reduction in the moral socialisation and personal regulation of children by families. The criminal statistics recorded by the police during the war did not record the age of apprehended offenders and therefore were not presented separately for juveniles, but the widespread assumption was that the bulk of the property crime causing concern was committed by children and adolescents. Particular anxiety centred around the involvement of juveniles in looting, especially in London during the winter of 1940—1, which resulted in 4,584 cases being heard before the metropolitan courts during 1941 alone. In 1942, the International Committee of the Howard League ('a committee of men and women of thirteen

Table 2.1 Indictable offences known to the police 1939–45 (excluding offences against Defence Regulations)

	Larceny	Breaking and entering	Receiving, frauds and false pretences	Sexual offences	Violence against the person	Other	Total
1939	219,478	52,295	17,561	5,015	2,899	6,523	303,771
1940	225,671	49,340	16,998	4,626	2,424	6,055	305,114
1941	268,738	52,876	21,392	5,608	2,727	7,314	358,655
1942	267,789	56,166	21,079	6,766	3,050	10,039	364,889
1943	272,186	58,543	20,964	7,784	3,432	9,851	372,760
1944	297,930	73,890	21,922	8,079	4,162	9,027	415,010
1945	323,310	108,266	23,254	8,546	4,743	10,275	478,394

Source: *Criminal Statistics 1939–1945* (published 1947), Cmnd 7227, London, HMSO.

nationalities brought together by the fortunes — or misfortunes — or war')[4] began to meet in order to produce explanations for the problems of youth that were likely to be encountered after the war. In the introduction to their report, eventually published in 1947 under the title of *Lawless Youth*, the authors recall that they had 'visualised the problem, now a grim reality, of winning back for society, the children and young men whom war had made rebels and outlaws', and they commented on the need for the child care services and the juvenile justice system to be a means for reintegrating lawless youth into their families, and the means for giving support to those families weakened or broken by the experience of the war.

The 'grim reality' being referred to in 1947 was the increase in the number of indictable offences known to the police, which continued to increase into 1948 (see Table 2.2).

The source therefore of the allegedly increasing involvement of young people in crimes against property and persons was the effect of the war in dividing up families. This threat to the family was expressed in, amongst other things, the increase in the number of illegitimate births during the war from 25,942 in 1939 (4.19 per cent of recorded live births) to 64,064 in 1945 (9.35 per cent of live births). These increases resulted from the increased geographical mobility experienced by both men and women during this period, as many more women had the opportunity to leave home to work in factories and/or to join the armed forces, and the majority of men were fully mobilised and dispersed away from their own neighbourhood and community. In 1943 a Ministry of Health sub-committee reported on the problem of the unmarried mother, and recommended the appointment of domiciliary social workers to help deal with the unmarried mother and her child in the community.

The provision of domiciliary services was supported by the creation of state nurseries for young children on a previously unparalleled scale:

the partial mobilisation of women, the need for many of them to spend a large part of their day working in the factories, the absence of fathers on service, or relatives at

Table 2.2 *Indictable offences known to the police 1946—8*

	Larceny	Breaking and entering	Receiving	Fraud and false pretences	Sexual offences	Violence against the person	Other offences	Total
1946	310,650	114,690	8,130	14,080	9,329	4,062	11,548	472,489
1947	330,918	111,789	8,976	18,459	9,999	4,408	14,027	498,576
1948	349,358	112,665	9,044	19,326	10,922	5,183	16,186	502,684

Source: *Criminal Statistics, England and Wales* (1959), Cmnd 1100, London, HMSO.

work, and the destruction of houses by bombing required the state to intervene in another way in providing residential nurseries where young children could be given the care and attention impossible where family life had become non-existent, and where they could be protected from enemy attack.

(Heywood, 1959, p. 136)

The state's involvement in providing facilities for unmarried mothers and for working parents was now justified, therefore, as part of a project of providing a form of family life for children who would otherwise not experience it, as a result of the effects of the war (see Riley, 1979).

The better known measures taken by the state in evacuating thousands of children from major urban areas and other potential targets of enemy attack, taking them away from their parents and placing them in the temporary care of families in rural areas, were also important in wartime experience in underlining the importance of the family:

this does not seem to have been accepted until the wartime disruptions between 1939 and 1945 demonstrated its truth, the fact that the family still preferred to cling together as a fundamental unit in the face of every obstacle. In spite of carefully contrived plans to evacuate young mothers and children to safer areas, they refused to remain divided, and gradually, in ones and threes and then in groups and crowds, they returned to their homes and family circle.

(Heywood, 1959, pp. 134–5)

Support had to be given, both economically and 'ideologically', to families in trouble (in need of care and protection), and the attempt had to be made to create substitute family settings for children and adolescents whose real families were temporarily or permanently non-existent or unable to cope. Further action to support troubled and broken families occurred quickly after the election of the Labour Government in 1945, but the immediate spur to action appears to have been an individual incident. The level of maladministration and indeed repression in the existing child care services was graphically highlighted in 1945 by the death of 12-year-old Dennis McNeill from a cardiac failure resulting from violent attack from a foster parent and also from undernourishment.[5] The Monckton Inquiry, reporting on the incident, put the blame for McNeill's death on the division of responsibility for the child's placement in a foster home between two committees of local government as well as between two local authorities. By 1948, the recommendation of a committee of enquiry, under Dame Myra Curtis, into the regulation of the standards of the child care services recommended that formal responsibility be given to a single government agency (the Home Office). This was incorporated into the Children's Act of 1948. Child care was made the responsibility of a national state agency, rather than being left to voluntary and amateur care workers, and volunteer foster parents.

Weakness or inconsistency in the control exercised over children by the family was seen as an encouragement to delinquency, especially in the conditions of the wartime period. Lack of parental control left children prey to a variety of other malignant influences (for example the black market), and temptations were provided in the increasing opportunities there were for illegitimate gain (especially, during the early years of the war, from the looting of properties hit by the air raids). Hermann Mannheim commented on 'the indirect effect of shelter life, particularly on juveniles' and observed in 1941 that

> [juveniles] hardly ever go to the same shelters as their own families . . . parental control has become a thing of the past . . . and even the police experience great difficulties in tracing juvenile delinquents.
>
> (Mannheim, 1941, reprinted in Mannheim, 1955, p. 52)

I repeat that in nearly all the accounts of delinquency and crime written in the 1940s, the problems were seen as temporary. In the period of social reconstruction after the war the family would be restored and strengthened, and the sense of community experienced temporarily in the wartime period would be institutionalised as a permanent feature of social and economic relationships. Crime and delinquency, the expression of inconsistent family control and socialisation brought about by the war, would decline and lose significance in proportion to the success of social reconstruction.

In 1949, indeed, in the immediate aftermath of the Labour Government's Children Act and Criminal Justice Act,[6] the number of offences known to the police did decline (see Table 2.3).

The increase in the official crime rate in 1950 was almost entirely due to police activity in the pursuit of fraud and corruption in and around the black market. Otherwise, the official rates again appeared to provide firm support for Mannheim's arguments that the post-war crime problem was temporary, and that it could be reduced by the general process of social reconstruction, coupled with the effective intervention of treatment workers. Social order could indeed be realised via state support for the family and by economic policies providing personal and social security for the population as a whole (according to need). Healthy social relations and healthy personalities (the twin sources of order) were a product of effective social reconstruction, and not the continued attempt to produce social order through the imposition of law.

The threat to social order emanated, however, not only from juvenile offenders. The social democratic accounts of the 1940s were also preoccupied with a variety of so-called 'economic offences', involving adults as well as youths. Apart from the outbreaks of looting mentioned earlier, particular attention was given to a tripling in the number of cases of smuggling (with 16,000 interceptions or seizures in the financial year 1945–6). At the end of the war, attention was also focused on a large number of currency offences, which were known to have been the work of members of armed forces on the Continent, and also of British visitors to the Continent (see Mannheim, 1955, pp. 111–12). In 1949, Harold Silcock published a reinterpretation of the increases in crimes of theft between 1938 and 1947, and suggested that the 78 per cent increase over the period was in part to be explained as resulting from the activities of black marketeers and others. The value of the property stolen 'in transit' during this period, and later written off (notably textiles) increased from £2.5 million in 1938 to £13 million in 1947 (Silcock, 1949). The

Table 2.3 Indictable offences known to the police 1948–50

	Larceny	Breaking and entering	Receiving	Fraud and false pretences	Sexual offences	Violence against the person	Other offences	Total
1948	349,358	112,665	9,044	19,326	10,922	5,183	16,186	502,684
1949	301,591	91,445	7,206	17,358	12,015	5,235	15,019	459,869
1950	301,075	92,839	7,586	27,561	13,185	6,249	14,946	461,136

Source: *Criminal Statistics, England and Wales* (1959) Cmnd 1100, London, HMSO.

overall number of indictable offences of fraud and false pretences known to the police increased from 13,122 in 1945 to 27,415 in 1951, an increase of 108.9 per cent, by far the largest rate of increase of any of the offence categories (*Criminal Statistics, England and Wales*, 1959).

For Mannheim, these increases, like the delinquencies of youth, were products of wartime and immediate post-war conditions, and not, as Sir Cyril Burt and others in conservative circles within psychology were to argue, the result of ineffective repression of 'mendacity'. The prevalence of first offenders in the statistics on looting, smuggling, wartime profiteering, and offences against food control and lighting regulations, was a demonstration of the fact that these activities were engaged in particularly by juveniles and young adults, *temporarily* out of parental control, and presented with one-off opportunities for material gain. There was no evidence of any general outbreak of 'pathology' or of any general commitment to a criminal career (although commitments of this kind might eventually result, in the absence of proper governmental initiatives to control the economic offences of the more powerful):

> Looting and the various types of profiteering are nothing but more pronounced forms of general patterns of anti-social behaviour which remain unpunished in times of peace, and their perpetrators, though public nuisances, do not therefore rank as professional law-breakers. In other words, the juvenile looter may represent only a further stage in the normal development of the slum child who is used to picking up things lying about on the pavement, and the war profiteer is only the somewhat more unscrupulous war edition of the smart businessman who, under normal circumstances, manages to keep to the right side of the law.
> (Mannheim, 1942, reprinted in Mannheim, 1955, p. 102)

Mannheim insisted on it being the duty of the courts to enforce existing laws against the 'white-collar' criminal, and in particular fraud (which he saw as economic gain won without productive effort):

As long as the extreme dangers resulting from this type of anti-social behaviour are not clearly realised, and as long as legislators and administrators of criminal justice fail to take appropriate measures against white-collar crime, it is nonsensical to expect the penal system to be successful in its fight against the ordinary thief and burglar and small fry.

(Mannheim, 1946, p. 119)

The legitimacy and effectiveness of Labour government initiatives across a wide range of issues were therefore connected with the enforcement of law against economic offenders as much as against the 'ordinary' thieves and burglars: 'It is becoming clearer every day that social reconstruction and the future of crime are largely dependent on the attitude of society towards the control of economic offences' (Mannheim, 1946, p. 120).

A report in *The Times* some two years later makes clear what Mannheim had in mind (for the immediate post-war period of 'austerity') in urging action on economic offences, and the importance for Labour of the enforcement of law 'without fear or favour':

On 4 May . . . Mr Gaitskell, in his capacity as Minister of Fuel and Technology, during the second reading of the Motor Spirit Regulation Bill, informed the House of Commons that the loss of petrol to the black market was estimated by the Government at 100,000 tons a year. (The Vick Committee, which had just reported, had a figure of 160,000 tons.) He continued that this [was] 'a moral scandal which should not be tolerated. We have a remarkably high standard in such matters and the petrol black market is an unfortunate lapse from that standard. It is surely wrong that people should benefit from the black market at the expense of fellow-motorists who are playing the game and obeying the rules.'

(*The Times*, 5 May 1948)

One of Mannheim's concerns in his definitive text on *Criminal Justice and Social Reconstruction* was to urge an extension of the criminal law into the 'world of business'. He thought it worthwhile to examine the use of law for this purpose by the Soviet Union to see what lessons could be drawn for Britain (Mannheim, 1946, pp. 195—9). In any such expansion of law, of course, most business people and capitalists would have nothing to fear: the 'economic offences' being targeted (of black market fraud, currency offences, etc.) were all presented as dishonest and immoral departures from normal, honest capitalist endeavour. Such dishonesty and immorality was more likely to occur, and less likely to be noticed and prosecuted, in a market that was uncontrolled by the state, and also unpoliced by the law.

So these economic offenders had to be apprehended and prosecuted in order to defend the larger project of social reconstruction. Failure to pursue the offenders would mean that the young people who were not under parental control would gravitate to these alternative 'role models', and that they too would be attracted to the illicit and parasitical pursuit of wealth, in defiance of the sacrifices and austerity being endured by the mass of the population, who had been promised social reconstruction and a general economic recovery.

The social democratic criminology of the 1940s was therefore very clearly committed to the defence of a specific conception of social and moral order which would *in law* allow various forms of state intervention into families and also into the world of business. If this failed, over the period of social reconstruction and later, to produce social order in the long term, this is not attributable to the amorality or lawlessness of social democracy's original commitments. It may indeed be attributable to the inability of social democratic economic and social policy to produce the real economic and social conditions for such an orderly and moral community to arise. And that particular failure may derive, in no small way, from the loss of nerve of the original post-war Labour government in and around 1948, the 'climax of Labourism' described by Ralph Miliband, from which the Labour Party has not since recovered. Miliband speaks of a fatal flaw in the assumptions of many of Labour's supporters in 1945, namely that the measures of 1945—8 were 'the beginning of the social revolu-

tion to which [they] believed the Labour Party was dedicated'.
Instead, Labour's

> leaders took these achievements to *be* the social revolution.
> Of course, they would readily agree that there was still
> much to be done to consolidate the social revolution. But,
> as far as they were concerned, the bigger part of the task
> had, by 1950, been completed. And they therefore were
> genuinely impatient with the argument that there remained
> a citadel to be conquered. They believed it to be already
> occupied.
>
> (Miliband, 1961, p. 308)

The 'disorder' that began to emerge after 1950 — with adult
crime statistics rising from 1950 onwards, statistics on juvenile
delinquency beginning to rise exponentially from 1955, and
considerable public anxiety beginning over the violence of
the Teddy Boy and of youth generally at around 1953 — may
therefore be understood, in part, as a product of the unfinished task of social reconstruction. They were expressions of
the continuing social divisions between working-class youth
(and some working-class adults) and 'authority', divisions
produced by the continuing existence of a fundamentally
divided class society.

Contrary to contemporary attacks from the Right, social
democratic criminology was nothing if not moralistic in the
offences it prioritised and the explanations it advanced of
such offences. Indeed, it is likely that the problems experienced by social democratic criminology derive in part from
the limitations of such a moralistic frame of reference.

The explanations of juvenile delinquency advanced by
Mannheim depended, as we have seen, on the theory of inadequate or inconsistent socialisation and a theory of corruption, operating together. Once the account had identified
the existence of a cohort of inadequately socialised youth, a
space was, of course, opened out in official criminological
debate and also in everyday common-sense journalism for a
full-scale investigation of various types of moral corruption
present in the population.

Mannheim himself, always in close touch with official policy-making circles,[7] identified the importance of members of the armed forces who had either deserted or been demobilised from the Continent. Many of these seemed to have developed great skills in smuggling, fraudulent conversion and other sophisticated economic offences. So far as these deserters were concerned

> Very soon after the onset of the crime-wave, the view was expressed by the authorities and the press that the rise in crime was largely due to the activities of this group of outcasts of whom, according to official estimates, there were about 20,000 at large (as against 80,000 after World War I). Unable to get identity cards and ration books in the legal way, they were said to be living largely on their wits, and always ready to commit even serious crimes.
> (Mannheim, 1947, reprinted in Mannheim, 1955, p. 114)

Mannheim notes that the attempt to encourage the deserters to return to normal life in the community by the granting of amnesty was largely unsuccessful, because of 'the force of retributive tendencies in the population'.[8]

For commentators with 'retributive tendencies', deserters were obviously not the only source of poor example and corruption affecting the youthful population. In 1947, *The Justice of the Peace and Local Government Review* moved from a discussion of desertion to note 'the presence in the country of a fairly large number of aliens of various nationalities, refugees and others, whose activities may not always keep them on the right side of the law'. The article continues:

> We do not wish to say too much on this subject, because we are uncertain of the real facts, but we do feel strongly that as far as this class of person is concerned the Courts have a special duty. The Aliens Order 1920, Article 12(b)(a) and the third schedule of the Order set out the circumstances in which a Court may recommend to the Secretary of State that a convicted alien be deported. We feel that it is the duty of the Courts at the present time to approach this question of recommendation from the standpoint that

it is for the alien, if he can, to show cause why he should
not be recommended rather than for the court to consider
why he should. We should not at any time keep in this
country aliens who refuse to obey our laws unless there are
strongly mitigating circumstances in their favour, and at
the present time, it is doubly important to get rid of them,
and so leave the police free to deal with the native criminals
who cannot be deported.

(*Justice of the Peace and Local Government Review*, CX(2)
12 January 1947, editorial on 'The Crime Wave')

As always, once the scapegoating of a particular segment of
society begins, for its alleged role in 'moral decline', the
'undermining of authority', or officially recorded crime, the
nature of the debate over causes tends to shift ground. Causa-
tion is thought to have been established — the corruption of
the youthful, the naive or the disturbed by outsiders is seen
as the self-evident explanation of the presence of pathology
(crime, deviance, dissent) in an otherwise healthy society. As
always, conservatives were quick to open out this space, and
a variety of reports in the press speculated at length on the
relationship between the presence of 'aliens' in the population,
especially from Poland and Eastern Europe, and the crime
wave. Little attention was given to the fact that these migrants
were the subject of considerable discrimination by the British
host society. But social democratic attempts to identify the
source of corruption as the criminality of the powerful were
in this way being successfully challenged and qualified by
essentially nationalistic accounts, stressing the connection
between crime and aliens.[9]

In the last years of the war and in the immediate post-war
period, the source of moral corruption were the 'spivs' and
the 'drones'. According to *The Daily Telegraph*, these terms
derived from the racecourse fraternity of the 1890s, but in
the 1940s they were applied to sharp practitioners, con-men
and other skilled operators on the margins of legitimate and
illegitimate business practices: it was alleged, in characteristically Labour style, that the spivs and drones were making
' "easy pickings" at the expense of the wider community'
(Hopkins, 1963, p. 100). According to one later commen-

tator, public anxiety was excited, in the main, by the more violent and 'really' criminal of the spivs. When the spiv appeared in the form of the 'wide boy', he met with a rather more tolerant, not to say admiring, public response: it was a 'cocking of the snook' at the rigidity and bureaucracy of the 'age of austerity'. Alan Deacon observes that the spiv, as a black marketeer, also actually provided nylons, chocolates, and other luxuries which people *wanted* to buy as a means of mitigating the overall atmosphere of austerity, and that spivs were often admired as 'exploiting a clumsy bureaucracy rather than [their] customers'. In addition:

> Arthur Helliwell's tales of 'spivery' made his Sunday column of the *People* the most widely read in the country [while] the cartoonist, Osbert Lancaster, and the comedian, Arthur English, made the flashily dressed 'wide boy' a national character.
>
> (Deacon, 1980, p. 446)

In a situation of national shortage of labour, however, the government had to act against what Prime Minister Clement Attlee called 'a section of the population which serves no useful purpose' (*Hansard*, 6 August 1947), and particular attention was given to the drones, the able-bodied but unemployed 'idle rich' of whom it was felt there was one million, 'most of whom spent their time in gambling dens and night clubs' (Deacon, 1980). If the drones were idle, the spivs were also likely to move out from the black market into other forms of crime, especially in the bad company they encountered in the black market.

Thus the continuation of property crime and also particular instances of violence were usually attributed, in official social democratic circles, to the corrupt and corrupting influences of deserters and black marketeers and, latterly, the spivs. In 1948 *The Times* observed that the deserters

> had been taught the techniques of violence in wartime and were bitter enough to exercise them now; indeed, London in 1946 attributed nine per cent of all crimes to them.
>
> (Hopkins, 1963, p. 150)

This commentator continues, in terms familiar to readers of Chapter 1 of this book, by remarking that

> By 1950 a legal paper had stated that the ordinary citizen no longer felt safe in his own home, and the Lord Chief Justice had earlier cited cases of old people trembling, often with good reason, when they heard a knock on the door at night. The statistics showed that every large school in the country could hope to have on the register a couple of active criminals who had no fear of the police.
>
> (Hopkins, 1963, p. 150)

Even the emergence of evidence of corruption at the highest levels of the civil service and industry could not be allowed to cast doubt on the essential health of social democratic order. In 1948 a series of public accusations were made by 'a promoter of business contracts', Mr Sidney Stanley, a Polish emigré, né Kohsychy, to the effect that junior ministers in the government and civil servants had taken special favours from industrial and commercial representatives in exchange for the firms which they represented being ensured government contracts. In the face of Conservative accusations of corruption in the government, an investigatory tribunal was established under the chairmanship of Mr Justice Lynskey, and the Labour government's Attorney-General, Mr Hartley Shawcross, chose to open the cross-examination of Mr Stanley and other witnesses personally. This was the first occasion in the history of tribunals on which government ministers had chosen to exercise this power. Mr Justice Lynskey himself opened proceedings by remarking that the 'whole question' facing his tribunal was to decide what could be counted as 'legitimate business' (Gross, 1963, pp. 284–6). But the tribunal did not spend much time on this question, concentrating instead on clearing the names of government ministers who had been placed under suspicion. In the end, no criminal charges were laid against any members of the government, but Mr John Belcher, Parliamentary Secretary at the Board of Trade, resigned after the publication of the tribunal's report, and Mr Stanley was deported, to criticisms that this was too severe a punishment and suspicions of a desire to have Mr

Stanley removed from the public eye.[10] Individual corruptors
had been identified, while the routine practices of the state
vis-à-vis private capitalist industry had been effectively rescued
from a detailed public scrutiny. This is also, of course, to
reassert that the 'economic offences' which were recognised
in 1940s social democratic criminology were indeed the
offences which were 'abnormal' to the routine practices of
capitalist production and distribution. They were the offences
of fraud located on the *fringes* of routine business or actually
in the illegitimate businesses involved in the black market.
These were the activities which were seen to be providing a
corrupt example to youth: there was no fundamental contradiction between the *normal* business of capitalism and moral
or social dislocation.

Thus social democratic criminology in the 1940s depended
as much on a specific theory of moral corruption as it did on
its socially reformist theory of inadequate socialisation. But
we should emphasise that the recognition of amoral or corrupt
influences was never connected, in social democratic criminology, to orthodox classical utilitarianism. The influence
exercised by the black marketeer or the corrupt capitalist on
youth did not operate at the level of *will*. Rather this 'moral
influence' worked alongside the economic deprivation experienced by individual youths and their inadequate early socialisation to produce an anti-social, criminal outcome.[11] What
was involved was the interaction, in a scientifically observable
fashion, of different causal factors. So the 'moral sense' of an
individual was an environmental, economic and social factor
primarily, and not a question of choice.

Social democracy and the enforcement of law

In this 'materialist—environmentalist' theory of social order,
the use of law either as a deterrent to crime or as punishment
proportional to a convicted person's 'responsibility' was
simply beside the point. The role of the legal institution,
instead, was to act as an arena for adjudicating the type of
treatment that would be most effective in particular cases. In
the previously mentioned report of the International Com-

mittee of the Howard League, the Howard League's Vice President contributed an essay on juvenile justice, in which she argued that

> the treatment of young offenders as well as of other children in moral danger, should be dictated by the special needs of the individual case: the 'offence', where such exists, will be regarded as a symptom.
>
> (Fry *et al.*, 1947, p. 20)[12]

The quest for the transformation of the juvenile court into a treatment tribunal and for the abolition of legal tests of 'guilt' and 'responsibility' was to continue until 1969 and the passage of the Children and Young Persons Act. It was a campaign that was waged most strongly by professionals working in the newly reformed child care services, discussed earlier, and by liberals working in areas of mental handicap and mental illness. Among the most vigorous proponents of this post-war revolution in the court's functions, however, were Fabians like Lord Longford and Barbara Wootton, whose influential *Social Science and Social Pathology*, published in 1959, argued for a *complete abandonment* of concepts of responsibility. What was required was 'choice of whatever course of action appears most likely to effect a cure of any particular case' (Wootton, 1959, p. 251).

The effective construction of social democratic order depended not on the unremitting enforcement of law, therefore, so much as on the proper diagnosis of symptoms in individual cases. So other Fabian writers of the 1950s, writing of the problems involved in diagnostic work, advanced on earlier, 'environmentalist' wisdoms on the broken family and identified the existence of 'multiple problem families'. Many of these problems were 'relational':

> The parents of many [delinquents] are not equipped to cope sensibly with the pressures and problems of the modern world. Many are educationally backward . . . [They are] parents with little insight, with few of the skills required for the care of children in the modern world and

without the self-confidence and poise needed to seek advice and follow it.

(Stewart, 1962, pp. 18, 25)

A 'Darwinian' realism is evident here, which seems to have been constructed in part in recognition of the existence of working-class people who did not take proper advantage of the opportunities given them by the welfare state and social reconstruction.[13] As a social democratic form of realism, it was to serve several functions, in explaining the continued existence of crime and delinquency in the aftermath of social reconstruction, and also in allowing for troublesome people and criminals to be incarcerated either in mental hospitals or in prisons. It also did service during the House of Commons debates on capital punishment in the 1950s in allowing certain Labour MPs to draw on a long-standing Fabian perspective and to argue for the retention of the gallows in effect as an instrument of social hygiene.[14]

The well known social democratic distrust of law as 'class law' is only a part of the explanation for post-war social democracy's emphasis on treatment and the beginnings of the campaign to transform the court into a 'family service' (see Clarke, 1980). The seeds for the creation of a new community and a modern social democracy had been sown by the welfare state reforms of 1945—8 and by the entry of the state into the management of the economy. It was now the task of professional social workers, aided by 'social science', to identify and where possible to correct the problems that were preventing families and individual family members from experiencing the full benefits of citizenship in the welfare state. Where correction was impossible, however, incarceration was necessary in order to defend the good order of the welfare state. These were difficult decisions, but for social democrats like Barbara Wootton they were essentially diagnostic decisions, to be taken by expert, state-employed psychiatrists and social workers. They were quite inappropriate for adjudication in law.

Social democratic attitudes to law were similar to their attitudes towards capitalism. On the one hand, social democrats stood in some awe of the legal system and of legal rules and precedent generally, impressed by the complexity of the apparatus whilst ignorant, like all non-professionals, of the detail of its procedures and rationales. This feeling of awe was compounded by the insistent assumption that the law's mysteries were a form of ruling-class deceit, and that the essential function of the law was the preservation and reproduction of ruling-class power and the existing distribution of property. The response of post-war social democrats to law was, therefore, confused. For a moment, in June 1946, it looked as if the logic of *democratising* recruitment to the courts might be pursued when the Home Secretary, Chuter Ede, announced the establishment of a Commission on the Justices of the Peace (the magistrates) to

> review the present arrangements for the selection and removal of Justices of the Peace . . . and to report what changes, if any, in that system, are necessary or desirable to ensure that only the most suitable persons are appointed to the Commission of the Peace.

For two years or so, a certain nervous anxiety was detectable in the pages of the *Justices of the Peace and Local Government Review*. But the Commission's report, published in 1948 and enacted in 1949, was hardly a fearsome attack on the traditional methods of selection of magistrates. The power exercised by the political parties over appointments was qualified by the recommendation that the major criterion for selection should be 'fitness for discharge of judicial duties' and by the recommendation that the local advisory committees, which nominated individuals for the Bench, should be drawn from 'different sections of the community'. A statutory age for retirement was established for the first time, and set at 75.

The major thrust of social democratic activity in relation to law has been not towards democratisation but towards modernisation and professionalisation (see Williams, 1951). Social democratic lawyers have concurred with Conservative lawyers in seeing the law as chronically out of date, but they have differed from Conservatives in recognising that the 'law's delays' in righting itself could pose serious problems for the larger project of social reconstruction. Family law in the late 1940s was in need of considerable modernisation in order to improve the legal position of children of broken families; industrial law needed revision to take account of the increase in the size of a white-collar working class; and commercial law needed to be updated in the aftermath of nationalisation and other changes in the state's relationship with business. Social democrats also differed from Conservatives in recognising that this project of modernisation was unlikely to emerge out of the self-activity of judges and lawyers. In a collection of essays on *Law Reform Now*, published in 1963 in advance of the election of the second postwar Labour government, the essential logic of social democratic legal argument was pursued to its conclusion:

> The problem of bringing the law up-to-date and keeping it up-to-date is largely one of machinery; and if the machinery is to work efficiently at a time, such as ours, which is a time of thorough and rapid technological and social change, it must be kept in continuous operation and minded by full-time personnel.
>
> (Gardiner and Martin, 1963, p. 1)

One of the first initiatives of the Labour government elected in 1964 was to establish the Law Commission, with the express function of investigating the legacy of English law in discrete areas, and recommending how the often contradictory principles established could be made coherent and 'codified'.

So the essential argument of social democrats towards law, as towards capitalism, was that the tiger could be tamed through state intervention. And just as state intervention in a capitalist economy would ensure that the processes of production and distribution could be reorganised according to *social need*, so state intervention in law would ensure that a modernised law would take the newly powerful interests (and *legal needs*) of 'the people' into account. As early as 1949, in the Legal Aid and Advice Act, the principle was recognised that it was a duty of the state to provide the services of a lawyer (in private practice) at public expense to people who had a legal problem but did not have sufficient means to pursue it.

By the middle 1970s, after the massive expansion of legal aid
provided for by the state for such purposes and the establishment of duty solicitor schemes, neighbourhood legal advice
centres and unofficial law centres financed indirectly by the
state, the social democratic plea for modernisation and codifi-
cation had been transformed: a modernised and codified law
was being taken to the people (who were experiencing a
variety of social problems) by professional lawyers whose
(extremely lucrative) business was *to transform these social
problems into legal ones* (see Bankowski and Mungham, 1976,
ch. 3). Once again, as in the transformation of child care and
juvenile justice, the fundamental reproduction of social
inequality, even in a welfare state, had been displaced onto
another 'terrain'; and the task of managing the problem was
given over to professionals in a position of dependency on
the state, and in an authoritative and unaccountable position
over their clients.

Even if the law required modernisation and was suspec-
ted of being at base an instrument of class power, this did not
mean that the social democrats of the 1940s were in favour
of withdrawal from law enforcement. It is true that the police
were in some disfavour in the immediate aftermath of the
1945 election. The force was still remembered for its role
during the General Strike and also for its defence of the
Fascist marches in the 1930s. In addition, the aristocratic
style still adopted by many chief constables, most of whom
were products of public shools, was very much resented by
the new Labour government and by a radicalised population
as a whole. The uniformed and hierarchical police force was
compared rather unfavourably by social democrats, and by
the population in general, with the much more representative
and accountable local auxiliary police and civil defence wardens of the wartime years.[15] Recruitment of new manpower
into the police force had been at a standstill in 1941—5, since
most potential constables were taken directly into the armed
forces; and the level of police pay had been allowed to fall to
around the national average. This remained the situation in
the immediate post-war period, and in 1949 there was a very
high number of vacancies in all forces, and especially in the
Metropolitan Police. The size of the police force actually *fell*

from 63,980 in 1939 (one policeman for every 648 in the population) to 60,190 in 1949 (one for every 727); and expenditure on the police also fell as a proportion of total government spending from 2.4 per cent in 1938—9 to 1.3 per cent in 1949—50 (Martin and Wilson, 1968, pp. 70—1).

This decline of the police was in no way the result of any concerted attack from the government. The Police Act of 1946 was actually of some help to the force, in introducing some efficiencies through amalgamation, in providing for new equipment, and also in providing support for the opening of the National Police College. But the fragile — cooperative but cool — relationships of the early post-war period eventually strengthened and warmed to the point where, by 1949, the government was able to accept the recommendations of the Oaksey Committee for substantial pay rises for police (bringing them well above the national average and having a rapid effect on the police's recruitment problems).

There is little doubt that the publicity given by the popular press to the murder of PC Edgar by an army deserter in February 1948 played a part in the improvement of the police's fortunes, and it may also be the case that the efforts of Sir Harold Scott, as Metropolitan Police Commissioner, to improve the image of the force by cooperation in the making of films like *The Blue Lamp* (in which policemen were depicted as folk heroes) had some impact on public opinion (see Chibnall, 1977, p. 270). Equally important, however, was the fact that the Labour Party in government came increasingly to need the help of the force, *politically*, especially after 1947. The renewal of Mosleyite activity in London in 1947 (which the Left tried to counter by breaking up Fascist meetings and marches) and also the spread of unofficial strikes through London and Merseyside docks during 1947—50 were both 'managed' by the Labour government in terms not of any new policy direction, but instead by the use of the police. On the Mosleyite question, the government gave support to the police's use of the Public Order Act of 1936, which allowed them to take the names and addresses of hecklers and to give them to the chairmen of Fascist meetings, in case they wanted to initiate private prosecutions (Cox, 1975,

p. 40). In the dock strike the government made use of the
Special Branch to obtain tape recordings of the meetings of
the unofficial Port Workers' Committee, in the attempt to
characterise the PWC as a communist cell. The PWC was
expelled from the Transport and General Workers' Union,
and in April 1951 seven dockers were tried for organising
strikes in contravention of wartime legislation still in force
(Bunyan, 1976, pp. 124—5). So the increasingly close relationship of the police paralleled the move in the first post-war
Labour government towards 'consolidation' of the reforms of
1945—8: it was exactly in this period that government economic policy began to 'retreat from planning' and to remove
'controls'.

But social democratic support for the police in the later
1940s was not merely politically strategic. Though unpopular
in their role as guardians of the 'public order' of class society
(in the General Strike and the Mosleyite activities of the
1930s), the police had always been (begrudgingly) in some
social democratic favour as supports to the community in the
preservation of the peace. The beat policeman was a court of
appeal in cases of domestic and neighbourhood dispute, a
firm hand in cases of trouble between local youths, and a
helping hand for the elderly or the indisposed. He was also a
useful resource in dealing with drunks.

For Mannheim, as for other social democratic observers,
the best response to the youthful 'crime wave' of the immediate post-war years was to increase the size of the police force.
This would have deterrent effects on juveniles as a whole, as
well as allowing for more of the minority of disturbed adolescents 'in need of care, protection or control' to be apprehended and handed over to the care of treatment workers. No
dangers need be feared from this, Mannheim argued in 1947,
since

> The English police, and, in particular, the Metropolitan
> Police Force, have always been counted among the most
> efficient forces in the world, and they amply deserve all
> the praise bestowed upon them . . . according to the Home
> Secretary, [however] the total male strength of the Metro-

politan Police is 14,850 as compared with an authorized
establishment of 19,740.

> (Mannheim, 1947, reprinted in Mannheim, 1955,
> pp. 112—13)

So social democratic criminology in the 1940s gave considerable support to the police, who were encouraged to direct
their attention towards preventative work with juveniles but
also to bring juveniles to court when necessary. The enforcement of law in the community was an essential part of the
'consolidation' of social reconstruction, as well as being closely
integrated with the apprehension of disturbed young people
in need of the help of social work professionals.

Encouragement was also given to the police in their role as
detectives, especially in working on fraud, 'fiddles' and on
black market offences — the 'rackets', an area of expertise in
which the police took great pride in the 1940s (Hart, 1951).
The police themselves were by no means immune from the
general climate of reconstruction and reform: there is evidence
of considerable internal conflict between the more authoritarian chief constables and their staff, and also a number of
accounts which display the detective as the hard-working
defender of the new social democratic community, burrowing
away in pursuit of the predatory crimes of the powerful (see
Martienssen, 1951, ch. 8). The number of people found guilty
of 'frauds and false pretences' increased sharply, as we indicated earlier, from 13,122 in 1945 to 27,415 in 1951.

The relationship between the police and the first post-war
Labour government, like that government's relationship to
the law, was increasingly collaborative and consensual. The
police force was urged to intensify its activities in areas of
peace-keeping and the control of economic offences,[16] but
the day-to-day policies and operations of the police were left
under the control and discretion of police professionals. The
accountability of police to the local Watch Committees,
qualified as that was by the recognition that chief constables
were responsible primarily to the Home Secretary, was left
untouched in the Labour government's legislation in the
criminal justice field.

The elaboration of treatment

We have already underlined the importance of the nuclear
family to Labour's project of social reconstruction, and shown
how a reformed child care service was given the responsibility,
in the early post-war years, for rebuilding the lives of children
of broken families, in order to equip them for citizenship in
the new social democracy.

This quite politicised conception of family treatment was
given the full support of psychiatrists and other specialists.
John Bowlby, in particular, was extremely active in support
of social reconstruction.[17] Bowlby announced his support
for the interdisciplinary science of 'sociatry', developed by
Moreno, an American psychiatrist, as a guide for post-war
mobilisation. According to Bowlby (1947—9, p. 47), psychiatrists and doctors should join together and act as 'doctors to
social groups' in order to unleash the 'terrific drive that there
is in people towards achieving better personal and group
relationships'.[18]

Bowlby's commitment to scientific social democracy (anti-
cipating the later work of Wootton and Longford) was
announced in the year after the publication of his best known
study, *Forty-four Juvenile Thieves*. That study became
famous for its finding that seventeen of the forty-four boy
thieves studied had suffered some early or prolonged separation (in the first five years of their lives) from their mother or
father. Bowlby concluded that the delinquency of his adoles-
cent thieves resulted from the experience of 'maternal deprivation' (Bowlby, 1946). In that work, and even more influ-
entially, in *Child Care and the Growth of Love*, published in
1951 and written for the World Health Organisation, Bowlby
was concerned to provide 'scientific' arguments for the importance in child development of a child's 'earliest ties to his
mother'. As Packman observes in her authoritative history on
post-war child care policy in Britain, the publication was well
timed (it was helpful to government departments wrestling
with the problem of homeless and deprived children). It
presented 'a message [which] appealed to the heart as well as
the head . . . [being] readily translated into layman's language

. . . Few research studies can have had such a favourable
launching, nor such a profound impact' (Packman, 1975,
p. 23).

Bowlby's support was being given, in other words, to a
form of social reconstruction that depended on the reassertion
of motherhood in the nuclear family.[19] As Elizabeth Wilson
has observed,

> The theme of latch-key children was taken up in the popu-
> lar press and neglectful working mothers, their values
> perverted by materialism and greed for more and more
> possessions, were blamed for juvenile delinquency.
>
> (Wilson, 1977, p. 64)

The preparation of children for adulthood in the new social
democracy and in any society was seen to be a 'natural' and
biological responsibility of the mother. The task of the professional treatment agencies, working with youth, many of them
staffed by women, was therefore to provide a form of substitute mothering, while the task of doctors and psychiatrists
working with troubled or disturbed adult women was to
re-equip them for their natural roles within the family. In the
multiple-problem families discovered by the Fabians in the
1950s, many of the relational problems being experienced
arose out of the inability of women to perform their natural
roles (because of a personal inadequacy or out of ambiguities
in the division of labour in families containing working
mothers).

Equally important an assumption in the treatment worker's
vision was the almost metaphysical view of 'full citizenship'
in the new social democracy. Very little attention was given
by social democrats or by liberal professionals to the real
character of the juvenile or adult labour market in the immediate post-war years. It was a surprising silence, since the
post-war period did witness a rapid decline in the average level
of wages being earned by many young workers (as compared
with the wartime period) and also a considerable increase in
the number of low-paid and casual jobs in the labour market,
especially in the service industries. Many young school-leavers
were confronted with a specifically *juvenile* labour market

(rather than being able, like the preceding cohort of school-leavers, to work at adult jobs for adult wages) and a labour market in which there was little security or little sense of worth and identity. At the same time, of course, the number of jobs described as being available for women was declining very rapidly, and girl school-leavers were increasingly forced into unskilled jobs on production lines and in specific service occupations (like hairdressing), which had very few prospects for advancement and which did not provide any particular training. These developments in the labour market were largely hidden from the public eye of the media, which were much more interested in the alleged 'affluence' of teenagers at the upper end of the labour market, exploring the rewards of the new white-collar jobs or of apprenticeships in success-ful craft industries. The social democracy produced by social reconstruction had its own hidden effects on relations within the class and between sexes.

Thus the 'treatment' elaborated by social democratic psychiatrists was recommended as a support to a *particular* (often hidden) form of social order and a *particular* concep-tion of the role of the family and wage labour in that order. So also were the various forms of treatment which were elaborated in the juvenile and adult penal systems from the 1940s onwards. Throughout the 1950s, a climate of 'reha-bilitative optimism' extended throughout 'the system', and the particular presenting symptoms in individuals' social behaviour were all seen as being in principle amenable to treatment. Experiments in treatment were initiated in Borstals, with the introduction of group counselling techniques at Pollington and elsewhere, and even in prisons (in the exten-sion throughout the system, from 1956, of the so-called 'Norwich system', involving greater freedom of association between prisoners and less intensive supervision by staff).

In the period of the Conservative governments from 1951 to 1964, the commitments of professional workers to rehabili-tation and treatment were increasingly separated from the original commitment of 1940s social democrats, to a society of 'social justice' built around care institutionalised in the community. Delinquency and criminality were increasingly disconnected from the broader social contexts of the economy and the broader structure of class and power, and increasingly relocated into a psychodynamic theory of maladjustment. The 'liberalism' of the professional resided more and more in his or her claim to care for the client's personal (rather than social) needs, and the key to successful rehabilitation was seen to lie in the quality of the relationship between the state worker and his or her client, rather than in the quality of the relationship between the state itself and 'the people' or, indeed, between the owners of capital and the sellers of (waged or domestic) labour.

Social democracy and social control in the later post-war period[20]

Social democracy's increasing accommodation to the ideologies of liberal professionalism has, over this period, had two overriding and long-term effects.

First, social democracy has increasingly justified its own elaboration of treatment and social control in the rhetoric of the state and of 'authority'. By this I mean *inter alia* to point to the continued use, by liberal experts from the 1950s onwards, of an increasingly private language and private knowledge to describe and legitimate their activities. In the treatment of mental illness, for example, an array of apparently neutral terms was constructed and defined in the Mental Health Act of 1959, each of which conditions was primarily defined by the administrative-legal decisions taken in individual cases. On the boundaries of education and psychiatry, the Committee on Maladjusted Children, reporting in 1955, described maladjustment in an entirely circular fashion when it took maladjustment as a reference to children who

> [are] developing in ways that have a bad effect on [themselves], and cannot without help be remedied by [their] parents, teachers, and other adults in normal contact with [them].

In juvenile justice work, many workers in approved schools and elsewhere came increasingly to justify their practices as a part of experimental research programmes in social science, evaluating the impact of particular types of treatment on particular types of offender. The criteria being used to evaluate the impact, when announced in the scientific language of the research report, were often mysterious, a part of the professional's private knowledge, but they always reduced in practice to the effectiveness of a programme in reducing reconviction. They were measures, in other words, of the effectivity of a programme in encouraging young offenders to adapt to family life and the labour market as currently organised.

Some of this work depended on the quality of the relationship that could be encouraged voluntarily in the relationship of the worker and the client. But nearly all the relationships were in fact compulsory. 'Permissiveness' and 'client-centredness' occurred within a larger set of coercive parameters. The after-care given to ex-convicts was offered in their own interests (to help them to re-adjust to the world outside prisons), but it was compulsory (failure to accommodate to a probation and after-care officer could result in a return to prison). A family's failure to accommodate to the suggestions of field social workers attached to them in preventative work could result in a court ruling to take the children away from the home. The clientele of the liberal professional was, indeed, 'conscripted' by the state into the care of the professional.[21]

The critique of the post-war expansion of professional social control has taken several different forms in recent years. The initial impetus was a libetarian reaction against the untramelled authoritarianism of the care worker and, in the work of R. D. Laing, David Cooper and others, the 'violence in psychiatry' (Cooper, 1965). In the work of labelling theorists and anti-psychiatrists, the interventions of care agents were indicted for their intolerant and absolutist attempt to correct the behaviours of deviants (see Schur, 1973). These deviant behaviours were often seen by labelling theorists as entirely authentic and unpathological. In any case, they argued, the attempt to correct them often resulted in deviants being stigmatised and labelled, and confirmed in their deviant careers.

Later critiques of 'social control' have retreated to some extent from the celebration of all acts of deviance, and have argued instead that the advance of correction, rehabilitation and treatment has more to do with the expansive logic of the social work, educational and medical professions than with real, popular needs (Friedenberg, 1976). The actual form assumed by social control (as institutional or non-institutional, intensive or extensive, etc.) may depend upon fiscal considerations (especially given the larger crisis of state expenditure), but the fundamental trajectory is given by the tendency for social control bureaucracies to expand. They have also quite correctly argued that the 'dispersal of social control' throughout society is occurring without any proper adjudication as to whether a law has in fact been broken. The dispersal of social control demands encourages a 'blurring' of the traditional legal defences of the individual against the unwarranted intrusions of the state (Cohen, S., 1979).

Writing primarily of the expansion of new forms of 'community treatment' during the late 1960s and 1970s, Stan Cohen has written of the coming, in Britain and North America, of Foucault's 'punitive city'. His image is of new forms of community-based forms of social control, operated by social workers and always justified as a means of 'diverting' or 'decarcerating' people from prisons or other institutions, spreading out throughout society into a 'correctional continuum' that is somehow present at every waking moment and in every social space. So, for example, the boundaries between a preventative pre-deliquency programme, a treatment programme for children who are in trouble, and an after-care programme for children released from care programmes into the community, have become increasingly blurred. Cohen fears that

> We are seeing . . . not just the proliferation of agencies and services, finely calibrated in terms of degree of coerciveness or intension or unpleasantness. The uncertainties are more profound than this: voluntary or coercive, formal or informal, locked up or free, guilty or innocent. These apparently absurd administrative and research questions — when is a prison not a prison? is the alternative an alternative? who is half-way in and who is three-quarter way out? — beckon to a future when it will be impossible to determine who exactly is enmeshed in the social control system — and hence subject to its jurisdiction and surveillance — at any one time.
>
> (Cohen, S., 1979, p. 346)

In the accounts presented by Foucault and Cohen, the reality of the liberal state is the extension of surveillance and discipline throughout society.

Critiques of this kind concentrate on the illiberal character of insensitive over-reactions of so-called liberal-professionals. They do not give their prime attention to the contradiction between the advance of professional treatment and the fulfilment of real social needs. But the systems of treatment run by unaccountable and apolitical professionals, employed by the state, are a *distorted* expression of the original programme of social reconstruction articulated in the late 1940s, as well as being to some extent a display of the particular limitations of that programme. That is to say that the programmes are presented *as if* they are generally to do with the defence of the community and, therefore, with 'social justice', but they are organised *in practice* as ways of surveilling and containing troublesome youths and as ways of 'policing the family'. They are not programmes defending a *universal social interest*, so much, as a heavily financed support for the *existing form* of the labour market and the *existing form* of the family. They do not and could not realise the just demands of all youths or all women for just and equitable roles in the economic and social life of society.

Their repressive and disciplinary quality is given — not primarily by the urge to power of professionals — but by the necessarily authoritarian defence of particular conceptions of the role of the family in the reproduction of sexual roles (of women, in particular) and in the preparation of youth for the adult labour market. The *form* of discipline is given by the requirements of social relations in a capitalist and patriarchal society.

The second effect of post-war social democracy's accommodation to authoritarian and statist forms of compulsory rehabilitation is the association of social democracy with 'disorder'. Nearly all professional criminologists now admit, and the New Right enthusiastically proclaims, that rehabilitation does not work. It works neither in the narrow sense of correcting individual offenders nor in the broader sense of providing order between the classes and/or the generations.

From the late 1950s onwards, the scales devised by Mannheim and Wilkins to predict the chances of re-offending by different kinds of young offenders sent to Borstal no longer seemed to work (Mannheim and Wilkins, 1955). The reconviction rates of the Borstals, approved schools and detention centres increased, as did the failure rates of programmes offering alternatives to institutionalisation[22] Throughout the 1960s, outbreaks of trouble among working-class youth, ranging from the mods and rockers events of 1961–4 to the emergence of the skinheads in 1968, increasingly suggested that the promised orderliness of conventional social democracy could only be assured by a reversion to the use of containment and coercion. The emergence of a rebellious and critical counter-culture and student movement amongst middle-class youth pointed to what for the conforming population were the disabling and disorderly consequences of earlier 'permissive' education and child-centred psychiatry and child-rearing.

The attacks that have been made on the failure of professional liberalism as a guardian of social order have resulted in confused responses from the Left. The Labour Party has taken up the hopeless position of arguing that the increases in crime (and therefore the sense of disorder) are inevitable, being a feature of the development of any complex industrial society (Labour Party, 1979). Reference is made to the increase in crime rates in all modern industrial societies. This defeatist acceptance of the form of social arrangements as being unreformable and as an unavoidable consequence of 'industrialisation' was treated with proper contempt by television and radio journalists during the 1979 election, and gave assistance to the Right in its attempt to articulate a highly moralistic and radical critique of the inadequacies of welfare and of liberalism.

Liberal professionals (like the British Association of Social Workers) and liberals generally have responded to these critiques by arguing, rather incoherently, that the disorderliness of youth arises out of the *inadequacy* and *underprovision* of social welfare, while the more 'realist' Labour Party centre has argued for a reimposition of moral discipline by the family. Both responses misunderstand the significance of contemporary youthful delinquency as an expression of the contemporary 'crisis of social reproduction'. They have no understanding of the increasing contradiction that exists

9

between the family form (especially its patriarchal, working-class form) and the real economic and social opportunities that are available to youth. Like the working-class Labour supporters interviewed by Jeremy Seabrook, the traditional Labour politician is unable to understand the irrelevance of the traditional family form to youths or, indeed, to women. Youths who reject the opportunities made available to them in the welfare state are merely 'ungrateful' (Fyvel, 1961).

What neither the liberal Left nor the disciplinarian centre seems to realise is that the reproduction of a genuine social order requires a constant interaction between state activity and developing and changing social needs. A welfare state which works on the principle that woman is naturally dependent on man and also currently *depends* on the expulsion of large numbers of youths into worklessness is not meeting the real needs of women and young people to be self-generating members of the human species. A socialist politics which reduces the question of need simply to *economic needs* (for wages or for pay-outs at the social security office), or to the *needs for care* (given by a professional social worker), has no understanding of the range of hopes (for change or growth) or fears (of defeat and demoralisation) that currently characterises the relations of the classes, the sexes and the generations. A socialist social policy must be directed at the realisation of these social needs by the state, rather than at some nostalgic call for familiar but ineffective forms of discipline.

Notes to Chapter 2

1. Stuart Hall has recently argued that the SDP may have 'real effects in preventing that reshaping of the Left and of Socialism which alone can provide a real alternative' [to right-wing reconstruction] — 'permitting, instead, Labour ... to recompose itself along familiar lines. A Labour Government, succeeding to its third rotation in power, under such conditions, would certainly neutralise Socialism for a very long time to come. That, after all, may be what Social Democracy is *really* about' (Hall, 1981, p. 13).

2. Labour politicians were also indicted for their alleged failure to support the police, and again it was suggested that this failure arose out of fundamental features of the philosophy of social democracy (see *Politics Today*, 7, Conservative Research Department, 17 April 1978). My examination of the policy adopted by the Labour

government of 1945—51 towards the police, and also my examination of Hermann Mannheim's observations on the police, should show the true social democratic position (in all its contradictions).

3. The right-wing argument about the relationship between 'majestic' law and the moral order is always posed most clearly by Conservative defenders of capital punishment. Law must be terrible in its consequences in order to deter evil people in the population from intentional evil deeds. (For an examination of Conservative and social democratic ideologies at work in the debates around the abolition of capital punishment, see Ian Taylor, 1981, ch. 2.)

4. The International Committee of the Howard League appears to have been an ad hoc creation of European social democratic criminologists based in London in the early 1940s, exiled by the events leading up to the war. Included on the committee were Grunhut from Germany (later appointed to Oxford from where he campaigned for the reform of the juvenile court) and Grabinska and Radzinowicz from Poland (Radzinowicz was later to become the first Professor of Criminology at Cambridge.) Each of these figures exhibited quite clearly what Perry Anderson has called 'an elective political affinity with British social democracy', like the 'white emigrés' in adjacent philosophical and social scientific areas (Malinowski, Wittgenstein, Popper, Eysenck and Isaiah Berlin) (see Anderson, 1968). On the International Committee, however, the clearest influence was that of Mannheim. It was probably due to Mannheim's influence that Harold Laski, as chairman of the Labour Party, suggested to the Home Office in 1942 that a Royal Commission on crime should be established in order 'to create the atmosphere of large scale social change' (Lodge, 1975, p. 12). Mannheim had been a friend of Laski ever since his arrival in Britain, and had dedicated his book *Criminal Justice and Social Reconstruction* to Laski, who in turn had sponsored Mannheim's successful application for a lectureship at the London School of Economics.

5. The description of the existing child care services as 'repressive' and 'chaotically maladministered' appeared in a famous letter written by Lady Allen of Hutwood to *The Times* in 1944. Her denunciations of the 'Poor Law mentality' dominating British child care were fully supported by the Curtis Committee in its report of 1946.

6. The Labour government's Criminal Justice Act of 1948 was a contradictory piece of legislation. It substantially increased the use of probation with both adults and juveniles (with the intention of reducing sentences in prisons and the various juvenile institutions); abolished 'hard labour' in prisons; abolished corporal punishment throughout the penal system; introduced remand centres (to be used instead of prison in the pre-trial containment of 17—21 year

olds); and legislated to give financial support for 'new treatments' for offenders, as yet undeveloped. An editorial in *The Times* of 31 July 1948, evaluating these measures, concluded that the guiding principle of the Act was 'that there must be no despair of humanity'. It was a little more complex than that, however, as the Act also legislated, to the great dismay of the Howard League, to introduce the detention centre for young offenders, and also failed to legislate, as had been widely expected, for the abolition of capital punishment.

7. A common complaint in the editorial pages of legal journals in the 1940s was that criminologists like Mannheim had greater inside knowledge of impending legal and penal reform than the legal profession itself. This 'imbalance' of professional representation in government circles was to be corrected by the Conservative government of 1950–9, with the parameters of expertise being broadened to include the police and the judiciary, and the patronage of government being extended away from the LSE and towards Leon Radzinowicz and his small criminological department within the Cambridge University Faculty of Law.

8. The scapegoating of deserters as the source of the post-war crime-wave was aided by the well-publicised involvement of deserters in two police killings, in February 1948 and in July 1951, when four policemen died. Steve Chibnall notes how 'the killing of policemen has played a particularly prominent role in the development of law and order crises since the war, becoming a potent symbol of lawlessness' (Chibnall, 1977, p. 54).

9. The incipient racism of the Conservative press and certain spokesmen in the Conservative Party on the aliens issue was to be repeated in the early 1950s, in the attempt to equate the alleged growth of public prostitution with a spate of Cypriot and Maltese immigration (see Smart, 1981a). This ever-present racism was supported, as it still is in many Conservative circles, by an overwhelming lack of interest in the penal and social policies of other countries. In the debates over capital and corporal punishment during the reading of the Criminal Justice Bill, Lt Col. C. Gage, Ulster Unionist MP for Belfast South, who had acted as an Assistant Deputy Judge Advocate General with the Canadian forces in Belgium during the war, commented on the use of statistics in countries where capital punishment had been abolished as follows:

> I am not impressed by the argument as to statistics in other nations. It is an attractive argument and, at first blush, one would like to accept it, but the psychology of criminals differs with nations as well as with people.
>
> (*Hansard*, vol. 449, 14 April 1948, col. 1063)

10. The parallels between the subject matter involved in the Lynskey Tribunal and that of the investigations into the affairs of John Poulson during 1974—6 are obvious. Indeed, where Edward Heath in 1973 designated the activities of 'Tiny' Rowlands of Lonhro and John Poulson as evidence of 'the unacceptable face of capitalism', Judge Lynskey remarked in 1948 that the 'whole question' facing his tribunal was to decide what could be counted as 'legitimate business' (see Gross, 1963, pp. 284—6). The difference between the two cases is that the allegations of Sidney Stanley resulted in a full-scale investigation by tribunal, with a spirited and well-publicised defence of the government by Hartley Shawcross, who opened the cross-examination of Stanley. Three connected reasons can be advanced for the government's concern to 'clear the air'. The Stanley allegations were used, by some Conservatives and by some sections of the mass media, as evidence of a corruption that they argued was an inevitable result of creating a government state apparatus for economic planning and initiative. (The view of Rogow is that opportunities for illegal gain, along with many other problems being experienced economically at the time, arose out of the inadequacies of the government planning machinery, and, in particular, the government's attempt to use methods developed in wartime for the regeneration of a peacetime economy.) A second reason for the government's activity in the tribunal, however, was its determination to continue what it saw as a project of moral reconstruction (a task that would be rendered less legitimate if Stanley's allegations were to go unanswered). Thirdly, the economic climate of 1948 was one that continued to require 'equality of sacrifice' — as evidenced in the continuing campaigns against spivs, drones, racketeers and others, and, most crucially, in the imposition by Sir Stafford Cripps of a wage freeze, and the continuation of shortages and rationing. The Poulson allegations occurred in a very different 'conjuncture'. But it is clear from the findings of the House of Commons Disciplinary Committee in 1977 that a full and open tribunal of Lynskey proportions could have been embarrassing to both major political parties to a fairly senior level. The Labour Party could have suffered to some extent, in so far as that Party continues to claim that it is engaged in the *moral* re-ordering of society rather than simply the *management* of the relations of capital and the state.

11. In a later social democratic text on *Crime and the Penal System*, Howard Jones was quite explicit on the status of 'moral influence' when he observed that

> There is no reason why [arguments insisting on punishment on a moral basis] should prevent the criminologist from continuing

with his researches on a completely empirical basis. If moral
restraints are important, they will be vindicated.

(Jones, 1965, p. 144)

Jones chides Hermann Mannheim for the doubts he expressed on
the complete acceptance of a deterministic conception of punishment as cure. In *The Dilemma of Penal Reform*, Mannheim had
argued, heretically for a social democrat, that

> to divorce the idea of punishment by the State from moral
> considerations has, in the long run, proved a fatal error. Only on a
> moral basis is it possible to argue with the law-breaker.
>
> (Mannheim, 1939, p. 21)

12. The idea that the offence was a 'symptom' and the idea that treat-
    ment should not be restricted merely to offenders were both to
    find a place in the famous section 1(2) of the Children and Young
    Persons Act of 1969. The influence of the 1947 report of the
    International Committee of the Howard League on Labour Party
    and social democratic thinking is nowhere on record, but it is clear
    that the arguments advanced as the reform of the juvenile court in
    1964 in the Labour Party's study group pamphlet, *Crime: A Chal-
    lenge to Us All*, were very similar to those originally advanced in
    1947. As Tony Bottoms (1975) has shown, the 1964 proposals
    were the basis for the 1969 Act, subsequent to strategic revision by
    senior officials in the Home Office Children's Department.
13. On the long heritage of Darwinian and eugenic thinking in the
    Fabian version of social democracy, see Stedman-Jones (1971,
    pp. 352–3). In 1891, Sidney Webb argued that competition between
    communities rather than competition between individuals within
    communities was now 'the main field of natural selection'. It was
    therefore vital that 'the community should fortify the strong rather
    than succour the weak'. H. G. Wells and George Bernard Shaw later
    extended the logic of this argument further and argued for 'sterilisa-
    tion of the failures'.
14. The retentionist sentiments of some working-class MPs were sup-
    ported by George Bernard Shaw in a letter to *The Times* (5 Decem-
    ber 1947) in which he argued that 'dangerous insanity, instead of
    exempting from liquidation, should be one of the strongest grounds
    for it'. For an examination of social democratic attitudes to capital
    punishment, see Ian Taylor (1981, ch. 2).
15. There was certainly considerable hostility amongst some Labour
    MPs towards the amalgamation of the small police forces that was
    legislated in the Police Act of 1946, and Labour and Tory members

united to press successfully for an amendment to prohibit any
county or county borough force being combined with a police
authority larger than itself (Hart, 1951, pp. 63—4).

16. There was evidence of some continuing difference of view between
the government and police chiefs on the question of the proper
extent of the 'police task'. A Home Office committee, appointed
by Home Secretary Chuter Ede on 30 Aug 1950, 'to investigate
the performance of police on "extraneous" duties', refused to accept
that the traffic-policing functions of the police (which had substantially increased in the line with the increases in motor vehicles in
use after the war) were not 'within the ambit of police work proper'
(*Report of the Committee on Extraneous Duties*, 1953, para. 5).
Chief constables and other witnesses had argued before the committee for police to be relieved of these duties, in order that they
might concentrate on the pursuit and control of 'real' criminals.
The Committee on Extraneous Duties withdrew some already
anachronistic responsibilities from the police (in the area of tax
control), but argued that 'uniformity in the extra duties performed
by police forces is neither necessary nor desirable' (para. 40(i)).
For this committee, the police force was a 'peace-keeper' in the
most general sense, with a proper responsibility for traffic and
domestic problems, as well as for crime control, and for the policing
of industrial disputes and political demonstrations.

17. Bowlby's work on family separation and its effects was in some
ways a replication and a popularisation of the work done by Anna
Freud and her associates on children of broken families in her
Hampstead nursery (see Burlingham and Freud, 1942, 1944).

18. Bowlby was obviously aware of the similarity between society's
claim to act as a doctor to social groups and the claims made by
national-socialist social philosophers in Nazi Germany. But his
argument was that it was precisely because of the emphasis on
'legal, religious and philosophical techniques' that Nazi authoritarianism eventually failed. According to Bowlby,

> it is science which is bringing to the aid of the traditional and
> not very effective legal, religious and philosophical techniques
> for making people good, powerful techniques for achieving the
> very ends [the philosophers] value.
>
> (Bowlby, 1947—9, p. 47)

19. While it did not actually prioritise the importance of the mother to
the nuclear family as the proper subject of good social work,
Bowlby's influence did place an overwhelming emphasis on the

quality of individual relationships in families as a central topic for social workers engaged in the prevention of delinquency, mental illness and other disturbance. Jean Heywood puts the point simply and straightforwardly:

> The effects of Bowlby's work . . . tended to confirm social workers in their emphasis on individual relationships and it was not until 1965 that two sociologists, Peter Townsend and Brian Abel-Smith, published their discovery of poverty in the welfare state.
>
> (Heywood, 1978, p. 203)

20. The discussion and critique of the development of social control in the 1960s and 1970s presented here is a highly abbreviated version of the account in Ian Taylor (1981, ch. 6), since, as I indicated in the Introduction, the primary purposes of this book are not to present a full-blown historical account of post-war crime policy and ideology. I am more concerned here to identify the *general parameters* of social-democratic ideology in the Labour Party *vis-à-vis* crime, and these were clearest, in my view, in the work done by social democrats in the 1940s. Hence that is the period I have given most attention in this chapter.

21. The idea of the clientele of the welfare state being 'conscripted' involuntarily into a dependency on the professional state worker (in part to do service in providing a rationale for the state worker's occupation) is taken from Friedenberg (1976, ch. 1). It also echoes the late Alvin Gouldner's observations on the prime function of the welfare state being the post-war employment of the non-commercial middle class (Gouldner, 1970, pp. 76–82).

22. The percentage of boys released from Borstal reconvicted within three years increased from 55 per cent in 1950 to 65 per cent in 1956, and research by Little (1962) has demonstrated that this increase in reconviction could by no means all be attributed to changes in the quality (i.e. the previous institutional experience) of the boys being received into Borstal. By 1964–6, 60 per cent of all boys released from Borstal were reconvicted *within eighteen months* (Bottoms and McClintock, 1973, p. 265). The percentage of boys released from approved schools who were reconvicted within three years increased from 57 per cent in 1958 to 68 per cent in 1964 (Home Office, *Report on the Work of the Children's Department 1964–1966*, p. 51, *1967–1969*, p. 42).

3

The Reconstruction of Socialist Social Policy

The question of how to effect a transition from capitalism to socialism has become all the more urgent in Britain, as the baleful effects of Thatcherism on social and economic relations have become ever more apparent. In the absence of any serious prospect of the emergence of revolutionary movements which have the capacity to destroy the existing state apparatus and replace it overnight with alternative social forms, socialists have come increasingly to give serious attention to the construction of transitional or 'prefigurative' programmes, which have the function of posing socialist answers to the human waste, poverty and insecurity that are now once again, quite clearly, an integral feature of the capitalist form of production and its associated social relations. These prefigurative socialist programmes must clearly encompass the entire field of social policy, in order that they can challenge the right-wing arguments now active in all the social policy areas, and also in order to generate socialist responses to the wide variety of social needs that are experienced across the social structure. I shall deal in a provisional way with the questions of the family and youth later in this chapter.

The construction of a transitional socialist criminology is an urgent necessity for two reasons. First, as we saw quite clearly in Chapter 1, the law and order issue is a major and influential element in the social ideology articulated by the Tory Party under Margaret Thatcher, and it is therefore a means of creating a significant electoral base for what would otherwise be politically impossible economic and social poli-

cies. So the law and order question in its broadest sense
(including street crime and also terrorism, trade unions and
their relation to law, and the question of public order and
demonstrations) have been used in such a way as to justify
some expansion of the *coercive* apparatus of the state, while
simultaneously allowing for heavy cutting of public expenditure on social security and on social work. These 'candy floss'
expenditures are now portrayed as being economically luxur-
ious, as well as ineffectively managed and liable to be subject
to 'scrounging' or to other forms of unintended appropria-
tion.[1] Many of the agencies that have been cut *were* authoritarian, bureaucratic and a nuisance to working-class people,
but many others (such as hospitals, nurseries, day care centres,
clinics and battered wives' refuges) are or were essential to
particular working-class groups and areas. Perhaps more con-
sequentially in the long term, the ideological work that has
been done by the Right on the question of crime and law and
order has been very successful in adding a negative connotation in popular rhetoric to notions of 'welfare', 'care' and
'treatment' and also to 'collectivist' state responses to social
problems generally. In the absence of a popular transitional
socialist criminology, the law and order issue has worked
powerfully as an ideological support for Thatcherism.

A second reason for urgency in the creation of a transitional
socialist criminology is that crime will be a *real* social problem
the more that Thatcherism is allowed to have its effects on
the lived social relations in Britain. Crime is also likely to be a
worsening problem, in the sense that street thefts and crimes
of violence generally are likely to escalate as unemployed
people become more desperate in their quest for economic
survival and in their need to establish identity. Some early
demonstrations of this have been the heavy increases in crime
that were recorded in industrial areas of the North of England
during 1980: offences known to the police in South Yorkshire
increased by 11.7 per cent in that year (*The Star*, Sheffield,
30 January 1981), and in the annual report of the Northum-
berland police force, it was revealed that 49 per cent of all
detected crime in the area in 1980 was committed by unemployed people (*The Guardian*, 15 April 1981). In February
1981, the Assistant Commissioner for Crime for the Metro-

politan Police, Mr Gilbert Kelland, revealed at a press conference that

> after three successive years of falling or static crime rates
> in the capital, serious crimes rose last year by 5 per cent . . .
> The steadily rising tide of crime figures over the last 20
> years, which seemed to have been checked since 1977, was
> now in flood again.
>
> (*The Guardian*, 20 February 1981)

Further evidence of the effects that unemployment can have
(coupled with the general consequences of living in demoralising housing and dislocated neighbourhoods) has been
provided by the increase in suicide and divorce rates, both of
which are especially marked in areas of high unemployment.
The breakdown of trust between young blacks and the police,
which exploded into the riots in Bristol in 1980 and Brixton
in 1981, and the accelerating increase in racist attacks and
murders by young whites, are a further expression of the
deep social divisions that are further encouraged by unemployment. No analyst of Thatcherism, whether of the Left or
the Right, has yet identified any basis in that ideology for an
attack on the institutionalised racism that resulted in the
massive rates of unemployment that have been experienced
(disproportionately compared to whites) by blacks generally
since the 1960s and which have now risen to astronomical
heights, especially in inner-city areas and in South London.[2]
   The Prime Minister and the Home Secretary have both
indicated their belief that racial conflicts arise primarily as a
result of mistrust and subversion rather than out of material
deprivation or structured discrimination,[3] and they have
expressed their full support for the police and, by implication,
the ability of the police to contain the 'difficult' racial and
crime situations that exist in many of the inner-city areas.
Some chief constables have, however, become increasingly
anxious about the responsibilities being placed upon them
not only in the policing of race relations but also in the maintenance of social order generally. The Chief Constable of
South Yorkshire, Mr James Brownlow, defended himself
against criticisms of a decline in that force's clear-up rate in

1979 with the aggrieved observation that 'the police could not control the number of murders, industrial disputes, missing persons or hooligans' (*The Star*, Sheffield, 27 October 1980). By implication, these were all matters that could in his opinion be affected most by governmental economic and social policies[4] and, in particular, the contribution these policies could make to harmonious social relations and to general economic well-being and social peace.

There are few signs of such policies in the rhetoric or in the programmes of the present British government. Even more seriously, close analysis of the economic theories on which the present government policies are entirely based shows that these theories have no conception of social or economic community other than that of the competitive and individualistic market place, held together by coercion and moral appeals. This is precisely the kind of free enterprise ideology which is dominant in countries like the United States, Hong Kong and the Far East generally, all of which have massively higher crime rates than those of Britain, and much of whose crime takes the form of acquisitive individualism not stopping short of violence. In the free enterprise United States, the homicide rate in 1976 reached 156 per million (in the same year as it was 9 in Britain), and in 1981 murder emerged as the leading cause of death for males between the ages of 15 and 44 in New York City, ahead of road accidents, cancer and heart disease. ('Murder USA', *The Sunday Times*, 14 December 1980). Crimes of violence have been increasing in the United States throughout the last decade much more rapidly than in Britain, and in 1980 they increased by 13 per cent, the largest increase since 1968 (*The Guardian*, 2 April 1981). And yet the United States (especially at local level) has the kind of economy which most closely approximates the entrepreneurial social market economy at the core of Thatcherism. These are the sets of social relations to which the present government in a utopian manner aspires: hardly the most promising of visions for an already troubled and divided society.

Popular support for Thatcherism is obviously premised in part on the widespread acceptance of the need for alternative economic policies to those pursued by the governments of the post-war period. That is to say, Thatcherism's popular base seems to derive from the collapse of social democracy as popular ideology and in this case particularly from the failure of social democracy *as economic policy*. Members of the 'monetarist' inner ring of economics ministers in the Thatcher government constantly reiterate the refrain (without persuasive social democratic objection) that 'there is no other way'. A socialist analysis of the failure of social democratic (Keynesian) economics is required. Any such analysis could not simply be an analysis of Keynesianism to provide a level of affluence for workers (in some senses, it did do that for a period): it would have to be an analysis of the failure of Keynesianism, during the post-war boom, to *abolish* the insecurities of boom and slump under capitalism, and *to prevent the ultimate return*, in the 1970s, of a more fundamental recession occasioned by the declining rate of profitability in Western capitalist industries. Putting this another way, it would have to be an analysis of the failure of Keynesianism to yield the New Jerusalem of social and economic security and of political egalitarianism which its social democratic rhetoric anticipated.

We cannot offer that economic analysis here (see Rowthorn, 1980). But we can none the less identify some important features of post-war social democracy, discussed in Chapter 2, which have contributed to popular estrangement from socialist politics generally and which are in need of revision. In particular, we can clearly see the need for a challenge to social democracy's assured alliance with professionals and experts as the basis for social policy construction and, very closely connected with this, we can identify an urgent need for a fundamental revision of the 'authoritarian statism' which has characterised Labour's economic and social policies alike. We can also see that the challenge which is posed to these *must* be informed by a clearly visible alternative social strategy that makes sense to the various social interests and publics which now constitute the working class and the unemployed class in Britain. The 'reforms' promised by any future Labour government must make sense *popularly* as a potential solution to the real living problems of these various constituencies.

Socialism and the professionals

The account I presented in Chapter 2 of the activity and ideology of liberal-professionals was in part intended to highlight the great gap that has developed between the *needs* recognised in the psychoanalytic ideology of many social workers on the one hand, and the Poor Law ideologies of state officials working in social security offices on the other; and the economic and emotional needs that people experience in a class society. Following the great American sociologist, C. Wright Mills, I see these professionals as being intent on a constant *reduction* of the unremitting experience of deprivation, loneliness, institutional racism, sexist exploitation in personal relations, and real anxieties and fears — which in truth the *majority* of the population of a class society experiences — into the immediate and minimal material needs or presenting pathological symptoms of a minority of individual client cases.

The limited and specific visions of professionals were given considerable support by the Labour governments of the 1960s and 1970s. But the alliance of social democracy and the liberal-professional is now under quite widespread challenge, especially from the women's movement and from the various kinds of community organisations that were spawned by the New Left in the 1960s. The basis of this challenge is the failure of the professional agencies (caught within their own very narrow and ideological conceptions of need) to respond to the social needs experienced by particular 'client populations' like working women, ex-convicts, inner-city blacks or, in particular, the unemployed. It has been from among these voluntary and unofficial groups and 'fragments' (and not from the professional agencies of the state) that the rape crisis centres, battered wives' refuges, claimants' unions and latterly the various anti-cuts campaigns have emerged. And it is from these groups (rather than the liberal race relations industry, financed by the state) that the major opposition to the growth of racism in Britain's working-class areas has derived. The re-entry of these socialist fragments into the Labour Party is currently one of the objectives of Mr Tony Benn,[5] as well as being a significant area of discussion among the fragments themselves (see Rowbotham *et al.*, 1979).

Thus the professionals could not or would not deal with the specific needs of particular populations (for example, for an end to sexual or racial harassment, to the real depressions and anxieties of life in the inner city or in high-rise flats, or to discriminatory police practices in particular areas). Their failure to meet particular needs was often compounded and made more burdensome to clients by the increasing power which these professionals could wield over the clients' lives. This has been especially marked, of course, in the personal intrusions that are routinely practised by staff of the DHSS in the search for women welfare recipients cohabiting with men, and in their general search for 'scroungers'. But bureaucratic procedures and alienated relationships with clients are also quite common in local authority social service departments, and even the general expansion of new 'liberal' measures in social work, like intermediate treatment or preventative work with children deemed to be 'pre-delinquent', has not been by any means universally experienced as a welcome form of state benevolence. There is a *real* basis to the accusation so frequently made by the Right that bureaucracy and impersonality are inevitable features of the expansion of the state.

But the bureaucratic and impersonal character of many professional agencies in the welfare state does not arise out of the fact that they are state-provided public services as such. It arises out of the particular *form* that the welfare state has assumed in practice. Far from being free spending and all-powerful agencies drawing irresponsibly on the public purse and intervening unaccountably into the lives of the citizenry at large, most welfare agencies are extremely hierarchically and bureaucratically organised with very few areas of 'freedom' for their workers. Social workers, health service workers and teachers tend to work according to very similar procedures and rules, because these are the procedures they have been taught and also because these are the procedures that are enforced by the workers' superiors in the professional hierarchy. So individual workers in the professionalised welfare state are accountable in some detail on the financial and other decisions they take, *but only to other professionals*, and very, very rarely to the clients they serve or care for. It is not surprising, therefore, that the professionals of the welfare state are seen popularly as staff belonging to someone else rather than as being accountable to ordinary people and to clients.

The popular conception of the welfare state professional as mean and repressive is, of course, accurate in the sense that the largesse allegedly available through the welfare state in the post-war period had been extremely effectively controlled and curtailed by legislation and by fiscal decisions made during the frequent economic crises of the post-war period. Health, education and social welfare have all been modestly financed, compared to the support that has been given to these services in many other capitalist societies.[6] Equally important, the development of the welfare state during the post-war period has always closely reflected the compromise of reform Conservative and centrist Labour politics that dominated the period until 1974, and has therefore always reflected the primary concern of consensus politicians with the restriction of welfare to the meeting only of *immediate* needs. Welfare has rarely been used as a means to any fundamental equalisation of resources between groups and is never seen as a fundamental right. All of which is to insist, following the authors of *Beyond the Fragments* and *In and Against the State*, that the British welfare state, even as a provider of some of the people's needs for care, material support, medicine, etc., is a part of *the capitalist state*, and that it is therefore an incredibly contradictory form (see Rowbotham *et al.*, 1979; London–Edinburgh Weekend Return Group, 1979).

The restrictiveness of the British welfare state and the professionals working within it is in part a function of the role of containment and pacification the welfare state has been asked to perform within British capitalism: it is not a function of welfare state professionalism as such. But the ideologies that have been developed within the welfare state to defend the positions of professionals have also played a part in distancing the professional from her or his client and in mystifying the relationship by pleas to the special knowledge or skill which the professional is supposed to possess. One example of this would be the relationship of the average

NHS doctor (usually male and middle class) to the average working-class housewife, but another, often even more poisonous, example would be the relationship of the average DHSS junior payment clerk to his or her client. The essential similarity of the latters' class positions would in most cases be completely silenced by the clerk's attempt to impose his or her 'judicial' authority over the supplicant claimant.

The answer to these contradictory features of the 'social democratic' welfare state cannot be simply to argue for 'deprofessionalisation'. Many of the professionals involved in welfare, like doctors and nurses, are in fact very highly skilled and have specialist professional knowledge, although to say this is by no means to deny the need for dissemination of much more preventative health education, especially among working-class people, or indeed to deny the need for much more 'self-help' and even collective medicine in the population as a whole. So also do community lawyers or people working in housing action projects have a particular specialist knowledge, which can be of concrete use to people needing legal help or help in finding housing.

For very many people, though, the long-term experience of living in subordinate positions in a class society *has* quashed the sense of identity and self-respect which are essential to the search for health, or sometimes for any attempt to change one's life chances; and for very many more it has destroyed the will and the knowledge which are undoubtedly required in becoming a client of an essentially bureaucratic and hierarchical welfare state and in learning about one's material or other entitlements. Thus in any attempt to provide people with the basic needs they lack, the help of professionals (from health workers to community lawyers and social workers) may for a long time remain essential.

It is clear, however, that welfare state professionalism as currently organised is far too limiting on its workers and its clients and contradictory in its practices to be a prime site of prefigurative struggles for socialism. What is required is that the limitations in professionalism must be challenged in concrete and particular struggles within the welfare state. Social workers working with juvenile delinquents or with the young handicapped, for example, are currently in an impossible position if they act in a conventionally professional manner, trying to prepare their charges for opportunities of the work-place, as the logic of the government's economic policy has effectively destroyed the labour market for young people with such handicaps. The nihilism and violence that are currently quite common amongst adolescents in residential care, therefore, cannot always be attributed to some expertly reformable pathology.

Workers in the National Health Service also face enormous problems of morale if they continue to accept the limits of professionalism, as the effects of governmental economic and social policy begin to display themselves even more tragically in people's physical and psychic conditions (as well as in the violence which people increasingly do to each other), and also as the waiting lists for treatment lengthen. The contradiction between the health worker's personal commitments (to the prevention and treatment of disease) and the logic of the larger capitalist order and its governmental defenders must become more intense. We can anticipate that the gap between the existing practices of welfare state professionals generally and the need of their clients will diverge even more markedly than before as Thatcherism continues to have its different and specific effects throughout the population.

The needs felt by women who have been forced to return to lives of domestic labour by the collapse in the opportunities available to them will differ enormously from the needs of black populations experiencing the combined effects of the recession (of which they are unequal victims) and racist attacks. Neither of these groups' needs can be met by traditional forms of professional assistance, and it is not at all clear how calls for the intervention of professionals would be popular among women or the black community. But these *are* needs for welfare, properly defined, and there are ways in which professionals can organise people who would perhaps otherwise be isolated or defeatist with their welfare problems. The precedent for this observation must be the community development projects, established by the Labour government in 1967, which were enormously successful in reaching into particular localities and forging struggles (of tenants, workers, communities and other movements) where previously there would have been only grievances. The CDPs were eventually closed in the mid-1970s as a result of pressure from corporate and commerical interests in the areas in which they had been established. But in my view there is no inevitability in such matters: there is a real sense in which the ever-present misery that has been visited on certain parts of Britain by unemployment and public expenditure cuts makes it more difficult for governments or local authorities to close all projects that are working with the heavily disadvantaged and, in particular, those that are working with black groups and with women.

These comments on professionalism are very provisional, and it is certainly not my intention in this book to place too great an emphasis on the importance of liberal-professionals in prefigurative struggles for socialism. What is clear, however, is that the *traditional* alliance of conventional social democracy with liberal-professionals has to be jettisoned: too much of liberal-professional work has proven to be harassing and alienating to working-class experience, and too little of it has proved to be effective in solving the specific problems of the class.

Socialism and the authoritarian state

In a recent series of essays, Stuart Hall has brilliantly shown how the Labour Party in government in the 1960s and 1970s increasingly allowed itself to take on the part of authority and the state *against* the people. He attributes this posture in particular to the 'corporatist' economic policy initiated by the Labour governments of 1964—70, which was continued later by the Callaghan government.

Needing to find a means, in changing and less auspicious circumstances, for managing the high level of economic expectation generated by the rhetoric of the preceding 'age of affluence', the government of Harold Wilson was able to explore a connection that had not been open to Harold Macmillan or Lord Home. The 'secret' was

> to expand productivity: to make labour more productive —
> which in conditions of low investment meant raising the
> rate of the exploitation of labour. The potential sharpening
> of interests between the classes could . . . be dampened

down by subsuming everyone into the 'higher' ideological
unity of the national interest.

(Hall *et al.*, 1978, p. 236)

This 'higher ideological unity of the national interest' was to
be achieved by drawing

all sides into an active partnership with the State: to make
labour and capital equal 'interests' under the impartial
chairmanship of the 'neutral' state; to commit each side to
national economic targets; to persuade each to regulate the
share which it took out of the common pool; and thus to
establish a tripartite corporate bargain at the centre of the
nation's economic life . . . Each party had its constituency;
each its duties — principally of discipline. Capital defended
business, and would be rewarded with profits. Labour
defended the working man and would be rewarded with a
higher standard of living. The State represented 'the rest' —
the nation — and stabilised the contract enforcing it on the
community.

(Hall *et al.*, 1978, p. 236)

There was, in brief, 'the construction of a *disciplined form of
consent*, principally under the management of the corporate
state' (Hall *et al.*, 1978, p. 237).

The consequence of Labour's commitment to the corporate
state strategy has been a general commitment to 'statism' in
governing Labour circles as a solution to economic and social
problems generally, even as the specific decline of British
capitalism has accelerated and the general onset of world-wide
recession emerged. In the various social conflicts that have
arisen (between capital and labour, police and blacks, police
and youth, social security and claimants, etc.), Labour, when
in government, has been unreservedly 'with' the state and
against the people. In this way Labour has allowed itself to
be identified *as* the state, in circumstances where the state
has been widely experienced 'not as a beneficiary but [as] a
powerful bureaucratic imposition' (Hall, 1979, p. 18), and
also in circumstances where the state is self-evidently unable
to provide any real solution to people's problems in living.

Instead of interrogating this dissatisfaction with the state and instead of allowing space for critics of the state and for the various movements (like the CDPs, the women's movement, black representatives, etc.) that have arisen to fulfil needs that were unfulfilled by the state, Labour has tended to equate any dissatisfaction with 'statism' with Tory reaction. This has been a crippling long-term error, for

> the monopoly of the state and its policies, in alliance with the state-oriented fractions of 'big' capital, by social democracy has opened an effective, alternative space of operations for the 'radical right'. . . [They have] capitalized the disorganized discontents of the popular classes. [They have] constructed an alternative 'bloc' organized around the powerful themes of 'anti-statism', 'anti-collectivism', 'anti-creeping socialism' *and* 'anti-the-power bloc' (i.e. social democracy in power).
>
> (Hall, 1980, p. 171)

This is all done, especially in the speeches of Margaret Thatcher but also in the ideological support given her editorially in the popular press, in the name of a new and authoritarian 'populism'. It is a populism which connects the expansion of the state under social democratic governments (primarily Labour, but also the consensual Tory governments of the 1960s) with the continuing failures of the British economy, by virtue of the restrictions this expansion of the state has put on 'initiative' and by reason of the tax burden it has involved for 'business'. It is a populism which also speaks continually of 'common sense' and of 'human nature' (rather than the use of planning, research, etc.) as the solutions to both economic and social problems. The Conservative Party's manifesto for the general election of 1979 made the 'philosophical' commitments of the Thatcher leadership clear when it observed

> Attempting to do too much [Labour] politicians have failed to do those things which should be done . . . we want to work *with the grain* of human nature, helping people to help themselves — and others.

Social democratic policies *are* highly vulnerable to populist attacks of this kind, in part because of the general inability of corporatist economic policies to conjure more than a continuation of failure in the economic affairs of Britain, but also in part because the form that statism has assumed has not been amenable to popular accountability and control. In turn, this lack of accountability has partly to do with the increasing influence of professionals in the state and their increasing interventions into the lives of working people (which I discussed in the last section). But this lack of accountability stems, fundamentally, from Labour's conception of how state power is to be exercised. The achievement of socialism, in this perspective, is taken to be equivalent to Labour politicians exercising influence in and through the state. No fundamental democratisation of the civil service or of the local and national state is necessary, and no fundamental revision in the representation of working-class interest groups and of Labour generally in state organisations (from the Treasury through to the judiciary and the police). Consequently state power *has* been popularly experienced — correctly — as power that is exercised by 'them' over 'us' (even if the 'they' in the popular accounts are merely the people in local town halls who are responsible for bus timetables or refuse collections). Even in the brave new Labour Britain of Harold Wilson after 1966, when the government had a workable popular mandate, it was always somehow 'their' state and never 'ours'.

The existence of this distance between the people and the state has demoralised working-class people who often — again correctly — feel that they could do better themselves. A good example is in the area of penal policy. Elaborate schemes for providing 'treatment' for juvenile delinquents at the hands of liberal-professionals are not demonstrably any more successful in reducing levels of vandalism in working-class estates than the much loved clip around the ear of the traditional working-class community. That such communities no longer exist in their pre-war form, and that such discipline could no longer work in quite the same fashion, does not detract from the fundamentally correct scepticism that working-class people have of liberal, professional, statist measures.

The housing that has been built for working people by professional architects throughout the post-war period was designed and erected without any significant popular consultations, and with characteristically liberal individualist disdain for the established patterns of working-class sociability. That housing now exists as a fundamentally authoritarian restriction, in many cases, on working-class life and leisure, in forcing the residents of high-rise flats and estates to retreat into private space. Lack of power here has meant that the class has been unable to influence state housing policy. Liberal social workers recommend measures of support (home helps, more frequent visits, cash coupons, etc.) for isolated problem families in need, which may amplify their problems through stigma, and which *could* have been much more effectively resolved *in conditions of community solidarity*. Lack of power here has generated a distrust of the *direction* of state social work. Clearly there are differences between the activities of liberal social workers, employed by the state, in trying to help a family or an individual in trouble; housing officials allocating houses or dictating conditions of residence; and child care workers 'treating' working-class kids. And there is a large difference between all of these state workers and officials of the DHSS investigating working-class areas for cohabiting claimants. All the same, the contradiction of the state acting, in a social democratic manner, *in lieu of the class*, rather than *at the behest of* local segments of the class, inevitably makes each intervention of the state, whatever its particular purpose, into an instance of the general uncontrolled power of the state.

Social democratic politics has to be reconstructed in a 'popular democratic' form. That is, the recognition of a state form as a necessary element in the administration of complex industrial societies has to be connected to the recognition of the state as a *site of popular needs and popular political rights*. The lack of such responsiveness to popular needs and rights in authoritarian statism is a major reason for the rise of the 'authoritarian populism' articulated by Thatcherite elements in the British Conservative Party, as well as by the radical Right in the United States.

Such a 'popular democratic' conception may have to begin

at the local level, as currently appears to be happening, for example in the opening out of the local City Council in Sheffield to local organisations and communities. And it will almost certainly have to happen around particular issues and campaigns that relate to popular social needs, such as the subsidised bus fare policy in Sheffield, or the struggles that have been mounted against the closures of valued local hospitals throughout the country.[7] But in order that it can effectively mount a challenge to authoritarian populism as a hegemonic conception of social order — in other words, as a popularly accepted, consensual form of socialist reconstruction — socialist democracy will have to evoke via thoroughgoing democratisation. The state itself will have to be democratised from within, by trade unionists and socialists, by feminists and by liberal-radicals who have found the previous form of state power authoritarian and oppresive, and who can now clearly see that the social democratic rationales for such a form of authoritarian statism are exhausted.

Socialism and reform

Such a conception of a democratic state form will obviously demand a revision of the ends to which social democratic politics have been directed throughout the period of the post-war 'settlement'. This is not the place to enter into a doctrinal investigation of the long-standing debate between 'reform' and 'revolution' in socialist thought, but what *is* clear is that the version of reformism which has been dominant in influential social democratic circles during the post-war period is no longer a coherent option.

In place of this reformism, which has tended to manage and therefore to reproduce the social relations of class society, there has to be inserted a politics which will diminish and eventually abolish these long-standing and anachronistic divisions. These divisions include not only the fact of class itself, but also the independently effective facts of patriarchy and racial division. Only this kind of politics can authentically claim to represent a universal interest. Populism, of whatever form, is always in the end a form of ruling-class politics,

102 Law and Order

advanced when historical contingencies do not allow the
ruling class to 'represent itself' as a natural form of authority
and when the economic conditions are such as to necessitate
a direct attack on the accustomed support for the Left
amongst organised labour (see Laclau, 1977). Utopian though
such a radical conception of the abolition of social division
may currently appear, it is no more impractical or desperate
an option than the social reconstruction implied by Thatcherism.

The character of social democratic reformism is crucial in the
specific ideological struggles taking place, for example, over
crime and law and order. That is to say that the changed
economic conditions that have been created by the demise of
Keynesian solutions to capitalist economic problems, along
with the changed ideological conditions that have been
created by the attack on social democracy by the radical
Right, demand an entirely new set of responses from socialists on all fronts, including those the Right claims as its own.

A key element of this reconstructed socialism, in the area
of crime policy, must be a revival of a commitment to crime
control. The Left must relinquish its accustomed posture of
agnosticism on the effectiveness of particular kinds of crime
control measures and also modify its libertarian revulsions to
all forms of policing, control and containment. In particular,
the Left must declare itself to be in favour of the proper
policing of established working-class residential areas and also
areas of black settlement. The character of the policing should
be decided in conjunction with local residents active in local
community groups, and regular reports should be submitted
by police to enlarged local authority police committees, on
which should sit democratically elected representatives of all
community groups, and especially all minority group organisations.

The Left should also declare itself in favour of the effective
policing and control of the inner city and of all public space
in the city. The bus and railway stations of most major urban
areas in Britain are now major centres of vandalism, public
drunkenness, and sexual and other forms of assault. It was
and is no part of any socialist criminology to argue that
behaviours of this kind (however patterned and discriminate

they may be) are evidence of an authentic socialist diversity (they are an expression of the brutalisation of the underclass in an old class society), and it is no bourgeois apologetic to argue for the defence of the mass of the population from the real harassment and the real dangers of the late capitalist city.

The point about the demand for effective policing is that it is contradictory to the existing direction of police practice, which is continually moving in the direction of the defence of public order *as defined by the state*. The demand for effective policing speaks to specific urgent needs of particular segments of the citizen population. In particular, it echoes the increasing demands of Asians and West Indians for protection from racial attacks, of women from attacks by men, and of working people in general from the cohorts of skinheads and unemployed youths who currently patrol some of the urban space of Britain. The reform of the police, and the subjugation of the police to effective democratic accountability to communities it polices, is therefore no mere liberal flourish: it is an essential part of any programme of winning the support of a fragmented 'community' for social democracy (rather than for the strong capitalist state) as a guarantor of public order. Future reform of the police must be made responsive to the *real* needs for law enforcement (defined by local communities) rather than taking the form defined, undemocratically, by the state. A socialist conception of policing would be one that intervenes in the current debate between the two competing versions of policing (the authoritarian statist version of community policing and surveillance spoken of by John Alderson (1979), the Chief Constable of Devon and Cornwall, and the authoritarian populist conception of police as a 'fire brigade' and morality patrol spoken of by James Anderton, the Chief Constable of Greater Manchester) and speaks instead of policing as a popular *community institution*. It is a conception of law enforcement which Hermann Mannheim understood in the 1940s as an essential precondition of legitimate social democratic reconstruction: it would be an essential precondition of any more fundamental socialist reconstruction of the future.

Socialist reconstruction (like Thatcherism) requires effective policing in order to work. But, unlike Thatcherism, it would obviously not be able to work on the basis of policing alone nor indeed on the basis of any penal measures arrived at merely for the purpose of containment or discipline, The central point about an effective *socialist* reformism must always be its ability to transform the fundamental exploitation of labour by capital (and this must always be the *first objective* of its activity and initiatives) and also its ability to end the effects of this exploitation in lived social relations (one in which is the kind of interpersonal violence which occurs of urban areas). In other words, for socialist reformism to win a popular legitimacy, it must begin to win an economic struggle by abolishing the dependency of production on capital, and it must also win an ideological struggle in its ability to prefigure and thereby anticipate everyday lived social relations of a more human form.

So a socialist policy towards reform must be predicated primarily on its transformative economic policies; socialist policies of reform, for example in the area of law or welfare, must properly be formulated in terms of this initial premise. This is to say that policies towards the reform of law or towards policing cannot be substitutes for the initial, fundamental economic and social reconstruction. Demands for the democratisation of policing, therefore, are not in themselves a part of an integrated programme of socialist transformation, and they are not, and cannot be, substitutes for any such programme. So socialist reform strategies of the future must be integrated in order to avoid the danger of a piecemeal and unprincipled approach to the reform of discrete elements of the state apparatus.

The notion of an 'alternative economic strategy' is becoming much more widely understood and canvassed at the present time, as monetarist policy wreaks havoc on industry, on jobs and on investment for the future. Though subject to different interpretation and emphasis, the alternative economic strategy is formulated in terms of the centrality of human need. It is concerned with the organisation of production for socially useful purposes, including the creation of useful and supportive employment and also the fulfilment of widespread and urgent human needs. In particular, theorists of the alternative economic strategy, writing about contemporary Britain, point to currently unfulfilled demands for medical care, for operations and hospitalisation, to the need for alternative sources of food and fuel energy, for a new and more varied housing stock, and to pressing needs for new forms of community leisure provision, all of which could be met by a producton system established to meet collective needs rather than private profit.

Organised social democracy, in the form of the Labour Party, currently has no alternative *social* strategy, however, except in the shape of some reflex desire to defend the existing apparatus of the welfare state.[8] At the time of writing, there are some signs of a process of rethinking of social policy on the Left, especially in pamphlets (e.g. *In and Against the State*), in new journals (e.g. the *Bulletin of Social Policy* and *Critical Social Policy*) and in the very large conference on the welfare state held in London by the CSP collective in November 1980. For our purposes, one of the key questions in this process of rethinking will be the development of a social strategy similar to the alternative economic strategy which now exists on the Left, articulated around the changing and urgent needs of working-class people, women and blacks (young and old alike) rather than the interests of capital. It will have to be a social strategy which, unlike its Fabian predecessor, does not assume the appeal of the state and the family as the sources of community and individual expression for all citizens. It can only be out of such a social strategy (and out of the vision of an ideal socialist order) that sensible socialist reformism can emerge, and the incoherence of the 'modernising' or 'permissive' reformism of the recent past avoided.

Socialism and an alternative social strategy

(a) *The family*

In Chapter 2 we saw the centrality of the family in early post-war social democratic thinking and we were able to show that the significance of the family lay, primarily, in the contributions the institution could and should make to social order. Recent statements from the Labour leadership and publications of the Party do not suggest that developments in social relations in and around the family have had any serious effect on conventional social democratic thinking. When James Callaghan, as Prime Minister in October 1978, took time off from the management of the economy in order to send a message to a large national conference on vandalism (a message which was headlined in the London evening press), he announced that

> mindless destruction and damage is a danger signal of the *breakdown in the rules, standards and disciplines of the family and the country*, especially when they occur among the young.
> (*Evening Standard*, 31 October 1978, emphasis added)

Mr Callaghan continued by asserting that '*The Government can only do so much*. Parents bear a large part of the responsibility for bringing up their children properly.' He then linked this appeal to parents to bring their children up in a 'proper' fashion to a national mobilisation, declaring that there was a need for 'every person in the realm to help create a sharing, caring society which will make outcasts of violence and vandalism'.

Similar sentiments, less rhetorically expressed, find a place in the official Labour Party pamphlet on *The Deprived Child* (1973) and in the booklet on *Law, Order and Human Rights* produced for the use of parliamentary candidates in 1979. In the Callaghan speech, however, the primary objective appears to be to argue that 'social democracy' has done as much as it can in tackling problems of deprivation, urban decay and blight, and that any continuing vandalism must therefore be a product of other factors. In particular, Mr Callaghan, like Sir Keith Joseph in his popularisation of the notion of the cycle of deprivation as arising primarily out of pathological child-rearing practices in the underclass, invites his listeners to see the problem of youth crime as a product of faulty parenting in multiple problem families. This formulation propounds the internal dynamics of particularly disturbed families as the cause of social problems of crime and violence, especially in working-class communities, and detracts attention from the worsening conditions in inner-city areas, which in turn derive from the destructive logic of urban development in capitalist societies.

Callaghan's speech has at least two other ideological effects. It suggests that the existing direction of Labour government policy on urban development and social deprivation is very developed and far-reaching and that therefore any failings in such a policy could not be due to the policy itself (this allows the shift towards family pathology). But the Labour Party in government had a very limited, and fundamentally corporatist, policy towards the inner city and urban blight. That is, it has tended to use its own position of state power to direct money towards local authority schemes of urban renewal, many of which were developed in close collaboration with *local capital* rather than *local communities*; Labour governments and local authorities have tended generally to work only through existing, established interest groups. When one radical interest group, the Community Development Project, established by the Labour government of Harold Wilson, began to point to the frequent incompatibility of local capitalist and community interest, it was closed by the Labour government of James Callaghan.

Callaghan's speech also suggested that the problems experienced, often in a 'multiple' form, by certain families arose out of the inadequacies of the parents themselves. There is a traditionally social democratic reversion here to some absolutist conception of proper child-rearing, and in particular to the deferential proletarian notion of the family as an institution for inculcating bourgeois respectability and good order amongst otherwise unruly working people. But there is also a very limited and ideological conception of the 'family' and its relationship to wider social forces. It is almost as if the family stands apart from the social pressures and contradictions of late capitalist urban existence, largely unaffected by changes in the economic structure or moral order. There is no reference in Callaghan's speech to the massive effects on youth of the rapid decline in the casual labour market in the 1970s, or the consequences on women who had also entered the waged labour market in order to express themselves outside of motherhood and the nuclear family. Callaghan's rhetoric about the family is a rhetoric which literally *represses* the broader personal and social needs of women and also of young people, and instead speaks of the family as an institution which must *discipline* its constituent members, in the name of 'the rules, standards and disciplines of the family and the country'.

Gordon and Hunter (1977–8), in an insightful article on the successful use of a reactionary and patriarchal 'sexual politics' by the New Right in the United States as a means of gaining working-class support, have shown how this kind of defence of the family has a rational basis in the experience of the class. The family has historically acted as a 'vital source of economic and emotional support, as well as a basis for anti-capitalist struggles, as in strikes, community boycotts and [struggles for] cultural rights' (p. 13).

Moreover, the family has acted as an escape from the loneliness and disintegration of the wider social relations of capitalism. Finally, in the current period of inflation and fiscal crisis, the family has once again informally taken on a set of servicing functions that had earlier been taken over by consumer outlets and private and public health services:

> Many of the services that families provided – ranging from cooking to healing to entertainment – must be purchased or paid for through taxes, and the services paid for are an inadequate approximation of more personally provided services.
>
> (Gordon and Hunter, 1977–8, p. 13)

There is no doubt that the family has also had to take on these kinds of responsibilities once again in Britain in recent years, and that this has meant concretely that many women in both the middle and working class have had to readjust their expectations *vis-à-vis* the waged labour market, and to return to domestic labour. What is not at all clear, however, is whether this is a matter for celebration either among men or among women. There has been no significant attempt to articulate the defence of the family as a populist issue by the Right in this country of the kind that occurred in the United States, even though the defence of the family (specifically from 'moral pollution' of the media) has been the central slogan of Mary Whitehouse's National Viewers and Listeners Association. What has happened instead is that a traditional, social democratic rhetoric about the family has continued to be articulated by Labour leaders (as in the Callaghan speech) and by senior social workers. This seems to be the preferred alternative in Britain to generalised right-wing rhetoric regarding the collapse of family and social authority as a whole. What overall evidence there is on the family in Britain in 1980, however, suggests an astonishing degree of ambiguity, contradiction and pluralism.

Divorce *rates* have been increasing in Britain very rapidly over the last decade and a half, but so also have remarriages:

> In 1965, 11 per cent of the 370,000 marriages involved a divorced bride or groom; this increased to 22 per cent of the 426,000 marriages in 1972, and increased further to one in four marriages in 1974.
>
> (Leete, 1976, pp. 6–7)

By 1978 the total number of divorces reached 160,000 (as against 40,000 in 1966) and statistics over a period showed that one in three marriages ended in a breakdown. About 200,000 children a year experience a divorce between their parents (Dean, 1981).

Most leading texts on family sociology in Britain now start with a recitation of the definitional difficulties involved in any discussion. Thus, Peter Worsley *et al.* (1977) state that 'Uncertainties about the definitions of words reflect ambiguities in social relationships' (p. 168). They observe further that

> all of us, in society, are engaged in the business of defining 'the family' by the ways in which we think and act in relation to those whom we label as family and non-family.
>
> (Worsley *et al.*, 1977, p. 16)

Contemporary ambiguities surrounding the family revolve predominantly, though not exclusively, around the issues of the division of domestic labour and the connected question of gender identity. Research undertaken at the Birmingham Centre for Contemporary Cultural Studies into situation comedies shown on television in recent years shows that nearly all these comedies are taken up with jokes about the troubled areas of 'masculinity' and 'femininity' (including, centrally, the politics of housework), while analysis of popular women's magazines and of male pornography reflects a similar attempt to negotiate these changing definitions (Winship, 1980; Mort, 1980).[9] Most obvious of all, perhaps, is the work done around these questions by the five popular daily newspapers (*The Sun, The Star, The Daily Mirror, The Daily Mail and The Daily Express*), and in particular in their sponsorship of 'liberated', eroticised relationships between consenting heterosexual adults. This is not to say that tolerance has been extended towards all forms of sexual preference. Popular television shows and everyday popular humour are as anxious and antagonistic towards homosexuality as were popular newspapers in earlier periods; there is an almost universally negative reaction to attempts to lower the age of consent below sixteen; and there are stunning silences in popular discourse about the facts of lesbianism. The freedom granted to adult heterosexuals is paralleled by a *disciplining* and a *silencing* of other sexual characters (Pratt, 1981).

So far as heterosexual preferences are concerned the government of the radical Right has made no attempt to reassert a classically puritan posture, and neither has there been any direct attempt to re-establish the nuclear family ideologically as the only, natural or universal form of sexual or social relation.

So while we do not live in a society of mutual toleration of all forms of personal relationships for sexual preferences, we do not all live in families; and those of us who do live in families find the family to be an uncontradictory, unproblematic institution. The structure on which social democracy placed so much hope in the 1940s — the nuclear family — no longer relates to reality in quite the way it may have done then. In some respects this is simply to say, following researchers into popular youth culture in the 1960s, that the kinship group has lost some of its importance to the peer group, especially in the working class (see, for example, Downes, 1966); but, in other respects, it is also to point to the fractured and contradictory status of the family, particularly as an institution in which men, women and young adults all struggle for support, group membership and self expression.

The women's movement has developed major critiques of the repression of women in the family, ranging from studies of the differential socialisation of young girls and boys to investigations of the disadvantaging of women in the waged labour market and in the welfare state. Recent analytical work in the women's movement has resulted in the demand for the 'disaggregation' of the family, or, in other words, the dismantling of all laws and conventions which treat women as a part of a husband's estate (for tax purposes, or for purposes of social security, etc.) (see McIntosh, 1981). Radical feminists have argued that women should now break entirely with heterosexual relations, on the grounds that they are irretrievably patriarchal (Delphy, 1979), and groups of socialist feminists have once again initiated communal forms of child-rearing, in order to avoid having to retreat into the contradictory and privatised interior of the nuclear family.

Very little of this initiative in life-styles may be percolating into working-class neighbourhoods. But it is well known that the changes that have been occurring in the sexual division of labour, in particular in the increase of the number of working-class women in the waged labour market, has had effects within the working class. Statistics would suggest wife beating is either on the increase in the working class or that working-class women are far more willing to report the assaults being made on them whilst leaving their husbands and escaping to refuges (Pizzey, 1974; Dobash and Dobash, 1979). Psychiatric disturbances, in particular those associated with stress, continue to increase amongst women (as do crime rates). There is no open revolt against the family as a preferred form of living — most divorcees appear to want to remarry — but neither is there evidence that the family is a universally celebrated or romanticised institution, in the way that it appears to be in conventional social democratic thinking.

Our argument here is that any alternative social strategy by the Labour Party must begin to break with rhetorics that are defensive in a one-directional manner of the family, and begin to construct policies that recognise the rights and needs of individuals who may or may not choose to live in nuclear (or extended) families, who may want to live in 'serial monogamy', or who many want to live in broader kinds of communities. Anna Coote has proposed that the very conception of the family needs to be clarified, ideologically and in law, to signify 'the household where there are children (or other dependants in need of care) — regardless of how many adults happen to live with them, or what their marital status might be' (Coote, 1981, p. 7). She also argues for the recognition that parenthood is a male function no less than a female one ('a socialist family policy should be based on the principle of equal parenthood', p. 7). Thirdly, she affirms that a socialist family policy must include a commitment to the maintenance and expansion of social provision for families 'to include not only nurseries, but eating places, social centres, laundries, help for the elderly and the disabled, recreation centres and so forth — financed out of public money and controlled by the community'. Such social provision would enable fathers *and* mothers to work, and, especially if the facilities were democratically controlled and well funded, it would reduce the pressures on parents who do want to work. So, finally, it would make possible a family policy based on economic equality between families as well as within them. This could be ensured, in particular, by the provision of financial support for children irrespective of their parents' incomes (as with pensioners) and also by legislation requiring that male and female parents would be offered 'paid jobs on a genuinely equal basis — in terms of hours of work, pay and domestic commitments'.

The details of Anna Coote's proposals require discussion. The programme is not exhaustive, but it is a first move. It is clear that the legal and practical difficulties currently involved in departing from the nuclear family as a way of life are partly responsible for the continuing reproduction of unhappy existences within conventional nuclear families, although those families do also provide the material and emotional sustenance discussed by Gordon and Hunter. The Left must therefore avoid the trap of advocating a straightforwardly

oppositional or celebratory position on the institution of the
family. It should recognise the support that the family provides for many working people. It should neither be dismissive
of the widespread popularity of the nuclear family, nor be
too romantic or utilitarian as to the social and personal functions the family may perform.

Any such revision in social policy would have fundamental
consequences across the entire field of policy activity in a
future social democracy. In particular, the deprivileging of
the nuclear family would have fundamental effects *at law*,
especially in the already fluid area of family law. The patriarchal nature of some law has already been widely challenged
in recent years (especially in relation to divorce, rape and
prostitution) and in some other areas, for example the laws
governing equal pay or abortion, either the intent of the law
or its application are quite progressive (in supporting the
legitimate demands of women). In recent legislation on
domestic violence there has also been a move away from the
privileging of the nuclear family, as the same protection has
been extended to cohabitees as to wives. All of these changes
are excellent, but it is by no means the case that the motivation
informing these and other changes has always been that of
institutionalising the rights of women. Nor is it clear that
recent changes affecting the position of children of broken
marriages or of children in care are primarily and exclusively
concerned with institutionalising the rights of children in
every conceivable circumstance, even though there has
undoubtedly been a reduction of emphasis in law on the
rights than can be exercised by biological parents over their
children.

Carol Smart has summarised recent changes in family law
as involving a transition in

> the extent to which the law directly involve(s) itself in
> family life and in the modes of regulation that have been
> employed . . . On the one hand, the law has become more
> willing to invade the 'privacy' of family life (e.g. legislation
> on domestic violence, powers to vary the ownership of the
> matrimonial home) whilst it has abandoned to a consider-

able extent its negative and punitive response to extra- and non-marital relations.

(Smart, 1981b, p. 3)

The transitions are not, of course, equivalent to the recognition at law of the family as 'a living unit with dependants' or as an institution involving equal responsibilities for parenting and equal rights to work. They are transitions in the way in which the state recognises the marriage contract and also manages social and economic relations within the nuclear family form.

Any new socialist reformism that is going to recognise the rights of women and children and to challenge the patriarchal character of the nuclear family will have to go beyond existing legal struggles. The state should be called upon to give financial and other support to women's groups and to movements working in support of children's rights in order that they can afford to mount their own challenges to existing legal precedents. The state, in other words, must be required to give support to the struggle to recognise the different ways of life that people are currently engaged in as their *legal right*, and therefore as ways of life for which (providing no harm is done to others) they cannot be financially or otherwise penalised.

All of which is to say that the revision of social policy will clearly involve, as several other writers have already argued, the use of law as a specific arena of struggle. Women's struggles over disaggregation will have to take place at law, as will the various struggles involved in gaining recognition for living arrangements outside the nuclear family: and it is only at law that popular needs can begin to be recognised specifically as 'rights'. It is clear that the traditional socialist distrust of law is a posture which will not be very helpful in the creation and practical development of an alternative social strategy, and it is also transparent that the conventional Fabian insistence on the family as the cornerstone of the community can no longer be at the centre of the new social policy.

(b) *Youth*

A second area requiring immediate reconstruction in social

democratic thought is the question of youth, for reasons
which should be clear from my discussion of social democracy
in the earlier post-war period in Chapter 2. If we take the
pronouncements of the OECD and of Western governments
seriously, juvenile labour markets are going to be much less
extensive in the future than for some time in the past. The
new technology will virtually put an end to the need for a
large reserve army of labour, and the crisis of profitability
will force increasing numbers of lay-offs in competitive industries.

Post-war social democratic thinking about modern capitalism
has tended to assume a certain continuity in the character of
economic and social relations, including the relations of
production and employment. In a similar fashion, it has also
tended to think that a refurbished Keynesian capitalism
could continue to produce a surplus with which to fund a
variety of social programmes (including those involving job
creation funded out of state revenue). These two assumptions
have been the basis for many social democratic responses to
troublesome youth throughout the post-war period (in the
form of the Mobilization for Youth programmes in the United
States during the 1960s, and in the Youth Opportunities
schemes initiated by the last Labour government in Britain).
The state has subsidised an artificial labour market for youth.

Neither private nor public sector provisions can be expected
to fulfil this task once the current world recession and the
new technology have their full impact on levels of youth
unemployment in the West. The pessimism of new wave youth
culture is therefore likely to be justified, and, unless socialist
advances are achieved, the main political beneficiaries of the
recession are likely to be racist and Fascist parties, which have
recently recognised the primary importance of recruiting
within the massive army of unemployed and alienated youth.

What is abundantly clear is that the familiar response of
social democrats to the youth problem — as a 'temporary'
problem occurring for youth during the transition from
school to work — no longer makes sense of the social relations
of modern capitalism. There is likely in the near future to be
a large youthful sector in all the developed capitalist societies
which can have no realistic expectation of secure, long-term

employment. The full implications of this recognition cannot even begin to be grasped, culturally, politically or in social policy terms, by a Fabian and/or liberal-professional version of social democracy which speaks of youth only in terms of temporary economic deprivation or the pathological child-rearing practices of the problem family.

It is clear that a continuation of existing educational and social policies (predicated as they are on the potentialities of Keynesianism to sustain full employment) will become increasingly incompatible with economic 'reality'. We have argued that the response of socialists in such circumstances must not simply be to defend existing educational and social policies as such (which are by no means socialist in their conception or the detail of their functioning) but it certainly must be to defend the rhetorical commitment of educationalists to the provision of education for all children according to their abilities and needs — *irrespective of the realities of the market-place*. At the same time, it is obvious that the simultaneous arrival of the world recession and the new technology demand the articulation of new social policies in the immediate and long-term interests of youth. The prospect of short-term and long-term worklessness among youth, with all its disabling and dehumanising effects, has to be combatted by a new socialist politics which enlarges the scope of production (to meet the widely unsatisfied human needs) and thereby increases the number of opportunities that are available, while also moving towards a much more equal distribution of the work that becomes available. This in itself would also enable a substantial reduction of the working week for labour. The alternative to any such fundamental revision of the labour market is the continued reproduction of the nihilistic violence of the soccer terrace on the one hand, and, on the other, the frequently cynical, defensive commitment that both manual and non-manual workers exhibit towards their employment under capitalism. A continuation of the former will undermine the long-term possibility of social order in the public spaces of large post-industrial cities, as well as making the jobs of teachers and social workers quite impossible. So it is to some version of socialist transformation of the mode of production that teachers and youth workers must increasingly turn as a solution to their own everyday problems and the real problems confronting their youthful charges. The solutions offered by Thatcherism (the social market economy) and traditional social democracy (the succour of the family and the community) are no solution at all to the pressing problems confronting Britain's youth in the 1980s.

The construction of new policies for the distribution of labour according to socially useful purposes and according to need is an example of the kind of radical socialist reform which, we argued earlier, is going to be required in order to reconnect popular anxieties and aspirations to the project of socialism. But, whilst the long-term effects of this alternative social strategy would do much to mitigate the current hopelessness of workless youth and the routine alienation of youth employed in purposeless labour, in the short term there remains the real social problem wrought by the violence and nihilism of a massive rejected cohort of youth. The libertarian impulses of most democratic socialists have meant that state attempts at the containment or correction of violent or troublesome youth (from institutional lock-ups through to intermediate treatment) have been criticised from the Left as unwarrantable exercises of social control, militarisation and cheap labour, through to repression, but there have been some calls, in particular from Labour MPs from working-class backgrounds, for firm measures. Our argument is that the specifically penal discipline of the Borstal, detention centre and secure unit, and the casework of the professional social worker are both inappropriate as responses to contemporary social disorder. The use of penal discipline (as currently organised) on the young is as likely now as in the past, and just as likely as the penal discipline of adults, to result in enormous rates of recidivism and reconviction, as a result of the effects that prisons and penal institutions generally have in confirming the social 'marginality' and ideological rejection of their inmates. The use of measures of intermediate treatment for rebuilding moral character confronts the contradiction that the labour market for youth demands self-denial and automatism rather than self-respect. It also ignores the transparently immoral character of the unequal distribution of rewards under capitalism. And it does not in any case

satisfy the popular demands for retribution and social defence:
on the contrary, it appears to privilege children in trouble
over other children in deprived areas by providing them with
time out of the area (sometimes in the country) and with
new employment or leisure opportunities. So IT in this sense
may actually amplify the sense of inequality of reward in
capitalist society, and may encourage further division and
resentment within deprived areas, with consequent trouble
later.

Thus the conventional responses of the state to troublesome
youth have to be attacked — primarily on the grounds that
they will not be effective in their proclaimed objectives. The
Left is, however, in a more difficult position on the question
of the morality of the state's responses to youth. It has to
decide how to respond to the retributive demands and the
demands for 'social defence' that emerge from residents of
dislocated working-class areas, from public transport workers
and from elsewhere. The Left does want to use the argument
of social defence, as we shall see in Chapter 4, to argue for
policing that is adequate to defend the beleaguered black
communities in Britain and also to defend the right of women
to enter into public space at night. The Left may also want to
argue for the arrest, containment and even punishment of
violent activists of the racist and Fascist Right.

To do all this, the Left, if it is to be consistent and if it is
to be taken seriously in its programme for the reform of the
existing state, will have to argue for some form of containment and control of really violent and troublesome youth.
What is absolutely crucial, however, is, first, that any such
'correctionalist' politics must *continually* be linked to demands
for restructuring of the labour market, discussed earlier (in
the name of social justice), and secondly, that such correction-
alism must proceed according to the criteria of popular justice.
That is to say, the Left must begin now to devise programmes
for the popularisation of the existing magistracy and also of
the form of legal representation received by youth in the
magistrates' courts. The monopoly of the political parties
over the Bench, and the monopoly of professional solicitors
and barristers over juvenile court proceedings, must be challenged by the introduction of lay magistrates and lay advo-

cates acting on behalf of working people against young delinquents or alternatively acting on behalf of youth. The courts must be transformed from being instruments of an 'alien' form of law and discipline (as they are now in popular experience) into institutions that at least suggest that justice is popular. Once this is achieved, then abstract utilitarian debates about the criteria in offences which ought to 'justify' punishment will become practical matters receiving some form of popular adjudication.

A similar perspective is required from the Left on the question of punishment itself. We have already suggested that the use of penal discipline and of measures of treatment for purposes of remoralisation are likely to be ineffective in relation to youth. But we do not necessarily believe that the segregation of troublesome youth into institutions is therefore unjustifiable. The community homes envisaged by the architects of the Children and Young Persons Act of 1969 did do important work with young people, especially in the early 1970s prior to the introduction of an anxiety over 'security' and prior to the collapse of the juvenile labour market, in raising questions about the quality of social relations (between the sexes, races, and adults and youth). They did take troublesome youths out of their own neighbourhoods, so answering local demands for social defence and retribution, although they did not permanently segregate the young people from their family and friends in the community. But they were irretrievably 'liberal' and middle class in their practices, and therefore were constantly negotiating the problem of the contradictory class locations of the staff and their charges. They were (and are) accountable for their practices only to the superior authority of local authority social service departments, who would judge their performance according to the criteria of liberal 'professionalism' only.

What is required by the Left is a popularisation of the everyday practices of youth control in liberal community homes, via the introduction of many more staff from generally working-class backgrounds and many more working-class heads of home, governors and visitors. (Each community home could be made responsible to a committee consisting in part of social work professionals but also elected representatives of the community from trade unions through to parents' groups.) Such a redrawing of the accountability of institutions for the control and treatment of troublesome youth could in principle prefigure a change in the 'professional' criteria by which these institutions are run, and their replacement by much more grounded and mundane criteria of class discipline, on the one hand, and authentic community care on the other. Obviously this reform would not have immediate effects, any more than has the introduction of parental governors into conventional schools, since the everyday presence of professionals in an institution will always give them more power and influence than the body of representatives to which they are technically accountable. So the demand for a popularisation of the *recruitment* of the professionals working in community homes is at least as important as the introduction of greater accountability in increasing the possibility of a break from the abstract liberalism of the professional, and introducing legitimate and authentic popular punishment into homes containing troublesome youths of overwhelming working-class backgrounds.

This demand for the popularisation of the community home would have several other important effects. It would provide a real rationale for closing the merely retributive and militaristic detention centres, and it could provide the basis for the radical reform of the Borstal, with its thoroughly anachronistic involvement in the puritan and masochistic traditions of the public school. The reconstruction of the community home into an instrument of popular justice and discipline (and an expansion in their use) could also be the basis for a genuine 'decarceration' from other institutions as well as for the abolition of institutions purveying the discipline of the ruling class on their working-class charges. It could also provide a genuinely popular alternative to the populist demands for the firm exercise of existing state power over deviants and dissidents which have emanated from the Right in recent years. It proposes an authentically popular justice as an alternative to the spurious populism of the discipline of existing ruling-class institutions.

Any call for this form of popular justice and discipline must always occur, however, in the context of the demand for social justice for youth, discussed earlier. Existing policies for youth must constantly be indicted for their failure to provide social justice. The demand for reform must also specify that the selection of youthful offenders for punishment must occur in the context of a public and popular democratic process of legal adjudication, dominated neither by the magistracy or police, nor by liberal-professionals. It must be authentically responsive to popular demands for justice and social defence.

Notes to Chapter 3

1. The reference to expenditure on social services as 'candy floss' expenditure was made by Councillor Ronald Wootton, Chairman of the West Midlands Police Committee, in March 1980. He was calling for these services to be cut in order to provide the finance for the extra 1,171 policemen requested by his chief constable (*The Guardian*, 6 March 1980).
2. As if in anxious anticipation of the later riot in Brixton, *The Sunday Times* in June 1980 reported that 52 per cent of boys and girls aged 16–19 on the job register at the local unemployment exchange were black. The blacks comprised only 30 per cent of the age group in the area (15 June 1980). In the week after the Brixton riot, a speaker at the National Association of Schoolmasters annual conference observed that there were only 13 job vacancies in Brixton for 784 young people registered unemployed (*The Guardian*, 23 April 1981).
3. See Chapter 1, pp. 24.
4. In this, the chief constable was shortly to be supported in the belated publicity given to a study of *The Effectiveness of Policing* by R. V. G. Clarke and J. M. Hough of the Home Office's own Research Unit. This collection of heavily researched essays was summarised in one report as demonstrating that 'if you are interested in crime control, you will not bother recruiting extra policemen because they will have little or no effect on crime'. Quite the contrary, 'the increase in *reported* crime exactly mirrors the increase in police expenditure . . . [because] more policemen always mean [that] more crime [is] recorded'. This increase in crime known to the police means more work for the courts, probation service and prisons, but it does not mean less crime or more social order (Malcolm Dean, 'The Police Evidence That Will Embarrass Mr Whitelaw', *The Guardian*, 3 December 1980).
5. In his speech at the Durham Miners' Gala on 12 July 1980, Mr Benn argued that the Party had to 'broaden the base of popular support

for the Labour Party *by seeking affiliations* from among the community groups, the women's movement, the ethnic communities and those who are concerned with the environment. [The Party] must speak for the new peace movement in Britain, and harness the radical tradition which is still so strong in rural areas . . . and [it] must persuade *all those who call themselves socialists* to abandon their sectarian isolation and join the Labour Party as loyal individual members' (emphasis added).

6. Expenditure on health in Britain in the early 1970s, at 4.9 per cent of gross domestic product, was less than the percentage of GDP spent on health in France, Germany, Italy, Canada and Sweden. Expenditure on social security (at 7.7 per cent of GDP) was less than in the United States, France, Germany, Italy and Sweden; and expenditure on education (5.6 per cent of GDP) was less than in the United States, Canada and Sweden. Overall social expenditure in the UK (at 18.2 per cent of GDP) was less than in all the other major European societies (and some 5½ per cent of GDP less than in Sweden). See Gough (1979, table 5.2).

7. There have been a large number of (considerably under-reported) struggles against hospital closures in Britain in recent years. The best known of these has perhaps been the struggle against the closure of the Elizabeth Garrett Anderson hospital for women in London, which began with a work-in November 1976; but there are many other examples of successful resistance to closures.

8. The absence of any systematic social policy thinking within the Labour Party was noted by the usually well informed *Guardian* Home Affairs Correspondent, Malcolm Dean, in September 1980. Dean noted that on questions of crime (meaning the specific issues of juvenile and young adult offenders and on sentencing) 'the Labour Party still has no collective view' and that the prison question was 'a policy field which through indifference and timidity the Party had always left to pressure groups'. He accepted that 'there is a private paper now in circulation but the All Party Parliamentary Committee on Penal Affairs has already pre-empted the Party with a radical programme' (Dean, 'Age of Uncertainty After the Reformation', *The Guardian*, 24 September 1980).

9. The way in which the popular media have reflected, negotiated and informed these changes in the sexual division of labour should be the subject of a major study in itself. For example, films on general release in 1980 appeared to legitimise male violence against women to quite an unprecedented degree (in 'The Shining' and 'Dressed to Kill') and could only be read as part of a 'male backlash against the growing power of the women's movement' (Root and Murray, 1980, p. 30).

4
Reconstructing Socialist Criminology

It should be apparent from the emphasis I placed on the populist appeal of the radical Right that I believe the reconstruction of socialist social policy generally must in large part arise out of practice. That is to say, I do not believe that many people will be, or can be, thrust into action against Thatcherism as a result of abstract theoretical work — for example into the nature of 'law', 'the state' or even 'patriarchy'. People are likely to deal with these questions in a vigorous and effective manner the more that they are directly affected and angered by the operation of the state (through the social security system, the police, or the courts), by institutionalised racism or sexism, or by unemployment.

Direct and practical involvement in democratic socialist policies as currently organised (therefore in Labour Party politics at local and national level) is essential in order that the objective of socialism can be reconnected to the various — frequently fragmentary — social groups which now make up the working class. Socialists in the Labour Party have to begin to take seriously the popular anxieties and fears which have fed and sustained the growth of the radical Right. They must begin to construct and articulate policies that prefigure a genuine social order for all.

Nowhere is this more clear than on the law and order issue. Repetition now of earlier idealistic versions of radical criminology would be an inadequate and irresponsible response to the popular anxieties that exist on street crime and on contemporary behaviours of youth. It is no longer the case that popular concern with these questions is a product of a 'moral panic' manufactured by some intolerant local bourgeois or by an over-sensitive press. The fears of violence of public transport workers and of people living in and around Britain's football grounds are real (even if it is also mistaken, as we argued in Chapter 1, to conceive of violence as an immediate danger throughout society). They will continue to be real until the brutalising effects of unemployment, specifically, and of class inequality, generally, are eliminated through a socialist transformation.

So the recognition of crime in popular consciousness must be taken seriously. But a practical socialist criminology cannot merely be a reflection of the common sense about crime that is common in the class. This common sense has a long (and not always honourable) history of use in the evolution of working-class communities and working-class families during the eighteenth and nineteenth centuries. It is a common sense which has made sense of, and normalised, the reproduction of one male working-class labour force after another and also, therefore, the reproduction of women and children as dependants of the male wage labourer, with all real power and authority centralised in the man. It is a common sense which explains almost all forms of dislocation in working-class life in terms of the weakening of this patriarchal form of authority. So crime and delinquency are explained in terms of the moral or practical failings of other parents, the weakening of discipline in schools, and latterly the dilution of the authority of the class by the arrival of members of other cultures in an area. Where women or girls are involved, the absence of a proper exercise of male authority is usually the additional explanatory factor.

This form of common sense cannot — by reference to its appeals for the restoration of traditional forms of class and gender discipline — restore the social conditions (and the repressive, if cohesive, form of social order) of earlier historical periods. It cannot, for example, abolish the new consciousness of alternative life-style possibilities which the mass media have displayed before working-class youth. In particular, working-class common sense, with all its deeply sexist assumptions (as evidenced most clearly in working-class humour), cannot make sense of the stirrings of women's consciousness in certain sections of the class, and it is certainly not a viable basis on which to build alternative family policies or alternative transitional programmes for women generally.

In other words, the plea for practical involvement in existing Labour politics is not a plea for a return to a conventional working-class materialism or common sense. Any new socialist criminology must be formed in the practical context, responding to problems that arise in popular experience of the existing penal and welfare systems and, in particular, to popular demands for policing and a sense of social order.

There are currently only five potential agencies in which to begin the task of constructing a practical socialist criminology. These are the prison movements, the police critics, the socialist lawyers and civil liberties groups, and the various organisations that have arisen within the women's movement. The established agency of critical academic criminologists is currently a poor sixth, with little obvious 'practical' relevance.

The prison movement: rehabilitation, abolition, justice

In July 1981, the daily population of prisons in England and Wales reached its highest ever figure of 45,500, nearly four times the size of the daily average prison population in the first year of the post-war Labour government in 1945 (12,910). It is true that the prison population was therefore smaller in 1981, in proportion to the number of offences known to the police, than it was in 1945,[1] but it is also quite apparent that this level of imprisonment was a savage indictment of post-war social democracy and the form assumed by its social reconstruction. It was, indeed, the second highest number of prisoners per head of population of any country in Europe. For every 100,000 people in the population, 89 people were in prison in England and Wales on an average day in 1980. This compared with 91 people (per 100,000) in prison in West Germany (in November 1979), 72 in France (in March 1980) and 69 in Luxembourg, 62 in Denmark, 54 in Italy, 47 in Belgium, 35 in Eire (all in April 1980) and 23 in the Netherlands (in January 1980). The daily average prison population in Scotland and Northern Ireland, however, was higher than any of these (at 94 and 162 per 100,000 respectively) (Mr Partick Mayhew, Parliamentary Answer,

1 June 1981). The British prison system was being asked, in 1981, to contain an impossibly high number of largely working-class convicts, most of whom (nearly 70 per cent) had been convicted of relatively minor and non-violent property offences (see Fitzgerald and Sim, 1979, p. 135). There was, in other words, a massive crisis of over-crowding resulting from the continued use of prison sentences by the courts for the containment of minor working-class offenders. Over 18,000 of these prisoners in 1981 were housed two or three to a cell, and many were locked up in their cells for long hours (sometimes up to 23 hours a day).

The living and working conditions in British prisons were not subject to much comment in the recent report of inquiry into the prison system, chaired by Mr Justice May and published in 1979;[2] but during 1980 and 1981 more and more reports suggested that a rapid deterioration was occurring. Many of the older prisons in Britain are relics of the 'great incarceration' of the early nineteenth century, and these were described in 1980 by a tutor at the Prison Staff College as 'stinking ruins' (Godfrey, 1980). Later in the year, Mr Duncan Buttery, the senior civil servant in charge of prison building, informed the House of Commons Home Affairs Committee that

> our existing estate . . . is suffering from years of neglect and problems of maintenance exacerbated by overcrowding, a shortage of work staff and a shortage of tradesmen. The whole estate, to put a not too exaggerrated a view on it, is collapsing around our ears.
>
> (*The Guardian*, 4 November 1980)

Early in the following year, the Director-General of the Prison Department, Mr Dennis Trevelyan, broke tradition by using the department's annual report as an occasion in which to present strong criticism of the financing of prisons and also the over-use of prisons by the courts. Conditions in British prisons, he wrote, were now 'a disgrace to civilised society' (*The Guardian*, 1 May 1981).

Within these overcrowded and officially 'disgraceful' prisons, other crises were developing. Perhaps the most important of these, for prisoners themselves, has been what

Fitzgerald and Sim call the 'crisis of containment'. This particular problem is in part a reflection of the rapid increase in the number of prisoners serving long-term sentences. The number of prisoners serving life sentences increased from 122 in 1957 to 1,274 in 1978, and, in addition, the average length of the sentences being served in prison increased by 50 per cent between 1965 and 1975. By 1978, '21 per cent of the average daily male prison population in England and Wales was made up of lifers and long-termers . . . [In] closed training prisons only, the proportion was 67 per cent' (Cohen and Taylor, 1980).[3]

Partly in consequence of this increase in long-term imprisonment, but also specifically in response to the spate of escapes from British prisons in 1966,[4] the British prison system was subjected to a very rapid *Inquiry into Prison Escapes and Security* (the Mountbatten Report). This inquiry recommended in favour of the classification (into four categories — A–D) of all prisoners on admission according to their escape risk and the danger they would pose to the public if they were to escape. It also recommended that the means for controlling the most risky and dangerous category A prisoners should be the establishment of a single top-security fortress prison, on the model of Alcatraz in the United States. This argument was, however, lost to proponents of a policy of 'dispersal', where category A prisoners should be contained in specified prisons throughout the regions.

The dispersal policy has been seen by many to be the reason for the massive increase in physical security which has undoubtedly occurred throughout the prison system. The new security measures introduced since 1966 have included

the introduction of dog patrols, the use of TV monitoring equipment, use of electronic gates, lights, infra-red cameras for night-patrolling, the creation of specialist units of prison officers (for example, security officers) and extra fences and walls. The impact of these measures has been felt in all areas of prison life, including the availability of visiting, recreational, association and education facilities, the reduction in the number of outside working parties, and stricter control and surveillance not only on the external prison walls and perimeter fences, but within the prison wings and on the cell landings. Thus, a person sent down for being drunk and disorderly may find himself being guarded by some of the most sophisticated surveillance technology available.

(Fitzgerald and Sim, 1979, p. 23)

In reality, the elaboration of security and containment has not been related in any straightforward way to the particular distributions of category A prisoners in the prison system. Rather, it is now a general feature of most prisons in Britain, and a feature which seems to result from a third identifiable crisis in the system, a crisis in the legitimacy of prison as such to prisoners.

The rapid development of prison movements and of direct action inside prison was common to nearly all Western societies in the 1970s. In Britain, the major event was the formation of the national prisoners' movement (Preservation of the Rights of Prisoners) in 1972, signalled in the simultaneous twenty-four-hour strike on 4 August that year in favour of the PROP Charter of Demands by about 10,000 prisoners in 33 prisons throughout Britain (see Fitzgerald, 1977, p. 157). This was followed by a series of individual incidents of revolt in Gartree and Albany prisons, and then by the virtual destruction of large parts of Hull Prison in the summer of 1976. The response of the Prison Department of the Home Office was to allow a series of trials of the rebellious prisoners by the prison governors and the boards of prison visitors, but also to move to create the infamous control units at Wakefield and Wormwood Scrubs.[5] The physical amenities in the new control units were austere to the point of being seen by some as experiments in sensory deprivation, but the key feature of the units was the construction of a regime (of a ninety-day period of solitary confinement, strict rules, and silence followed by the 'carrot' of another ninety-day period of 'modest' activity and association) designed to enforce conformity. Failure to conform at any stage would result in prisoners being returned to Day 1 of the first stage in order to serve their time again. The unambiguous function of these units was to

relieve dispersal prisons, for limited periods and as occasion

arises, from the pressure and strains imposed by the activities and influence of the small minority of prisoners who
from time to time deliberately set out to undermine and
disrupt the pattern of life of the prison in which they are
held and show by their repeated behaviour that they are
determined not to cooperate with the normal training
regime.

(Home Office Prison Department, Circular Instruction
35/1974)

The contradiction, of course, is that the 'normal training
regime' in the overcrowded and heavily controlled prisons of
the early 1970s was also losing legitimacy for the vast majority
of prisoners. Official prison policy no longer took seriously,
as it had certainly done in the 1950s, the idea that prisons
could seriously pursue any rehabilitative work, and, even
worse, for supporters of prisons' practical social role, no one
could even take seriously the effectivity of prison as a deterrent to crime. 1975 data showed that 88 per cent of a sample
of adult male prisoners discharged in 1973 had already been
reconvicted. Most prisoners know that their return to prison
is possible or even likely, and very few in 1981 any longer
have respect for the authority of prison officers who, in the
words of the Prison Department's own Director-General, are
more and more 'withdrawing to the perimeter', concentrating
on 'outside security' rather than on working with prisoners
(*The Guardian*, 1 May 1981). The crisis of legitimacy merges
into a crisis of the prison officer's authority over prisoners as
a whole.

The final crisis in prison identified by Fitzgerald and Sim is
what they call the crisis of 'visibility'. By this, Fitzgerald and
Sim are referring to the collapse in the ability of the Home
Office to maintain the conditions of overwhelming secrecy
that have characterised the management of prisons in Britain
throughout the last 150 years. The physical destruction of
Hull Prison in 1976 was impossible to disguise from the local
and national media, especially given the presence of prisoners
on the roof; and, of course, the events of the summer of
1972 were the occasion for a massive, if often shameless,
problematisation of the prison issue even in the popular
press.[6] But it is probably even more telling as a comment on

the character of the changes occurring within prisons that many of the stories appearing in the press (on the control units, on the use of drugs by the Prison Medical Service and, most recently, on the establishment of the so-called MUFTI squad by the Prison Service for the purpose of riot control)[7] have all been leaked to the prison movement and to the press by staff working inside prisons.

In 1980, there was a final recognition on the part of the Home Office of the impossibility of continuing with existing policies of secrecy, when a BBC television film crew was allowed into Strangeways Prison in Manchester in order to produce an excellent series of eight programmes into conditions in that prison. The significance of the screening of 'Strangeways' may, however, lie not simply in the long-term campaigns that have been waged for opening up the British prison system, but in the way in which the programme portrayed the problems in prison as an almost intractable human tragedy, without there being any clear discussion of solutions.

The programme did, however, recognise the demise of any rehabilitative optimism in prisons and it did portray a sense of the various crises which (following Fitzgerald and Sim) I have outlined here. The same cannot yet be said for the Labour Party (or perhaps for socialists in general).

Democratic socialist thought, in both its early romantic and later practical versions, has until recently remained faithful to the prison as a primarily *correctional and rehabilitative* institution working with *pathological individuals*. Writing in 1905, the utopian socialist Edward Carpenter identified the Conservative conception of prison as being a place solely for punishment, and then observed that

> mere *punishment* must be abandoned; . . . reform must go more and more in the direction of health — giving life in Workshops and on Farms. Healthy industrial life must be made the basis of the reformatory system. The feeble-minded and bodied must be treated for what they are, as the sad product of social errors; and must be given such occupation or work as they are capable of. The more able-bodied and capable must be trained with a view to their return to life in the outer world. Throughout, the funda-

mental connexion between labour and its natural rewards must be kept in sight, as the main engine of regulation and stimulus. And where a man has injured another in any way that can be estimated by money values, as by theft or personal violence, it would be well to make him realise what he has done by working off, in the Industrial House, the full value of the injury inflicted. This, so far from being a mere punishment, would be a fulfilment of social justice, and a help to the offender — having made compensation — to return to society again with a clear conscience.

(Carpenter, 1905, pp. 75—6)

Whilst Labour governments have rarely been so imaginative in practice as to place the connection between labour and natural rewards at the centre of their penal policies, they have none the less continually urged the replacement of punishment by reformation or rehabilitation as the goal of prison. One of the effects of this elevation of prison into a treatment agency, especially in the 1950s and 1960s, was the development of ideologies about sentencing, for example, which suggested that people were being sent into prison 'for their own good', for treatment. This celebration of prison treatment was most marked of all in the fourth edition of the Home Office's *Prisons and Borstals in England and Wales* in 1960, published at the height of R. A. Butler's period as Home Secretary, but it was a legitimating ideology that continued to have force even beyond 1966 (the year of the escapes and the Mountbatten Report), throughout the period of the Labour government of 1964—70. It was only really made fundamentally problematic by the prison revolts of 1972.

In 1976, *Labour's Programme* announced — for the first time in a Labour Party policy document — that 'there is growing evidence that custodial sentences are not only expensive but also rarely successful as a method of reform and deterrence'. It therefore asserted that the Labour Party 'believes that the prime purpose of prison is to protect society from those offenders who are a real danger to it'. Apparently accommodating to panics about the growth of 'dangerousness' in civil society, the Labour Party indicated that 'In cases of violence and other crimes which justifiably arouse great public concern, custodial sentences will still be available.'

Major reductions in the size of the prison population could none the less be achieved by reducing maxima for offences and by a considerable extension in the use of parole. So, in the 1979 campaign handbook on *Law, Order and Human Rights*, Labour Party penal policy took the form of a series of important, but quite technical, proposals on the reduction of sentences and on parole reform. In the same year, Mr Justice May's Committee of Inquiry into the Prison Services recommended the introduction of a new rule 1 which would specify the object of prison as that of 'positive custody', replacing the rule 1 in force since 1948, which had identified the objective of prison as being 'the training and treatment of prisoners [in order to] establish in them the will to lead a good and useful life on discharge, and to fit them to do so'. The replacement in 1979 of this rule by a rule emphasising 'positive custody' arose out of an (inevitable) recognition of the demise of rehabilitation in the practices of prison. But the other significance of the adoption of this rule must lie in the May Inquiry's rejection of the well argued and topical demand from two liberal criminologists in a memorandum specially prepared for the Inquiry for the adoption of a rule specifying the minimum standards governing 'humane containment' (King and Morgan, 1979).

At no point in the May Inquiry are the arguments clearly put, but it seems clear that the objection to a rule 1 which spoke of minimum standards of humane containment would be that it would enable prisoners to challenge the Home Office and individual prison governors through the law. The European Court of Human Rights and the United Nations have both laid down precise descriptions of the minimum conditions that should govern custody, and many of the cases brought in other jurisdictions have hinged on the 'humaneness' of particular custodial regimes. The May Committee avoids this justifiable alternative by speaking of 'positive custody' as 'an openness of approach and mind not only to the staff but to all public requirements as well as to interests of the inmates' (pp. 277–8). The naivety of such a vision, given the overcrowded and polarised prisons of the early 1980s, is breathtaking. But given its overall commitment to the prison as an institution protecting society from offenders who are a real danger to it', the Labour Party has mounted no challenge to the adoption of the new rule 1. It has instead been at one with Conservatives and with Home Office officials servicing the All-Party Committee on Penal Affairs, in urging that custody be 'positive', in the above, rather vacuous sense.

The bipartisan ideological agreement of the parties and official agencies generally on the purpose of prison have, however, been heavily challenged in recent years by the prison movements. Three connected accusations have been angrily and forcefully made. First, the prison movements have echoed critics of prison's reconviction rates by insisting that prisons by their nature do not and cannot rehabilitate. They are self-evidently not organised, staffed or publically evaluated as institutions purveying rehabilitation. But they have also insisted, secondly, that the alternative description of prison, as institutions for the containment of dangerous people, is also misleading and ideological. An overwhelming proportion of the prison population are petty (non-violent) property offenders (social nuisances), and as the British prisoners' union, PROP, asserted in its report to the May Committee of Inquiry, many of these who then get to be defined in prison as troublemakers (and often therefore as dangerous) are precisely those 'men and women who are prepared to stand up for themselves and for others' (PROP, 1979, p. 6). So the notion that prisons are like they are by virtue of the number of dangerous people in them is *ideological* in the sense of trying to *pathologise* the vigour with which many prisoners have challenged the legitimacy and authority of prison custody. This ideological construction is a process we appear willing to recognise in the case of George Jackson, who was a prisoner in Californian jails for ten years for a $70 theft, but who was later extremely articulate in his criticism of prison's claim to be a rehabilitative institution and in the politics of the black power movement. Shot dead in August 1971 'whilst escaping', George Jackson was a prisoner who had dangerousness thrust upon him. He has less well known successors in British jails today.

The concept of dangerousness is obviously a convenient

instrument for legitimising all kinds of repressive measures (from the use of tranquillising drugs through to control units) against rebellious or difficult prisoners. It also has the powerful extra connotation of legitimising the tight security that now characterises most prisons in Britain as a necessary element in the containment of a dangerous prison population. It is an ideological term therefore in that it legitimises existing practices, and it is also ideological in constructing a false description of the prison population. The vast majority of the prison population simply are not dangerous in the sense implied. Even more infamous convicts like Wally Probyn and John McVicar, widely thought to be violent and dangerous in their criminal careers, turn out to be very different in prison. And while the Krays and Richardson *were* systematically involved in violence in the course of their earlier careers, and there were grounds for seeing them, and others like them, as dangerous, they were a very small minority of the prison population. The notion that prisons have to be secure in order that they can effectively contain the dangerous is clearly an ideological construction.

The third accusation made by the prison movement therefore suggests that prison is neither primarily rehabilitative nor containing in its real social function. This is an argument that has been put most cogently of all by Thomas Mathiesen, the founder of KROM, the Norwegian prison movement, in a series of reflections on his experiences within that movement (Mathiesen, 1976). For Mathiesen, the prison has four quite specific ideological functions in advanced welfare state capitalist societies. The prison is, first, an institution within which a proportion of the unproductive population of late capitalist societies can be housed and controlled (its *expurgatory* function). In other words, the prison is a support to the factory and labour market as a part of the social control system of capitalist societies, oriented in particular to the control of the unemployed and the reserve army of labour. But apart from segregating its inmates, the prison also 'strips them', in Erving Goffman's terms, of any sense of personal identity and thereby attempts to deprive the inmate in his own eyes, and in others', of any legitimacy. The prison in this respect has a *power-draining* function. It deprives prisoners in advance of the legitimate right to criticise the existing penal system or social order.

Imprisoning largely working-class offenders, the prison also works to highlight certain kinds of behaviours as serious social harms (i.e. as imprisonable crimes), and to suppress popular interest in other forms of behaviour (by finance capitalists, factory owners and other powerful agencies). In this respect, the prison has the third important function 'of *diverting* the attention from the really dangerous acts that are committed by those in power' (Mathiesen, 1976, p. 78). Finally, the prison stigmatises its inmates in the eyes of non-inmates. In other words, the prison has a crucial *symbolic* function, in reproducing an imagery of the criminal set against the respectable, conforming population. It thereby divides working people at large within themselves along largely symbolic (rather than real) divisions; and because the prison is closed off and invisible to the mass of the population, it can do this ideological work without fear of being contradicted by the visible evidence.

Mathiesen's overall thesis is that the prison has the general, largely ideological (but latently economic) function of housing an 'expelled' population, which then becomes the object of anxious surveillance and coercive, controlling responses by the state acting on behalf of the employed, productive population. It is a function that has accrued to the prison in part because of the strength of social democratic politics in Scandinavia, and official Norwegian socialists' continuing insistence on the prison as an institution purveying rehabilitation.

Mathiesen's conclusion has been paralleled and echoed by many other recent analyses of prison and of the penal system as a whole. In the United States, the American Friends Service Committee, reporting in 1971, spoke of the criminal justice system in that country as being a system for the containment of the underclass (blacks, Chicanos, Puerto Ricans, Indians, women and youth) and the *obverse* of rehabilitation. In 1979, Jeffrey Reiman recognised that the continuing failure of rehabilitation in American prisons was none the less coupled with a continuing and increasing high level of investment in prisons. This had to mean that the penal system in the United States had another, specific and very important social function. He surmised that the penal system had the specific function of sustaining *pyrrhic defeats* in the struggle against crime (Reiman, 1979, ch. 1). That is, the system sustains defeats in what is said to be the continuing and difficult struggle of providing defences against crimes committed against the general population, and in particular against the poor. So each and every defeat of the poor (general declines in their living conditions and sense of personal security, recessions and slumps, 'real' crime, etc.) becomes the occasion for further state commitment to the penal system. More prisons are built, but street crimes and other social anxieties continue to escalate.

The effect of these circular ideological arguments, which translate the problem of social order into problems of law and order, is continually to increase the capacity of the penal system and hence to increase the likelihood of working-class people being subjected to later criminalisation. It is a particularly powerful process in a period of crisis in the relations of capital to the labouring and unemployed population, and in the crisis of community that this is translated into at local level. It constantly *appears* to anticipate the restoration of social order through the expansion of punitive law, including of course the expansion of prisons.

Both Mathiesen's and Reiman's arguments suggest that the prison and justice systems are incapable, in capitalist societies, of producing either rehabilitation or social defence. So the prison continually thwarts all the best rehabilitative efforts of more liberal and progressive prison staff because it must perform another social function — that of providing evidence of the need for coercive exercises of social control, in the form of failed, recidivist offenders.

It is an intriguing argument. It would, for example, explain the recent renaissance of ideological arguments about dangerousness in the criminal population; and it would also explain why the relevant state authorities rejected the Mountbatten Inquiry's argument for the segregation of the minority of troublesome prisoners into a single fortress prison in favour of a policy of dispersal. The dispersal of dangerous prisoners throughout all prisons makes an account available of the ongoing occurrence of trouble in each of these institutions.

This account says that the troubles in prisons result from the activities of dangerous offenders rather than from the crises of authority and containment that are affecting the prisons.

It is clear that state authorities *could* in principle transform prisons into institutions allowing much greater amounts of freedom and much greater internal democracy, with a consequent reduction in the brutalisation of prison's effects. The massive technology available to prison authorities could be used to provide secure perimeters to open spaces within prison (including private conjugal visits), rather than being used as at present to survey all aspects of the prison day and constantly to segregate prisoners in their cells, on their landings or by prison block. The level of investment is high (£242 million in 1979), having increased by some 15 per cent per year from the early 1970s (Central Statistical Office, *Social Trends*, 1979). The size of the industry is considerable (in January 1979 there were 14,976 male prison officers and 1,358 women officers in 67 different prisons in England and Wales, plus untold numbers of governors, Prison Department officials and other non-uniformed staff); and many of the prisons have been built in the post-war period.[8] So the condition of the 'penal estate' (its institutions, technological capacities, and staffing) is not unevenly bad: it is not the estate itself which ensures the defeat of rehabilitation or necessitates continual containment.

The need for prison to perform its function of 'expulsion', producing a population of 'dangerous' criminals in need of containment in the name of social order generally, clearly takes precedence in practice over reformative and ameliorative initiatives within the prison system. But there are both fiscal and strategic limits to the process of expulsion. The increases which have occurred in the numbers of imprisonable offences throughout the 1960s and 1970s cannot be allowed to result in proportionate numbers of admissions into prison, since any further increases in the size of the prison population might make the institutions literally unmanageable. Thus in September 1978 the House of Commons Expenditure Committee produced a report on *The Reduction of Pressure on the Prison System*, and in June 1980 the All-Party Penal Group produce a report entitled, simply, *Too Many Prisoners*.

Throughout the summer of 1980, the Conservative Home Secretary and the Chief Justice spent much of their time trying to persuade the judiciary and magistracy to reduce the length of prison sentences. The all-party group argued against persuasion, saying that 'the powers of the courts must be restricted by legislation' (*The Guardian*, 26 June 1980). Expansion of the prison system is, however, likely to occur in order to meet the increasing need for 'expulsion', and prisons will certainly appropriate an increasing share of public expenditure. The limitations on this process will derive from the general limitations on the government's structuring of the distribution of public expenditure.

None of these exercises has been primarily articulated around the prison as an institution purveying rehabilitation or an institution guaranteeing social defence. Instead, the concern has been with the pressure of the flow of offenders from the courts to the prisons, and the consequent managerial problems in prisons themselves. The concern has been with *managing* the continuing effects of (a necessary) social expulsion.

So the Labour Party's commitments to prison as a rehabilitative agency are obviously ahistorical at least (they made some more sense in the 1950s when reconviction rates were rather lower), and they are also a misunderstanding or a displacement of the true social functions of prisons in late British capitalism. Institutions which function to contain over 45,000 largely minor working-class offenders in overcrowded custodial regimes, with reconviction rates of over 80 per cent, are not the institutions of social defence described in recent Labour Party booklets.

As long as sentences to prison are administered by undemocratic and authoritarian law courts, as a consequence of discretionary decisions by an unaccountable police force, then prison will be a form of expulsion and punishment that has no fundamental legitimacy to prisoners themselves. Some individual prisoners may accept the 'justice' of their sentence, but prisoners as a whole will see themselves to have been victims of an unjust and impersonal system, characterised by double standards, and unresponsive to their own case (see Bottoms and McClean, 1976). This fundamental and intransigent feature of prisons will then be exacerbated by the more immediate, inessential, and intrinsically reformable features of overcrowding, lack of exercise, lack of contact between the sexes, censorship and lawlessness in prisons to produce an alienation from the state among prisoners that will be visited later on civil society. The impossible experiences of ex-convicts in the declining labour market will further undermine any incidental contributions made by prison to social order.

I repeat that rhetorical references to imprisonment as a means of social defence are ideological in that they massively exaggerate the intrinsic dangerousness of convict populations and also silence the contribution made by prison to disorder in civil society. They suppress the role of prison in brutalising and damaging inmates and therefore in producing anti-social behaviours among ex-convicts. Socialist rhetorics on prison should be directed to these effects of mass imprisonment (the contribution of prison to social disorder), and to a thorough-going reform of (unaccountable and undemocratic) legal and penal systems that make little contribution to popular social defence.

Prison movement critics have also argued that talk of reform of the penal system is a dangerous self-deceit. The American Friends Service Committee, for example, observed how

The criminal justice system has a phenomenal capacity to absorb and coopt reforms. Throughout the years reformers have won all sorts of concessions. Many specific abuses have been halted or diminished. But the system grinds on inexorably. No matter how many new police have been hired, how many new courtrooms and prisons built, the system has remained overcrowded. Reforms have not succeeded in getting the system off people's backs. Increased discretionary powers have not led to more equal law enforcement. The criminal justice system is not solely responsible for the level of crime and violence in our society, but few would claim that the system has functioned effectively to diminish these problems.

(American Friends Service Committee, 1971, p. 155)

Mathiesen, in a similar fashion, writes of the danger of advancing 'positive reforms' which are then taken up by the system in order to strengthen the existing system and to protect it from criticism and subversion. Many proposals to provide concrete alternatives to imprisonment have been accepted by authorities in Western societies and then been used in addition to, rather than instead of, existing measures of penal discipline. Many of the currently most oppressive penal institutions (for example, Attica and Wormwood Scrubs) have at earlier points in their histories been examples of more liberal forms of 'humane' correction.

Recognising the ideological character of the rhetoric of rehabilitation and the severe dangers of strengthening a coercive system with 'positive reforms', Mathiesen, along with the spokesmen of other prison movements, has argued instead for the abolition of prison. Only with such an abolition could there begin a successful and thoroughgoing transformation of arrangements for social control, because only in a society without prisons could the 'unfinished ground' be glimpsed, and new, democratic forms of social control initiated. In Mathiesen's abolitionist vision, going beyond social democratic penology will necessitate the self-activity of prisoners and their supporters against the fact of imprisonment as such; and it will also require mass, democratic discussion on the basic principles of social control in a socialist society.

The visionary conception of an 'unfinished' society determining its own future shape and trajectory through *mass democratic* discussion may be a possible political option in a small unitary society like Norway (although there must be some question as to whether Mathiesen underestimates the potential antagonism of Norwegian workers and peasants to the exercise of such libertarianism). It is certainly not at all clear how mass support for any such abolitionism could be generated in societies like the United States or Britain, where there is minimal opportunity for penetrating the dominant ideologies which operate at the level of the national state via exercises of abstractly libertarian or democratic rhetoric. What is really crucial in these societies is to connect demands for immediate reductions in the use of prisons to popular sentiments or *class rhetorics* about 'justice', referring both to notions of punishment in terms of real desert, and equality of consideration at law. A first move in going beyond existing consensus penology in Britain, for example, would be to argue that minor non-violent property offences should not be imprisonable offences at all, unless a judge and jury of the offender's peers should find reason to make a particular offence an occasion for such a disposition. Such a demand not only places a new and proper emphasis on the prison as being an institution of popular justice (i.e. an institution for housing offenders, of all kinds, who may have been popularly adjudged to need punishment or control): it also raises the question of the relationship of the sentencer and the judging agencies to their proper, popular constituencies. It speaks to the urgent and immediate requirement for the democratisation of law, to which I shall turn later.

To begin to think of prison as having a place only in a popular justice system has several implications. It disconnects socialist discussion from existing movements for conventional types of reform of the existing prison system, and also from rhetorics which speak of prisons as having even potentially rehabilitative capacities (retraining individuals for citizenry within the existing capitalist society). It also subjects notions like that of dangerousness to popular control and adjudication, to be applied personally to individuals by communities rather than generally to types of offender by prison administrations or the judiciary.

One immediate consequence of any such democratisation of the justice system should be a substantial reduction in the number of people being sent to prison. That is, popular rhetorics of justice would operate to redefine the bulk of the offences for which people are currently imprisoned as offences demanding compensation or other non-segregative responses. This was indeed the effect of the Portuguese revolution of 1974 on the size of the prison population in that country, as new popular courts released very large numbers of the property offenders who had been imprisoned by the pre-revolutionary courts of the Salazar regime into the community (see de Sousa Santos, 1976). The work of Moorhouse and Chamberlain (1974) in Britain on popular attitudes to property would suggest that a decarceration of petty property offenders would also be a feature of any popular justice system in this country, although the new system would be quite punitive towards other categories of offenders (for example, landlords in contravention of tenancy agreements, or employers in contravention of safety or wages legislation). The demand for the democratisation of the prison system anticipates a broader demand for democratisation of law in general and the building of popular legal institutions. The precise content of any democratisation programme for any specific institution — but especially for an institution like prison, which is so closed off from mass experience and scrutiny — must derive from groups which have particular experience of the institution, or from organisations which can authentically demonstrate that they are representative of such groups. In its report to the Committee of Inquiry into the United Kingdom Prison Services in 1979, the national prisoners' movement (PROP) made twelve recommendations:

1. The immediate opening of prison administration to public scrutiny.
2. The initiation of a massive and lasting reduction in the prison population.
3. A moratorium on all new prison building and the phasing out, in step with the reduction in the prison population, of existing prisons, starting with those remote from centres of population.
4. The promulgation of a new constitution for the residual prison system after consultation with all interested bodies and prisoners themselves. The constitution must start from the premise that prisoners should be guaranteed maximum freedom commensurate with their overall restriction. This means:
   (a) Freedom to move about the prison subject only to the minimum necessary security and control.
   (b) Freedom of communication between prisoners and outside bodies and persons (see 5, below).
   (c) Freedom to meet with visitors with the maximum frequency practicable and the minimum security necessary.

(d) Freedom to receive or circulate any document or publication available to the general public.

(e) Freedom to determine the organisation and running of their own lives to the maximum degree commensurate with security, including the right to organise and elect their own representatives.

(f) The right to know precisely the wording of all regulations and administrative procedures to which they are subject.

5. The immediate abolition, for all prisoners in all prisons, of all forms of censorship of the written or printed word.

6. Disbandment of the Prison Medical Service and the provision, for all prisoners in all prisons, of medical care by NHS doctors responsible to the local Area Health Authority . . .

7. The disbandment of educational services as a branch or responsibility of the Prison Department and the provision, for all prisoners in all prisons, of the right to education provided by the local education authority.

8. Provision of these and other specialist facilities to be made available through the relevant services operating in the local community and to be integrated, as closely as practicable, with local medical practices and the activities of local schools, universities, churches, ethnic groups, etc. Inspection and regulation of health and safety standards to be provided by the relevant statutory authority.

9. The right of all prisoners in all prisons to independent legal advice on all matters, including internal prison matters.

10. The right to independent fair hearings of all internal offences. All acts which constitute offences under the criminal law to be tried in the ordinary courts.

11. The removal, from all prison staff or those working in prisons, of the restrictions (or, as we would prefer to put it, the protection) of the Official Secrets Act on any matters not relating explicitly to security.

12. The local or at any rate regional placing of prisoners
     so as to facilitate family links; i.e. an end to the
     inhumane imprisonment of Irish prisoners in English
     jails and of the regular use of distant allocations as a
     means of putting pressure on prisoners and their
     families.

                              (PROP, 1979, pp. 14—15)

These demands are clearly not exhaustive. Revelations in
1980 about the special training of prison officers to engage
in riot control suggest the need to add a demand for the
immediate cessation of techniques of force in prison management; with prison officers, governors and prisoners (their
representatives) being introduced into common assemblies in
which the long-term and daily problems of management of
prisons are openly discussed and specific administrative
arrangements subjected to popular votes. Common assemblies
of this kind would also act as a check on the behaviours of
individual prison officers and help to prevent further incidents
of brutality and even 'unlawful killing' of the kind an inquest
decided occurred in the death of Barry Prosser in the hospital
wing of Winson Green Prison, Birmingham, in August 1980
(*The Guardian*, 16 April 1981). They may also have the
advantage of being a better means of managing prisons than
the existing hierarchical structure of Home Office, governors
and assistant governors operating as the 'authority' over
rank-and-file prison officers and prisoners alike: this was a
structure which was, after all, responsible for the long and
extremely bitter strike of the Prison Officers Association
during 1980.
   Democratisation of prison management may also be perhaps
the only way to force the final closure of the ancient prisons
which along with workhouses and mental hospitals are monuments to the 'great incarceration' of the early nineteenth
century, institutions which, as I noted earlier, are now described by the Prison Department's own officials as 'stinking
ruins' and a 'disgrace to a civilised society'. Democratic assemblies of prisoners and prison officers would surely insist on
the demolition of these prison buildings, and the establishment
of decent living and working conditions in any residual prison

system. The continued use of these relics has been beneficial only to the fiscal managers of the state.

The PROP demands could be a topic for lengthy examination in terms of their strategic utility in a socialist programme. Such an examination will not be undertaken here, because the central feature of the PROP recommendations is that they derive from PROP members' own detailed experiences of the injustices and deprivations of prison and that they are therefore formulated as *demands for popular justice*. It is this conception of justice which demands a massive and lasting reduction in the prison population and therefore a prison-building moratorium; and it is this justice which demands an end to the needless and often illegal petty deprivations which prisoners experience in jails. It is also this justice which allows, in demands 4 and 5, for more radical conceptions of the prisoner as an individual who should be free in all aspects of his or her existence, 'commensurate with [his or her] *overall* restriction'.

Thus the PROP demands are for a transformation both in the marginalising and dehumanising character of imprisonment under late capitalism, and simultaneously for a massive reduction in the use of imprisonment, by taking seriously the existing state's own description of itself (as both lawful and humane) in its relationship to its people. In this respect, the demands are classic examples of what have been called *transitional demands*: they make demands which are entirely legitimate in terms of dominant liberal democratic ideology, but they are also incompatible with the inequality demanded by the capital—labour relationship, and the criminalisations and expulsions that are demanded in order to protect that relationship of inequality. So the PROP demands pose the need for thoroughgoing social transformations.

It is only in moving towards transitional demands of this kind that organised social democracy can hope to compete with the populist rhetorics on law and order which have recently been appropriated by the Right; and it is only by making such a move that the relation between the law and order question and the question of social order can be posed in a popular fashion differently from the way that it is posed in authoritarian populism. For socialists to continue to argue

for 'reforms' of the prisons by informed penological expertise
or other existing authority (as do the Howard League and the
Labour Party's own new Committee for Justice) is to perpet-
uate the collusion of socialists with 'liberal' state bureaucrats
which we criticised in Chapter 3, and which has been thoroughly discredited by the radical Right. What socialists should
be doing is to argue for a democratisation of the prison system
internally and also for a massive reduction in the use of
prison. But they should argue the case by identifying the
contribution which this presently massive use of prison makes
to social disorder; and they should be arguing that the way to
reduce the use of prison sentences is by a fundamental democratisation of the courts and the introduction of 'the people'
into the process of 'doing justice'.

The police critics: accountability and popular demands for policing

Unlike prison, the police force does not generate its own permanent group of clients or consumers on a mass scale. The
police deal with the public, and with suspects and accused,
almost exclusively as individual suspects, complainants or
enquirers and accuseds (where the prison dealt institutionally
with masses of 'convicts'). Moreover, the police almost always
relinquish their individual charges later to other institutions
or agencies in the penal system rather than remaining responsible for them over any length of time.[9] So there are no
'natural' constituencies, made up of clients of the police, on
which to base a popular socialist conception of policing.
There is no equivalent to the prison movement.

This fact may be responsible in part for the historical tendency of the Left to adopt rather generalised oppositional
positions towards the police, although it is also clear that the
social democratic Left's attitude to the police in Britain has
been heavily influenced by the role played by the police
during the General Strike and also in the police's defence of
Fascist marches prior to, and just after, the Second World
War. It is primarily on the police as the state's main instrument for the maintenance of public order that the Left has
focused its attention.

There is, of course, every reason for disquiet about the developing logic of public order policing in Britain. The British police are now, *de facto*, capable of armed and coercive intervention into all kinds of 'public order situations' (from bank robberies and embassy sieges to massive but peaceful anti-racist demonstrations).[10] The frequent lumping together of all these kinds of events as 'public order situations' is indeed an example of the dangerous logic of what has come to be called either 'reactive' or (more dramatically) 'fire brigade' policing. A summary article on changes in policing in Britain during the 1970s in *State Research* described fire-brigade policing as

> a system of policing which because it places efficiency at the forefront, not only leads people generally meeting the police into conflict, but necessarily negates 'community/ preventive' policing in any meaningful way. It also relies on an ideology which designates part of inner cities as 'high crime areas' — those working class areas of high social deprivation and often large black communities like Brixton, Hackney and Lewisham in London, Huyton in Liverpool and Lozells in Birmingham — where policing is not a question of protecting the community but of keeping it under control. The same ideology also leads to the creation of specialist 'heavy' squads like Special Patrol Groups.
>
> The degree to which 'fire-brigade' policing has been adopted is indicated by the number of forces which have 'command and control' systems to ensure 'quick response time' to incidents . . . 27 forces either have, or will soon have, such systems. This indicates that 'fire-brigade' policing is not a passing phase but is now a permanent feature of policing. It is the means by which everyday policing in the community will be conducted in the 1980s.
>
> (*State Research*, vol. 3, no. 19, 1980, p. 148)

The concluding sentence of this analysis is contentious, but the coexisting and contradictory tendencies in contemporary British policing are put very clearly none the less. Fire-brigade policing as described here is firmly established in the police authority areas mentioned and in many others, and as a form of policing it has contributed to massive breakdowns in

relationships between the police and the public, of the kind
that surfaced in the riot in St Paul's, Bristol, in March 1980,
and was then evidenced in public opinion surveys like that
highlighted on the Granada television programme on 8 April
1980,[11] and, during 1981, in the riots in Brixton and during
the coroner's investigation into the fire in New Cross, London,
in which thirteen young blacks died.

'Community policing' is in part an attempt to prevent such
breakdowns. As a form of policing, it concentrates on the
attempt to prevent crime through the use of police patrolling
neighbourhoods, attempting to integrate themselves into local
communities and win trust. It is an approach which has been
most widely publicised by the Chief Constable of Devon and
Cornwall, John Alderson (see Alderson, 1979), but experimental community policing schemes are also being undertaken
in the West Midlands, in Gloucestershire and on Humberside.
Beat police have also been reintroduced, as a support (or
symbol) in other constabularies (like South Yorkshire) which
rely fundamentally on reactive rather than preventative
systems.

The response of the Left to fire-brigade and community
policing has been remarkably similar. Fire-brigade policing is
seen as evidence of the 'iron fist' of the state: an instrument
for the repression of the wide varieties of threat, disorder and
subversion which confronted capital and the state during the
1970s, and which influential groups clearly anticipate will
continue during the 1980s. Community policing is seen as a
confidence trick, the velvet glove enclosing the iron fist: it is
the means by which the state extends its capacity to survey
and thereby to control populations (for example, in inner-city
areas of Birmingham, Plymouth and Exeter) which might
otherwise be more difficult for police to penetrate. The fear
on the Left is that the data so obtained on the local black
immigrant population, on trade union militants, on social
security claimants, leaders of women's movements, and,
indeed, on the Left itself, will then be fed into the massively
improved computer technology that is now owned and controlled by the police,[12] and that this data will in turn be put
to use by an enlarged Special Branch[13] in the task of surveillance and containment.

The instinctual attitude of opposition adopted by the Left towards both forms of policing are based on a healthy distrust of uniformed and coercive authority in a class society. And the fear that both forms of policing are a potential threat to the advance of socialism does have a rational kernel. The recent elevation of police chiefs into media spokesmen on trade unions, public order and on social morality generally has left little doubt as to where the political sympathies of many chief constables lie. The widely publicised view of ex-Metropolitan Police Commissioner, Sir Robert Mark, issued during the general election of 1979, was that trade unions had achieved an influence in the state under the last Labour government which was similar to the power given trade unions by Hitler's National Socialists, and Mr James Anderton, the Chief Constable of Manchester, has made his own espousal of authoritarian populism quite public. For Anderton, the proper targets of modern policing should include 'social nonconformists, malingerers, idlers, parasites, spongers, frauds, cheats and unrepentant criminals' (quoted in Kettle, 1980, p. 43).

The police officers' own union, the Police Federation, was of course also very active during the 1979 election in support of a 'Letter to Candidates on Law and Order' (published in six national newspapers) which was remarkably similar in demands to those that were put by Margaret Thatcher during her Birmingham speech on the 'barrier of steel' (see Chapter 1). So the recent politicisation of the police gives considerable grounds for anxiety on the Left as to the direction of contemporary policing, whatever particular organisational form it assumes.

The memories of older socialist politicians extend back even further than the Depression to remind us that it was at the time that Labour councils were coming to power in the 1920s that changes were made in the structure of local police committees, ensuring that the operational accountability of the police should be with the Home Office only. In this way, the feared influence of socialist ideas on local police committees could be offset (Bunyan, 1976, p. 72).

This conspiratorial interpretation of the police has also been given credence by recent experience of the system for investigating complaints against the police, and also by the 'reforms' made by the Police Act of 1964, which established new Police Committees at local authority level which had even less control over police practices than the earlier Watch Committees. The Left's agnosticism has also been allowed by a continuing utopianism on the question of social control in future socialism: in the absence of any serious examination of this problem, conflict of interests in socialist society have been spoken of, abstractly, as being resoluble through merely administrative, rather than legal and enforceable, forms of regulation. We have been asked to think of socialist societies without police.

Two observations are appropriate. First, we have to remember that this agnosticism was not a feature of the original social democratic criminologies of the 1940s. Important and influential writers and propagandists like Hermann Mannheim and Harold Laski argued then for an expansion of the police force. But they did so in the specific sense of wanting to see an expansion of 'beat policing', directed in an avuncular fashion at the control of delinquency and petty property offences, and an expansion also of detective work in the control of the black market, fraud and parasitical business activity generally. They did so in a context in which the police force itself was affected by democratic and radical prejudices (*for* equality of material sacrifice in conditions of general austerity and *against* those who took advantage of their own privileged social position for their personal enrichment). There is also evidence to suggest that individual socialists were actively interested in the question of police accountability throughout the 1940s, but especially in terms of trying to influence police activity around the Fascist marches and the docks strikes in that period. It was during the 1950s and 1960s, a period in which the Left was generally uninterested in the question of the police, that the rapid amalgamations of police forces and the introduction of the new Police Committees were to occur, and earlier, the limited accountability of the police undermined.[14]

The second observation is that the Left's agnosticism on the police question has worked in an opposite direction to the 'realist' logic of working-class communities themselves. Indeed, working-class support for the police has appeared to increase the more that the traditional social controls of working-class community have been dislocated by post-war social and economic changes.[15] Sections of the white working-class populations living in particular parts of London, in particular, have in recent years come to demand the kind of reactive fire-brigade policing that is provided by the Special Patrol Group, in the sense of having constantly appealed for police action against what they (the white population) see to be a threat to 'their' community, in the form of mugging and even simply in the form of rowdy street parties. In 1970, when Judge Gwyn Morris went further and proposed the establishment of vigilante squads in South London, particularly to deal with the threat of mugging by blacks, he claimed to have received 'hundreds' of pitiful letters, notably from frightened working-class women; and for a time there appeared to be a real possibility of vigilante squads being created in Brixton and Lewisham.[16] In more recent years there has been increasing evidence of working-class support for a strong police presence on public transport and on football match days. Metaphorical and misled though the racialism of some of these responses may have been, there is no doubt that street crime and interpersonal violence *have* become a serious and fundamental problem in the everyday life of white and black alike in many of the more dislocated inner-city areas and also in metropolitan London.

There is also little doubt that the visible presence of uniformed police officers is a deterrent to unemployed youths who, for want of material alternatives, have recently taken to lives of street crime and hustling, or who live through their experience of aggro at soccer games. A police presence is a rational defence for working class and bourgeois, black and white alike, against the unforeseeable expression of contemporary youth cultural nihilism.[17]

A police presence is also demanded by the black population, although blacks have little confidence in existing police practices, either in relation to themselves or in relation to racialist groups. In some areas accusations have been made that the police 'collaborate' with the National Front and the British Movement. In part, this accusation arises because of the poverty of existing legislation on racist provocation in Britain (and the lack of political will to extend it), but in part it is

based on experience and observation of police tactics in dealing with the growth of the National Front and the British
Movement in areas like the East End of London. The Bethnal
Green and Stepney Trades Council complained in its 1978
publication, *Blood on the Streets*, that the Metropolitan Police
only took action on the presence of racist movements in their
own area when anti-racists organised to close the National
Front's headquarters in Shoreditch and to stop racialist leaf-
leting in Brick Lane. But in the ensuing confrontation, it was
mainly anti-racists who were arrested, which had the effect
of portraying the anti-racist Left as extremist and violent.
The same process was of course to be repeated, with widely
publicised effects, during the Special Patrol Group's intervention in Southall to protect the right of the National Front to
hold an election meeting on 23 April 1979. In both areas
there had been a pre-history of woundings and murders of
Asians by racists with very few arrests made and few public
announcements of concern from responsible local police
officers.

In 1979, police in London gave further support to the
anxieties among the black population by inaugurating a series
of night-time raids on private homes and on factories employ-
ing immigrant labour, as part of the search for illegal immigrants overstaying the time limits on their visas (*The Guardian*,
9 July 1979).[18] In 1980, the Metropolitan Police's 200-strong
Special Patrol Group was accused of harassing the black community as a whole during two periods of 'saturation policing'
of Hackney as part of an attempt to discourage street crime
in the area (*The Guardian*, 26 March 1980). Not surprisingly,
a multi-racial joint conference of the Asian, West Indian and
Pan African movements, meeting in London in July 1980,
called for the establishment of a new civil rights movement in
Britain, and also announced that blacks should no longer
cooperate with the police in recruiting, identification parades
and liaison work (*The Sunday Telegraph*, 6 July 1980). A
similar mood of non-cooperation and, indeed, an unexplicated
theory that the police are monolithically and inextricably a
part of a racist and anti-socialist state apparatus are both
apparent in many left-wing journals and circles.

This kind of conspiratorial theory of the police, however,

does not account for the sort of policing that existed in Britain, with significant social democratic support, in the 1940s, and neither does it explain the initiatives that have been taken by the police in recent months against the National Front and British Movement. In 1980 the police raided West Midlands BM members' houses and discovered hidden arms supplies, and in recent months they have strictly controlled and policed all Fascist marches and successfully demanded bans on some of the more provocative marches proposed. In April 1981, eight members of the British Movement were arrested at the start of a march in Sheffield by the South Yorkshire police using the Public Order Act's clause on the wearing of political uniforms. Initiatives by the police of this kind are clearly to be welcomed, although there should obviously be no illusion that the struggle against the spread of Fascist ideas can be won through support for firm police action alone.

Moreover, the antagonism shown towards the police by the black community (which obviously reached new heights in the Brixton riot and at the New Cross fire inquest early in 1981) does not in practice amount to a call for an unpoliced society. The black communities of Britain, like the white working class in the declining inner city, are torn between demanding effective social defence from the existing state police (from white racists and from black and white delin- quents alike) and attempting to build organisations for self- defence of the black community. By preference, the majority of blacks would undoubtedly opt for being policed by a force that was accountable to their community leaders and unam- biguous in its multi-racialism, neither of which qualities is a noticeable feature of the Metropolitan Police in 1981.[19]

A similar schizophrenia towards police is now apparent amongst women, in the working class and middle class alike. In the North of England in particular, throughout the late 1970s, large numbers of women had to reorganise their lives in order to ensure that they were never out alone at night (*The Guardian*, 17 December 1979); and, in 1979 and 1980 increasing numbers of women gave support to marches and demonstrations opposing the curfew which the West Yorkshire police attempted to impose on women in the wake of the murder of Barbara Leach in Bradford in September 1979. Protests were also made against the failure of the police to act against pornography shops and film shows in London; and women invaded and vandalised cinemas in London, Leeds and elsewhere protesting against films like 'Dressed to Kill' which depicted violence against women (*The Guardian*, 13 December 1979). One of the women's demands was for the more vigorous enforcement by the police and local councils of existing censorship laws to outlaw films which could be seen to legitimate male violence against women.

During the same period, other women's groups, and particularly the organisers of women's refuges (which shelter victims of violence within the family) also called for a greater responsiveness on the part of the police to women's demands for protection in domestic quarrels. Other calls were made, especially by women student leaders, for women to have the right to carry offensive weapons for their own defence, especially after dark, and also classes were arranged for women to learn karate in order to develop their own physical skills as a defence against men.

Thus within the white working class, among black workers and among women, the same contradictory attitudes towards police were becoming more and more apparent. But the criticism of existing police practices was decidely not made with a view to the abolition or withdrawal of any form of police were becoming more and more apparent. But the criticism made of existing police practices was decidedly not made sexes. The critique of policing from all these quarters was a demand for the radical reform of exisiting police practice and ideology, and for the development of a police that was adequate to the task of social defence in a divided and pluralistic society.

For these reasons, the orthodox and instinctual attitude of the Left to the police — of a *generalised* opposition to policing, coupled with an ambiguity as to the role of police under socialism — is unlikely to find much response among workers, white or black, or among women generally, especially in continuing conditions of high unemployment, social insecurity and increasingly contradictory relationships between the sexes. A socialist police policy is in need of immediate con-

struction, *for present conditions* as well as for some hypothetical socialist future.[20]

Such a police policy could not be based on a simple reversion to the social democratic form of policing envisaged by
Mannheim. The police institution (as we have tried to show)
is an entirely different institution to what it was in the 1940s.
From being primarily organised around unarmed beat patrols
and the maintenance of the 'Queen's peace' via the maintenance of close personal relationships with particular localities,
the police force has become a motorised and highly mobile
organisation with massive technological support and a routine
access to arms, working at one remove from the locality. It
has been drawn increasingly into fire-brigade forms of policing, in which specially trained units (like the SPG) act, like
the army, to enforce a state (rather than a particular, local)
definition of 'public order'. The links between the police and
the army, rehearsed over a long period in Northern Ireland
and displayed in other incidents in England (like the Iranian
embassy siege), are indeed quite close: the usually well
informed *Guardian* newspaper has argued that the existence
of the SPG is the last chance 'to keep the army off Britain's
streets' (16 June 1979). For *The Guardian*, the SPG is therefore to be supported because, although similar in its methods
to the army, it can still be called (unlike the army) to some
public account ('SPG: Keep It But Change It', *The Guardian*,
25 July 1980).

The police force is also much greater in size than at any time
in the past. From an establishment of 60,190 in England and
Wales in 1949, police numbers have expanded to nearly
124,600 in 1980, with a further 12,000 officers in Scotland
and 6,000 in Northern Ireland. (This has occurred at the
time of the loss of several functions, such as traffic control
and the transport of cash, to traffic wardens and the private
security industry.) The number of traffic wardens increased
from 336 in 1961 to 5,087 in 1977, while there were, according to the government, about 100,000 people employed as
'guards, patrolmen and watchmen' in 1979. The number of
civilians employed by the police in administration increased
from 10,984 in 1960 to 34,119 in 1977. Police numbers were
on the increase throughout the 1970s, but were accelerated

by the salary award made by the Thatcher government on its very first day of office. In the period between 1961 and 1975, total expenditure on justice and law almost doubled as a proportion of gross domestic product (from 0.8 per cent to 1.5 per cent), and the vast bulk of this expenditure (£1,075 million out of £1,764 million) was spent on the police. Policing is, in other words, a massively capitalised and central element of the modern state and is no longer a body of 'coppers' committed to the provision of social peace on behalf of local neighbourhoods. The accountability of this state apparatus cannot be 'thought' in the manner of Hermann Mannheim in the 1940s.

It is also clear that the 'community' to which Hermann Mannheim appealed, in his writing on a democratically accountable police force, simply no longer exists. These essentially working-class communities have been broken up and rehoused, and no equivalent sense of community has been created in its place in the new housing estates, high-rise flats or new towns which have replaced the older neighbourhood areas. Abstract appeals for community policing or for the accountability of the police to the community make as little concrete sense in such circumstances as the celebration of communities by liberal social workers which I discussed in Chapter 2. For the same reason, abstract references to the interests of the 'working class' (which are common throughout this book) will have to be filled in by more mundane explorations of the kinds of class and community representation that exists in the different parts of cities and their surrounding areas. It is on the basis of retrieving some sense of specific class and community interests that a more generalised reconstruction of socialist politics can proceed.

There are two main sources of the construction of a socialist police policy in the current period. On the social democratic Left there are the councillors who have been forced to confront fundamental questions about the character of policing because of the heavy fiscal implications for local authorities of central government policies on law and order. Lewisham Council, for example, refused in April 1980 to forward its £5.5 million share of the Metropolitan Police budget until it was given greater responsibilities in the decision-making

bodies of 'the Met' (*The Guardian*, 18 April 1980). South
Yorkshire Council in 1980 imposed cuts of £1.8 million on
its police — at a proportional rate to the other cuts imposed
by the national government on social services expenditure
(while refusing to implement certain other cuts, for example
on public transport subsidies) (*The Star*, Sheffield, 16 April
1980).

In August 1980, London councillors came together with
representatives of bodies like the National Council for Civil
Liberties (NCCL) to hold a conference on the policing of
London. The concerns of this conference were in part fiscal,
but it was apparent that there was widespread disquiet in
many circles as to the proportion of police energy and expenditure that was being devoted to fire-brigade policing and the
technology of surveillance (*The Leveller*, August 1980).
There is a political 'space' here, where the relationship between
the *technological* and *political* logic of policing itself and the
popular demand for policing (as a defence of community) has
become transparently contradictory. It is a political space
which was indeed filled by the Greater London Labour Party
in its manifesto for the local government elections in 1981.
The Times crime correspondent reported that

> a Labour-controlled Greater London Council would invite
> boroughs to join in establishing a police committee to
> monitor work of the police force as a prelude to it gaining
> power to control the police. A Labour GLC would cam-
> paign for a police authority consisting solely of elected
> members of the GLC and London Boroughs to have control
> over the Metropolitan and City Police Forces.
> (*The Times*, 13 April 1981)

The demand for control was also voiced by the South Yorkshire County Council, demanding legislation to oblige chief
constables to give local councils information on a wide range
of matters, a practice that is presently at the discretion of
chief constables and very uncommon in practice (*The Star*,
Sheffield, 26 March 1981).

It is a political space that demands the democratisation of
the police authorities established by the 1964 Police Act,

which are currently composed two-thirds of local councillors, and one-third of magistrates; and the extension of the accountability of the police to much broader interest groups in each community. This was recognised nationally in 1981 by the Association of Metropolitan Authorities when it sent a resolution to the Home Office demanding the removal of the non-elected magistrates from the police committees (*Morning Telegraph*, Sheffield, 19 March 1981).

The key area, however, is the present exclusion of policy questions from the powers of local authority police committees and the consequent restriction of the agenda of such meetings to fundamentally trivial questions. It was in order to retrieve some of the control over policy which was lost by local authorities in the 1964 Police Act that Jack Straw MP introduced his private member's bill into parliament on 11 March 1980. This Bill draws a distinction between day-to-day *operational decisions* like emergency calls or decisions as to which officers to deploy on particular cases (over which the authority would have no powers) and *general strategy issues*, i.e. what emphasis should be placed by a local police force on particular kinds of police work (where the authority would have power). The Bill includes two safeguards for chief constables, in allowing them to delay for six months changes in policy with which they disagree, and also in allowing disagreements to be arbitrated by the Home Secretary (see Straw, 1980), but it has none the less encountered a fierce and almost unanimous opposition from the police chiefs (see Malcolm Dean, 'Who Watches the Police?', *The Guardian* 25 January 1981). The Jack Straw Bill did receive a first reading in 1980, but was given no government time. It is apparently Mr Straw's intention to reintroduce the Bill during the 1981 session of parliament. The struggles over this Bill and any further Bills on police accountability may appear to be fundamentally liberal (nearly every state institution other than the police contains some procedure allowing public accountability, but this does not make them genuinely and popularly 'democratic'). The successful achievement of a genuine accountability of the police to law would still pose the problem that the *equal* enforcement of law does not, and could not in itself, bring about a socialist social order. Equal enforcement of existing law would reproduce a bourgeois form of justice rather than ushering in a society of real social justice in which the unequal relations of capital and labour, men and women, black and white, were abolished. But bringing the police under democratic control is a vital project for the Left, none the less, because by opening out the police to further public scrutiny, we increasingly 'problematise' the question of the relation between existing police practices and the demands and needs of the different publics for effective and legitimate policing.

A third aspect of the public problematisation of contemporary policing is the need to pose a further challenge to the existing system for investigating complaints against the police. This is important not only because of the increasing friction between the police and the various groups we discussed earlier — groups who are clearly unhappy with the character of the policing they receive — but also because of the public re-emergence of corruption within the police (as revealed throughout the 1970s by the continued expansion but slow progress of the Operation Countryman investigation into the Metropolitan Police).[21] The need for an adequate complaints procedure connects very closely to the question of corruption, as Malcolm Dean has observed, because

the most corrupt force in the country — the Metropolitan Police — has been the least accountable. The Met's line of accountability runs direct to the Home Secretary who even in Robert Peel's day was too busy to spend any time examining London's policing priorities once the force had been established.

(Dean, 1981)

Moreover, the ability to bring complaints about treatment received by the police would clearly be an important control on police practice with persons taken into custody. The widespread concern provoked by the revelations that 169 people had died between January 1970 and June 1977 while in police custody (Hansard, 26 October 1977) was only partially quelled by a subsequent House of Commons inquiry. Attention was again focused on the question of police practices with suspects in police stations by an extremely 'respectable' piece of research conducted by the Home Office Research Unit into techniques of interrogation in use in many police stations, and into the ways in which some police can later disguise or deny the use of violence with suspects.[22] By 1981, a clear division of opinion appeared to exist between the Police Complaints Board (who in 1981 asked to be given the power to supervise complaints made against the police for serious assaults, on the grounds that 'in a significant minority of cases investigations are not as thorough as might have been expected' (*The Times*, 8 April 1981)) and the Director of Public Prosecutions, Sir Thomas Hetherington, who believed that 'too many prosecutions were brought against police officers'. The complaints were brought, in his opinion, because 'there will always be elements of the community who are suspicious of police officers and the law and order establishment' (*The Guardian*, 20 April 1981).

Despite a lengthy period of resistance from the Metropolitan Police Commissioner and other chief constables throughout the 1970s, an independent element has eventually been introduced into the investigation of complaints by the Police Act of 1976, in the form of the Police Complaints Board. The Board's responsibility is to scrutinise complaint cases subsequent to the police completing their own internal proceedings, and to decide as a Board whether charges could be brought against police officers, irrespective of decisions already taken by the police not to prosecute. Prior to the creation of the Board, police spokesmen saw the introduction of this amount of independent assessment as a real threat to the integrity of the police and seemed to anticipate subversion of the police's decisions in disciplinary proceedings. But in 1979, the third year of the Board's operation, when the police themselves made charges on their own account in only 79 of 12,434 cases, the Board itself disputed the police decision in only 18 cases (0.1 per cent of cases). The police reaction to these statistics predictably interprets them as a measure of the number of unfounded complaints. So we are told by the Chief Constable of Kent in his annual report for 1979 that 'The complaints system is an expensive ploy for the ratepayers and yet another factor to inhibit police officers in the performance of their duties' (quoted in *State Research*, 18, 1980, p. 121).

Research undertaken by Ken Russell prior to the creation of the Police Complaints Board anticipated this outcome. Russell was able to show that police have developed a variety of strategies for discrediting complainants (for example, by describing them as mentally ill, criminal or drunk). According to Russell, this discrediting occurred in a 'sizeable proportion' of the cases he investigated in complaints proceedings in two police forces in England (Russell, 1976). Russell was not able to anticipate the precise limitations on the powers that were given the Police Complaints Board, but he was certainly not persuaded of the Board's ability to represent the public (or, probably more correctly, the various publics) in genuine grievances at their handling by the police.

The procedure established by the 1976 Police Act has at least four other major faults. First, the public have complaints against particular policemen investigated by other policemen, albeit senior officers from other forces. *Prima facie*, the suspicion must be aroused that many complaints are rejected out of professional solidarity. Second, the investigating police officer's report is not shown to the complainant before it is sent to the Director of Public Prosecutions. Thus there is no way that the public can check the accuracy or the comprehensiveness of the police dossier. Third, the DPP and his staff are prevented under English law from interviewing the complainant, the police officer or any eye witnesses; as a result the system for making complaints has been rendered impersonal and bureaucratic (see Meacher, 1980). Fourth, however, the procedure that was eventually constructed by the 1976 Act is one which effectively prevents the Board from bringing a disciplinary charge against police officers 'if the evidence required to substantiate it is the same as that required to substantiate a criminal charge which the Director has decided should not be preferred' (Police Complaints Board, *Triennial Review Report*, 1980, para. 13). In other words, the crucial decision of whether individual complaints should result in either criminal charges or internal police discipline remains a responsibility of the Director of Public Prosecutions. As the 1980 report rather self-consciously observes, this is 'an important limitation on the Board's powers'.

My earlier analysis of the demand being made for policing by various sections of the public would suggest that a complaints procedure with these built-in limitations must undermine the democratic accountability of the police. So a radical reform of the existing Board is clearly required. As a first move I would suggest that complaints (and suggestions for change) should be publically invited (via the local media, notices in public buildings, etc.) and handled, in the first instance, at the level of the local authority police committee. Sub-committees of this body should sit as public tribunals, adhering to formal rules of evidence, and recommendations to bring criminal charges or internal disciplinary charges should be made, *publically*, to the local representative of the DPP or to the chief constable, as appropriate.

Certainly, support for the police among working people is by no means uncritical or uncontradictory, as is evidenced by the emergence in recent years of popular working-class groups reacting against particular instances of police behaviour. The best known examples of this are the essentially local committees of working people which were established spontaneously in Birtley, County Durham, subsequent to the death of Liddle Towers in 1977, and in Huyton, Liverpool, subsequent to the death of Jimmy Kelly in 1979. Both Towers and Kelly were in police custody at the time of their deaths. The death of Blair Peach at the hands of the Special Patrol Group (death by 'misadventure') on 23 April 1979 also resulted in the establishment of an ad hoc committee, which has done a lot of valuable work in publicising the completely inappropriate use of the coroner (who normally works closely with the police) as a quasi-judicial agent investigating deaths in police custody.[23] The work of all these committees has been vitally important in revealing the degree of force that is sometimes used in arrests in some police areas, and also therefore in posing the urgent requirement that police forces should be open to regular, routine investigations by a broad, concerned local public.

These requirements have of course been apparent at times of major class confrontations like the miners' strike of 1974 (especially at the siege of the Saltley depot) and the Grunwick

dispute during 1977—8. On both these occasions senior police
have deployed extraordinary numbers of officers and very
considerable degrees of force in attempting to contain picket
lines and also in trying to harass strike leaderships. It is
extremely significant for my argument to notice that the
South Yorkshire police were much more restrained in their
handling of the effects of the 1979 steel strike in their own
area (particularly the enormous picket of the private sector
plant at Hadfields) since the South Yorkshire force are ultimately under the surveillance of an (untypical) local council
which treats the police authority as an important part of the
council's fiscal and political responsibilities.

The working class appears to be much more divided over
the police role in class struggles than it is towards the police's
role in crime control and social defence. And the police themselves are far less happy with their role as agents of the British
state *vis-à-vis* trade unions than they are on their role as
'peacekeepers' in the area of crime (see Reiner, 1978). It may
be that this political space can be opened up 'transitionally'
by socialists attending closely to the police question, in particular by stressing the common interests shared by police and
other white-collar workers, and also in making political connections on the questions of racism and sexism to blacks and
women employed in the force.

Any future socialist social order will clearly have to allow
full political discussion as to the proper character and the
legal scope of police action. The struggles that will continue
under socialism over the scarcity of resources will require
policing, as will violence within families and in public space,
property theft and a variety of anti-social activities from pollution to fraud: the question is what kind of policing will be
required, using what techniques and supported by what sanc-
tions? It is clear that if the police under socialism try to
develop a separate 'professional' ideology and separate practices they will have to be subjected to continual popular
scrutiny and the ultimate control of the local political community. The large amalgamated police forces may have to be
replaced by a patchwork of smaller police forces reflecting
the particular character of local areas. Any retention of fire-
brigade policing would have to be directly accountable at a

local level (unlike the existing SPG, with its literally irresponsible 'snatches' into local communities). Recruitment into the
police of a cross-section of all the interest groups in society
would have to be encouraged. The current introduction of
black and women police would have to be speeded up considerably, and political and legal initiatives would have to be
taken to ensure that these groups were not merely given token
tasks in the policing of inner-city ghettos or in the handling
of only women offenders.

In the current period of reconsideration of socialist assumptions, new perspectives on the police are urgent. Critics of the
police who emerge 'spontaneously' out of the working class,
as did the Jimmy Kelly Committee, must clearly be given
much greater voice in Labour Party and socialist debate and
in the formulation of future policy options. Generally, socialist leaderships must allow the 'police question' to become a
public *issue*. Hermann Mannheim's programme, conceived in
the 1940s, for a democratic and accountable police, oriented
to the apprehension of the powerful criminal as much as to
the street offender, was a clear demand for the reform of an
aristocratic form of policing, and its replacement by a social
democratic police; it was a demand based on a confident and
unitary working class, united for social reconstruction. It
made existing forms of police an issue in a specific and relevant fashion. Any modern alternative and socialist conception
would have to emerge from less promising circumstances, out
of a fractured class experiencing the worst effects of a recession, of racial strife and of cultural conflicts in family and
neighbourhood, and disunited ideologically by the failures of
post-war social reconstruction. But such disunity is no
ground for allowing debates about policing to remain mon-
opolised by the authoritative agencies of the state and by
senior policemen themselves.

The legal critics: taking the people to the law

Existing social democratic approaches to the question of law
have been either legal rationalistic and/or civil libertarian.

Many of the social democrats who have been interested in

the relationship of law to social order have tended to have essentially liberal concerns in wanting to encourage law reform on behalf of some hypothesised universal good. Throughout this century, the primary concern of such social democrats has been to widen access to the law in order to make the law available to the poor. The conception of law here has been that of a body of rules that can be used to arbitrate between conflicting interests in an essentially neutral fashion. In so far as law has operated otherwise in the twentieth century, and in so far as it has appeared to operate in the interests of property as against labour, it has done this because of the undemocratic and class-bound procedures of recruitment of judges and magistrates and the narrow and unsociological training of professional lawyers. Law has been an instrument through which the hierarchies of class society and the pre-eminence of propertied interest are reproduced, but it is not an essential feature of law that it must operate instrumentally in this direction. The remedy for this bias in law has been seen to be the reform of the class character of recruitment of legal personnel, and in particular, in some writing by social democrats, the introduction of a full-time professional magistracy and the radical reform of the training of the judiciary as a means of wrestling control of law from aristocratic amateurs. The anonymous author of the Left Book Club's critique of *Justice in England*, published in 1938, observed that

> just because [magistrates] are unpaid, it is easier for the governing class than for any other class to take on the work. In most cases, too, they can be relied upon to possess, consciously or unconsciously, the right class bias. Moreover, in courts, which have so much to do with the maintenance of 'lorandorder', the rough and ready methods of the untrained justice are much more efficient from an executive point of view. Impartial and well-trained professional judges would not merely acquit the innocent; they would acquit all those whose guilt was not clearly proved.
> ('Barrister', 1938, pp. 43–4)

'Barrister' was convinced that 'real improvements' in the

magistracy and judiciary would be opposed in powerful circles because it was in the interest of the governing class 'to keep all its weapons sharp for times of trouble' (p. 44).[24] Forty years later, assessing the political role of the judiciary in Britain in the post-war period, John Griffith could indeed still conclude that

> on every major issue which has come before the courts concerning industrial relations, political protest, race relations, government secrecy, police powers, moral behaviour — the judges have supported the conventional, established and settled interests. And they have reacted strongly against challenges to those interests . . . This conservatism does not necessarily follow the day-to-day political policies currently associated with the party of that name. But it is a political philosophy nonetheless.
>
> (Griffith, 1977, p. 213)

The narrow class character of legal decisions can be challenged, according to social democrats, by the persistent reform of the training of lawyers, by the provision of financial support by the state to enable much broader sections of the public to serve on the magistracy without loss of income, and ultimately the replacement of existing judges by much more broadly educated, socially aware individuals, drawn from the ranks of practising lawyers.[25] In the last two decades, this reform programme has expanded to encompass support for the use of state expenditure to subsidise the recourse to law by the poor and also to support the expansion of law centres in working-class and inner-city neighbourhoods 'taking law to the people'.

In this conception, the courts and the law itself are agencies that have had a class character historically, but which can none the less be reformed, largely as a result of state initiatives, to become means for resolving problems experienced in living by any section of society. Law reform activity by the state must therefore be a continuing process by and through which the law is constantly reformulated and consolidated, so bringing it into line with what social democrats would refer to as 'modern' conditions. It was this conception of law reform (as a modernising influence) which activated the Labour Party lawyers Gerald Gardiner and Dr Andrew Martin in producing a collection of essays, in 1963, demanding *Law Reform Now*, which led to the establishment of the Law Commission in 1965 (see Farrar, 1974, ch. 1), and it was this notion of law reform which continued to inform the Labour Party's claims to progress in law reform in their 1979 election campaign handbook (particularly in respect of modernising the law relating to women's rights in the family and divorce, and in landlord—tenant disputes).

This 'rational' conception of the law as a recourse for problem resolution in society as a whole has sat rather uneasily with many social democrats' civil libertarian perspectives on law. Classical civil libertarian perspectives focus on the dangers of repressive law, and in particular the use of law by the state to enforce and protect the interests of those with authority under existing social arrangements.

The National Council for Civil Liberties was founded in 1934 by liberals and radicals who saw a real danger of the encroachment of such a repressive law in Britain, specifically at the hands of the national government: and from that point onwards, the NCCL has tended to problematise law rather than to celebrate it in the manner of some law reformers. In particular, the NCCL has given prominence to the repressive character of most immigration law, to the sexist character of much labour law and some criminal law, and to the discriminatory and often repressive use of existing law by the police in their public order and crime work, without adequate legal controls. The overall emphasis in NCCL work over the forty-seven years of its existence, however, has been on conflicts between individual 'rights' and the claims of authority, usually identified with government or the state. Particular attention has been given to cases of individual members of particular minority groups (gays, gypsies, blacks, working women, etc.) who have been subject to discrimination in employment or in other respects, by virtue of their subordinate or minority status. The NCCL has also worked to publicise and to reverse censorious restrictions on the freedom of individuals to read and to view whatever books, films or theatre they want, and to be able to give expression to whatever opinions they may hold. Court cases have been fought in order to try and reverse the decisions of authorities in particular cases and if possible to establish new legal precedents. The ultimate reference point for NCCL activities has always been the sovereignty of individual freedom, with threats to such a sovereignty being seen to arise from the state, the government and especially from the judiciary and the police.

Thus the relationship between civil libertarians and social democrats has always been uneasy. Social democrats have given support to the expansion of the state in the regulation of civil society and economy (in the interests not of individuals but of what they call the 'community'), and have introduced laws which legitimate and structure this regulation, but they have also been uneasy about the additional powers accruing to the police and judiciary as a result of the development of the power of the state. So social democratic politicians have expressed civil libertarian conceptions about the powers of state-employed officials in the prison system, about police powers generally and also about the arbitrary discretionary powers that have accrued to social workers and doctors in the child care and mental health systems. But they have not tended to be so concerned about the 'rights' of individuals to contract out of closed-shop employment supported by state law or about the various 'rights' claimed by individual employers in the face of Labour government legislation on conditions of work for employees. The rhetorical references to threatened rights of individuals have rarely challenged the logic or effect of social democracy's support for state interventions in the body of civil society, on behalf of the social democratic community against its enemies. It has been an article of faith, for social democrats, that the state authentically represents the interests of working people at large, rather than an undemocratic intrusion on them, and the NCCL, caught in a libertarian version of social democratic theory, has tended not to question this 'statism' in any fundamental fashion.

Other versions of civil libertarianism are less sanguine about the beneficence of the state. Perhaps the most radical, though currently least known, are the critiques of existing law developed by the 'small society theorists' (see Christie, 1976). In this conception, the problem with law in contemporary society is not that it is an instrument of class rule in need of democratisation, nor either that it is a potential instrument of state repression or authoritative coercion. Rather, the problem with law is that *it has not been sufficiently widely institutionalised* and given an accessible, normal social form as an instrument for the discussion and settlement of the disputes that are inevitable even in simple societies and pervasive in complex societies. Specifically, what law and lawyers do is to steal the right of victims *and* accuseds in criminal cases to participate in the resolution of the conflict:

> in a modern criminal trial, two important things have happened. First, the parties are being *represented*. Second: the one party that is being represented by the State, namely the victim, is so thoroughly represented that she or he for most of the proceedings is pushed completely out of the arena, reduced to the triggerer-off of the whole thing. She or he is a double loser. First vis-à-vis the offender, but secondly and often more crippling by being denied rights to full participation in what might have been one of the more important ritual encounters in life. The victim has lost its case to the State.
>
> (Christie, 1976, p. 5)

Law is therefore unfamiliar and mystifying to the vast majority of citizens, who feel alienated and powerless at the workings of the legal system as presently established and cannot believe that such an instrument could work mundanely and democratically to settle ordinary problems of living to their satisfaction. Law is seen as an alien instrument of 'power' in society, in the same sense as are most of the disciplines through which the powerful rule society. It is a part of what Foucault called the power-knowledge form, through which elite groups ('they') naturally govern the mass of the rest of society ('us'). In this perspective, one means for demystifying both law itself and the discipline of the powerful would be to allow and even to encourage the elaboration of as many different forms and agencies of law as possible, of both a civil and criminal character, in order to 'secularise' law as part of the lived, experienced world of all citizens of society. There

are, however, some crucial silences in this version of democratising the law. In particular, the role of the state in relation to an expanded system of law is left unexamined, and
also the problem of avoiding an undemocratic expansion of
state legal bureaucracies tends to be unaddressed. Thus
it is not easy to see how the call for the expansion of law
by small society theorists would be any different in practice from the expansion of legal specialism and practice that
has characterised most capitalist states in the post-war period.
The rapid development of what is euphemistically called
public law — governing the relationships between specialised
and powerful agencies of the state and the rest of society,
and operating predominantly through closed tribunals rather
than open courts — is a good example of an extensive new
legal form that has no obvious, immediate relevance to the
problem of democratising the state. Small society theorists
have been conspicuously silent on the developments that are
occurring within the existing state, and on the relationship of
these developments to their own utopian alternative.

The other perspective on civil liberties under the law comes
from the radical Right, and has found expression in recent
years in the support given by sections of the Conservative
Party and the judiciary for a Bill of Rights, which would have
the function of limiting the power of the state in specific
areas of property and industrial law.[26] It is no great distance
from the orthodox civil libertarian focus on individual freedom
as threatened by 'authority' to an ideological position which
equates individual freedom with untrammelled egoism and
authority with the state form itself. In the view of Sir Keith
Joseph, arguing for a Bill of Rights in order to defend the
rule of law (in particular against pickets but also the closed
shop itself), 'The rule of law begins with the individual,
because individuals are real whereas society is an abstraction'
(Joseph, 1975, p. 6).

Socialists can clearly have no truck with analyses which
extinguish the facts of class and even of social structure itself
while attempting to establish egoistic (capitalist) accumulation
as an 'obvious', empirical fact of human nature and as the
basis of social order. None the less, the elaboration of the
original civil liberties position by the small society theorists

should be of more interest in highlighting the importance of 'socialist legality' (as a state form) becoming accountable to the community (and not just the state) in any future socialist society. This kind of analysis is also important in beginning to fill out what is meant by the abstraction 'community' in relation to crime and to law-breaking. Christie, for example, rightly insists on crime victims obtaining a much more active role in the resolution of conflicts in court than they do under the existing state judicial system, and he also rightly insists on a much greater degree of lay participation in the legal process than the current system allows. His distrust of legal professionalism stands in marked contrast to the sanguine support for professionalism and training in the social democratic penology of Hermann Mannheim. Christie's call for the extension of law as a popular and familiar form must also be taken as a serious goal in any socialist transformation of the legal apparatus, for the alternative would indeed be the perpetuation of a rule of law justified in terms of its 'majesty' (in other words, as a form of domination) rather than its accessible and useful character (as an authentic form of problem resolution between competing parties in a democratic society).

We can illustrate this with concrete examples. A crucial terrain of political struggle over the legal apparatus at the time of writing is that of the jury, for as E. P. Thompson observes, 'the jury box is where the people come into court' (Thompson, 1978, p. 130). In 1978 Labour Attorney-General Mr Samuel Silkin QC revealed to the House of Commons that there had been twenty-five cases over the previous three years in which the Director of Public Prosecutions had allowed checks on the records of potential jurors (in the Criminal Records Office, Special Branch records and in inquiries of the local CID). Twelve of these cases were said to have involved terrorism and another two were official secrets cases, including the infamous ABC trial, eventually lost by the state. The introduction of jury vetting (albeit under a set of 'guidelines') cut away at the English common law principle that accuseds should be tried by their peers 'selected at random, without respect to their beliefs or opinions and . . . subject to no influence of state' (Thompson, 1978, p. 129). The principle of random selection was established in the early Middle Ages, partly because of the large numbers of possible citizens who could participate in trials by jury as informants on a case, but also because a randomly selected jury was thought more likely to reach a balanced and just decision in a contested case than a judge, who has no one to challenge his prejudices. The jury system was therefore a product of continuing popular struggle against absolute forms of power, whether vested in the monarchy or in the gentry. It was one of a series of 'pacts' that was struck by the English ruling class with the people in order to win their consent to its rule.

The introduction of jury vetting — originally in a Home Office circular of 10 October 1975 — by a *Labour* Attorney-General is an expression of the depth of the commitment to the defence of the state that exists in some quarters of the Labour Party. Panels of juries were allowed to be investigated by the police, through a search of their records, for 'disloy-alty', in cases which 'broadly speaking' may have involved 'strong political motives' (Harman and Griffith, 1979, p. 24). The 1975 guidelines were not debated in the Commons (on the grounds that they were merely administrative), nor were they published in Archbold (the standard text for practition-ers in criminal law) — and the Home Office continues to refuse to release the circular to the press — but they were circulated to all chief officers of police, to the Director of Public Prose-cutions and to the prosecuting counsel in every case where vetting had taken place. In effect, the principle of the random selection of a jury from among peers has been modified to allow the state to pack the court — and this transformation has been accomplished without any significant debate by the legislature.

A Private Member's Bill to ban jury vetting, brought by the Labour MP Alfred Dubs, was given an unopposed first reading in the Commons on 20 November 1979, but was not given government time, and did not reach the statute book. So the vetting of juries continued after the election of the Thatcher government in 1979, and was used, for example, in the trial of three anarchists charged with the theft of explosives in the winter of 1979–80. Computerised records on ninety-three potential jurors had been vetted without their knowledge by the Special Branch, and the police discovered information on nineteen of them 'which might be useful to challenge a juror' (*The Guardian*, 20 September 1979). The acquittal of these defendants met with bitter criticism from the serving judge, Alan King-Hamilton QC, and an angry correspondence between the jury and the Attorney-General, Lord Hailsham (*The Guardian*, 1 and 13 February 1980). The introduction of jury vetting is just one instance in a recent sequence of attacks on the jury as a popular institution. Increasingly, the jury has been transformed by the state as a part of the apparatus of prosecution and punishment. In 1967 the Criminal Justice Act abolished the 'requirement of unanimity', allowing verdicts by ten out of twelve jurors if the jury fails to reach a unanimous verdict after a minimum of two hours' deliberation; and in 1977, through an apparently innocuous report on the distribution of criminal business (The James Report), about 8,000 cases a year (mainly thefts of less than £20) were taken away from the crown court (where they would be tried before juries) and given instead to the magistrates' court. Therefore 8,000 defendants a year could be tried only on a summary basis before magistrates, where previously these defendants could have gone to a jury of their peers in order to judge their guilt.

Two observations are in order about the recent struggles over the jury. First, although the removal of the requirement of unanimity, the withdrawal of jury trials from certain cases and the introduction of jury vetting are all major intrusions into the common law principle of democratic trials, there have also been victories for defendants of the jury. In 1973, the judiciary directed that members of the jury could no longer be questioned — in order to be challenged — on their religion, political beliefs, racial origins or occupation, and later in the same year jurors' occupations were removed from the list from which the prosecution and defence would select a trial jury.[27] In March 1980, the court of appeal ruled that jury vetting was 'unconstitutional', although by a two to one majority it also ruled that it had no legal authority to intervene to obstruct the vetting order made in the crown court case under consideration.[28] This strengthening of the principle of randomness has occurred concurrently with other measures which have undermined it. So there is no inexorable logic in operation here undermining the democratic form of the jury and ineluctably transforming it into a part of the apparatus of the strong state. But there *are* serious challenges to the jury from the state,[29] and they require a clear political response.

Our second point is to underline the imperfections in the existing role of juries, which have after all been a functioning part of a bourgeois legal system, and to demand a clarification of socialist thinking on the jury. The jury should not be supported on the grounds of any tendency it may be thought to have to acquit, since the objective of a socialist justice policy, responsive to working-class demands for order and also responsive to popular theories of justice, must be the democratisation, and not the avoidance, of justice administration. Picciotto clarifies one of the implications of thinking of the jury as a popular justice institution in this sense when he writes:

> To try to make [the jury] an instrument for anything that could move towards popular justice would mean much more than to ensure that the jury is 'randomly selected' (whatever that may mean): for a start it needs an effort to turn that randomly selected group of stony-faced individuals into an actual collection of human beings, whose job is to look at a human problem.
>
> (Picciotto, 1979, p. 173)

To argue in defence of the jury as the main area 'in which the people come into court', as does Edward Thompson, therefore requires an attack on the sacred rituals and the alienated and impersonal ecology of the British courtroom (an attack which Thompson fails to mount). Instead of being directed to its task by professionals and lawyers, a jury should be allowed to 'find the facts' in whatever way it deems fit, including cross-examinations from the jury box, within the general parameters of appropriate legal precedents. Popular discourse must take precedence over a purely legal form.

It is also clear that the defence of the jury should not be utopian as to the current impact of jury practices. Research on the jury in North America shows beyond any doubt that 'minority groups have historically been unfairly subjected to jury lawlessness' (Brooks and Doob, 1975, p. 180); and in Britain, Dashwood (1972), amongst others, has documented the insecurity among the black community towards jury trials, and the consequent demand for all-black juries. According to Baldwin and McConville (1979), in the most important piece of empirical research undertaken in Britain in recent years into the operation of the jury system, the evidence indicating that 'juries are moved by racial prejudice' is 'suggestive' (p. 81). They also show that juries convict on questionable evidence 'with a surprising frequency' (in at least 5 per cent of cases of conviction, according to the measures they adopt) and they do this mainly in serious cases, where convictions led, in the main, to immediate custodial sentences (pp. 127–8). The explanation offered for these questionable convictions is not altogether clear (amounting to the jury's 'sympathy' or lack of sympathy for defendants) but their clear conclusion is that a substantial improvement in the access of defence lawyers to the elaborate system of appeals courts and procedures is an urgent necessity.

The jury is therefore no automatic guarantor of 'justice', but neither is it the site of mischievous or irresponsible injustices (as the police have frequently claimed). On the basis of their recent research work, Baldwin and McConville

remain firmly convinced that the number of serious miscarriages produced by jury trial is, in numerical terms at least, of slight significance compared to the number of injustices encountered in those cases in which defendants are induced to plead guilty following some form of plea bargaining or other form of negotiated plea settlement.
(Baldwin and McConville, 1979, p. 130)

It is precisely when 'justice' is done out of sight, by professionals acting on what they say is their clients' behalf, that real injustice is most common. So the defence of even the existing jury system is important in keeping the machinery of law visible and accountable to a random selection of the population: the extension and demystification of the jury system and of courtroom procedures generally is an essential element in the creation of a socialist criminology and penology of a genuinely popular character.

It should be self-evident that any such socialist penology would require a sustained attack on the existing methods of recruitment of both the judiciary and the magistracy. A reform of the judiciary is demanded not only in order to 'modernise' judicial decision-making, by allowing much younger lawyers onto the Bench, but also it is required in order to make the judiciary much more representative of the social, sexual and racial divisions in society. John Griffith observes that

> there are those who believe that if more grammar or comprehensive schoolboys, graduating at redbrick or new glass universities, became barristers and then judges, the judiciary would be that much less conservative.

He thinks, though, that

> this is extremely doubtful for two reasons. The years in practice and the middle-aged affluence would remove any aberration in political outlook, if this were necessary. Also, if these changes did not take place, there would be no possibility of their being appointed by the Lord Chancellor, on the advice of the most senior judiciary, to the bench.
>
> (Griffith, 1977, pp. 208–9)

This seems unduly pessimistic and certainly does not take into account the likely future demands, not just of 'comprehensive school*boys*' (*sic*), but of British-born blacks and women in particular for entry into law and onto the Bench. It certainly is unhelpful to accept defeat on the question of the composition of the judiciary in advance, when other major capitalist societies, like the USA, Canada and West Germany, have been successful in democratising recruitment into their judiciaries, with the effect of wrenching law-making out of its traditional class location. How far the reform of the judiciary's *functions* in the making of law should proceed is a serious strategical question for socialists: there are certainly good grounds for attempting to retain the independence of the judiciary even from an elected government in a socialist society, since the judicial use of public law is the best guarantee of the defence of different social interests in socialist societies, and the best defence against the degeneration of state socialism into authoritarianism by a state bureaucracy (see Hirst, 1980). What *is* clear is the urgent need for an attack on the existing monopoly of the traditional English ruling class on recruitment into the judiciary.

The last reform of the magistracy, the local representatives of law, resulted from the Royal Commission into the Justices of the Peace, established by the first post-war Labour government, and which, after much trepidation on the Bench, reported in 1949. Its most radical proposal was to reduce the compulsory retirement age to 70. So the immediate problem of reforming the present system of recruitment remains. This system is nowhere defined or described by Act of Parliament, and its operation is shrouded in secrecy. In practice, local advisory committees, made up of magistrates from each county or county borough, prepare lists of names selected from lists submitted by the main political parties, and forward these to the Lord Chancellor. From these lists, the Lord Chancellor makes his appointments. The objection to this system, apart from its complete lack of popular accountability, is that it reproduces a magistracy chosen from among the senior officialdom of local politics or from their contacts in the local social and political structure. It is, indeed, a form of local patronage from within the existing local structure of state power operated by an unaccountable national state. As a consequence, the magistracy, which has a vast range of powers ranging from the granting of warrants to the police for arrest, to adjudication (with the assistance of the trained clerk to the justices) of points of law, tends unsurprisingly to become 'prosecution-minded'. D. N. Pritt observes that

> in most courts [there is] a strong tendency to make orders which the police ask for (especially on questions of releasing accused men on bail, where the police often want to keep them in custody, not because there is any fear of their disappearing but in order to spend hours 'interviewing' them — occasionally, too, because they want in effect to

punish them by keeping them in prison for a week or two for offences for which, even if they are in the end found guilty, they would only be fined and imprisoned), and also to accept the evidence of police officers even when there is grave doubt of its reliability.

(Pritt, 1971, Book 2, pp. 71–2)

The magistracy as currently established and recruited is clearly an integral part of the state apparatus at local level, and therefore it relates, ideologically and functionally, to other elements of the state apparatus like the police. A socialist penology which tries to break from a purely statist conception of socialism, in order to make the existing structure of state power accountable to the range of popular interests, would have to devise a radically different system for the selection of the magistracy, such that the composition of the magistracy would much more accurately reflect the occupational, class, racial and sexual divisions of the locality. Stipendiary magistrates, who are responsible only to the Lord Chancellor's office, should be abolished, as part of the move away from a reliance on state professionals as the agents of social democracy.

The democratisation of the magistracy would not in itself solve all problems in the relationship of law to the citizenry. In particular, it would not solve the problem of how the complexity of modern law can be handled by a representative but legally untrained local Bench. This is already a problem, however, in respect of the existing magistracy, who are often prevented from acting in a 'lawless' manner only by the intervention of the clerk to the court. The existing magistracy is further disadvantaged as an instrument of local justice in being far removed from the lived problems of the sections of the local community (the majority of the local population) who are not involved in the higher echelons of local state power, in commerce or in trade union bureaucracies.

To some extent the discussion here of some selected aspects of the existing *apparatus* of law flies in the face of contemporary Marxist discussions as to the character of the legal *form*. That is, attempts to speak to the radical reform of the courtroom, the jury, and the judiciary and magistracy, would be described as 'idealist' or utopian in ignoring the extent to which these institutions are merely frameworks within which, crucially, *bourgeois social relations* are reproduced but in an abstract and neutral *legal form* (see, *inter alia*, Jessop, 1980). According to this kind of analysis, the key to an understanding of law is an understanding of the precise ways in which law *necessarily* reproduces the unequal and exploitative relations of the classes in capitalist societies (albeit, sometimes, in a 'complex articulation').

The recent revival of interest in the work of the Soviet legal theorist, Pashukanis, has been important in drawing attention to the importance of the form of legal discourse in this reproduction to class relations. Pashukanis shows how law is built around bundles of rights and duties ascribed to legal subjects, and also around processes of reasoning that are attributed by lawyers to 'reasonable' or rational individuals (see Pashukanis, 1978). Once this general legal form is established, as it has been from the earliest days of capitalism the generalised rhetorical references to individual rights and duties and to the reciprocity of contracts between individual and society will always be resolved in courts specifically, in relation to the particular relations existing between owners and producers of commodities. That is, 'the [particular] relationships [between] legal subjects are . . . the projection back on to individuals of the social relationships between things involved in commodity production' (Cotterrell, 1979, p. 112).

We want to avoid being drawn into the more abstract theoretical debates that are occurring on the academic Marxist Left, even though these debates are clearly pertinent to our purposes in rethinking socialist strategy. It is simplest to say that our major objection to theories of the legal form as a *necessary reflection* (in the abstract) of relations between commodities is that they do not identify or prioritise law as an arena of political struggle. Socialists do need a conception of law's relationship, as Pritt put it rather starkly, to the 'class war'; and Marx himself was clearly convinced in his *German Ideology* and in other works that such a relationship did exist. Marx's earliest years were spent in the study of law, as well as in practical and political interventions in struggles occurring in the German courts on the customary rights of peasants on common land, on the importance of laws defending the 'freedom' of the press (from state censorship), the importance of the jury in political and other trials, and a variety of other legal questions. He concluded, quite unambiguously, that 'a people's statute book is its bible of freedom' (Marx, 1842). The danger in the abstract, functionalist accounts of law in some contemporary Marxist writers is that they frequently present law and legal institutions as an impenetrable and secure element in the apparatus of class domination, and that thereby they discourage the use of legal interventions as a useful move in political struggles. To say this is not, of course, to deny that one of the achievements of bourgeois law is to displace the *class* struggles that are constantly occurring in capitalist societies over commodities into disputes between *individual legal subjects*. The ongoing common law is the sum total of judgements made in individual cases contested in the names of individuals or individual corporate bodies (and not classes, sexes, tribes or castes): individuals are, indeed, 'interpellated' as the subjects of legal disputes that are in reality about the distribution of properties between classes and (because of patriarchy) between the sexes. So legal discourse is a mystification of the true character of social relations in a propertied, unequal society, but it is none the less an important (imperfect) instrument in the defence of the liberties of the classes and the sexes. The resolution to the mystifications in law lies not in an abstracted analysis of its overall functions, nor in a polemical dismissal of the inevitable class character of the legal institution: the resolution lies in the democratisation of law for the practical use of the various interest groups which constitute civil society.

The women's movement and law enforcement

Nowhere is the contradictory character of law, as an oppressive instrument of a particular social interest as well as an immediately important area of struggle, more apparent than in the relationship of law to women. I tried in Chapter 3 to show that the primary concern of the law has not been overtly with the enforcement of male rights so much as with the management of the nuclear family unit. This defence of the family unit has become more and more liberal, in that divorce and remarriage have been simplified, and also in that common law marriages now have in some areas (like domestic violence) as much protection at law as have civil marriages proper. Some of these reforms of family law have worked to the advantage of women, who previously might not have been able to go to law to divorce, or to obtain a legal injunction against a violent partner (Domestic Violence and Matrimonial Proceedings Act 1976).

Women have also gained the legal right under the Matrimonial Proceedings Act of 1970 to a fair division of the pooled matrimonial property (as decided by a judge) rather than having to accede to what, given a husband's superior earning power, is an already unequal distribution of property in the matrimonial home.

The anti-discrimination legislation of the 1970s (the Equal Pay Act 1970 and Sex Discrimination Act 1975) was important in attempting to prohibit gender discrimination in employment, education, advertising and the provision of public services, but the legislation failed to bring about any major changes in women's and men's wage rates in employment. Like the race relations legislation on which it was modelled, the anti-discrimination legislation put the onus of proof of discrimination almost exclusively on the victim instead of requiring proof of non-discrimination on the part of employers.

The procedural weaknesses of the anti-discrimination legislation was and is compounded by the number of exemptions it allows (such as the church, the forces and Northern Ireland) and also by the failure to establish rigorous machinery for enforcing new laws (see Sacks and Wilson, 1978, pp. 202–6). The new laws are also very rarely publicised in advertisements in workplaces, on television programmes, or in other public realms: they remain a part of that 'public' law that is known only to a few, and in particular to a few *middle-class* women. The anti-discrimination legislation has made very few inroads into social security law, which continues to operate (for example, in the income maintenance system) on the assumption that men are breadwinners and that women are housekeepers. The notorious cohabitation rule continues to allow the Supplementary Benefits Commission to withdraw benefits from a woman who is observed, by supplementary benefit staff, to be sleeping regularly with a man (the conclusion being that a woman who has a steady sexual relationship with a man is being financially supported by him).

The overall effect of family and social security law is not necessarily to encourage sexism (as the legislation on women's rights in domestic disputes displays) or even to celebrate patriarchy in a straightforward fashion. The laws do not work universally in the direction of male domination over women. But they do work in the direction of legitimising family life, which has the ultimate effect, given the structures of family life that are currently practicable in British society, of legitimising patriarchal relations — of dominance and dependency — between men and women. It is this articulation of family law around patriarchal relations (the domination of the head of the family over its members) that is challenged in contemporary feminist demands for the 'disaggregation' of members of the family at law.

The area of criminal law defining the character of sexual offences (especially rape) is currently a subject of a vigorous political debate, especially between civil libertarians, feminists and criminal lawyers, with what may be important consequences in the relations of men and women generally.[30] These consequences may or may not be beneficial according to *abstract* criteria, but they will certainly express some weakening of the straightforwardly sexist *assumptions* that have existed in this area of law in the past. This is an important development in providing a basis for women and men having a *formal liberal* equality in this area of law. As will be seen in my treatment of rape, however, the revision of the criminal law governing sexual offences may also, by the nature of its subject matter, require challenges to patriarchal relations as such.

Existing socialist thinking about these areas has been irretrievably patriarchal, precisely because of the overall prioritisation of the 'family' as the cornerstone of social order in reconstructed post-war social democracy. Discussion by male

Labour MPs of the 1957 Wolfenden Report on prostitution
and sexual offences, for example, were minimal: both topics
were unwanted intrusions into the public domain, and sexual
questions were for them essentially private matters, the pre-
rogative of the head of the household within 'his' family.[31]
Individual girls who were involved in prostitution were
inevitably seen as products of social and psychological deprivation. They had been deprived of the comforts of a psycho-
logically and economically secure home environment. So
C. H. Rolph (1955), writing for the Social Biology Council in
the 1950s, and Edward Glover (1969), reporting to the Institute for the Study and Treatment of Delinquency, both
wanted to emphasise the psychoanalytical significance of
prostitution to deprived (or fallen) women. Glover states:

> the fact that the prostitute barters her body for filthy lucre
> is psychologically speaking neither so surprising nor so
> unnatural as it seems. It is . . . one more proof that prosti-
> tution is a primitive and regressive manifestation.
>
> (quoted in MacLeod, 1980)

The fact of prostitution being a service for men, and often
for men married into social democracy's allegedly happy and
consensual nuclear families, was silenced. All analytical and
correctional effort was to be put into examining and saving
the women who, by virtue of pathology of personality and
social background, had 'fallen'.

Lacking any worthwhile social analysis of prostitution to
patriarchy, social democracy in the post-war period has been
almost entirely silent on the questions of rape and domestic
violence. In so far as these topics have ever surfaced, they
have tended to follow the same lines of 'sociological' and
'psychoanalytical' reasoning as Rolph and Glover. Women
who are raped and battered experience this fate because of
some feature of their personality and/or their sexual habits.
Violence in families is disconnected from the domestic division
of labour in the patriarchal family encouraged in post-war
reconstruction, as well as from the restrictions of women's
life-chances encouraged by the child-centredness of post-war
liberalism. Rape is then disconnected in turn from the unequal

power relations between men and women within the family
(which women may resist by withdrawal from sexuality), and
from the overwhelming emphasis placed in a patriarchal set
of social relations on the satisfaction of men's sexuality.
Rape is seen as an offence which women visit on themselves
by virtue of faulty upbringing and of being provocative to
men, rather than as a violent assertion by men of the power
of patriarchy — on women's own bodies and psyches.

One of the most telling indictments of modern (*sic*) capitalist societies is the restriction of vast areas of 'public space'
and large amounts of 'leisure time' placed on that half of the
population who are women. Specific areas of North American
and European cities (in the inner city, in certain parks, or on
isolated pathways) are increasingly defined as unsafe for
women to negotiate, especially at night, for fear of some form
of sexual attack. The hours of darkness have also become
defined as unsafe for unaccompanied women,[32] and both in
North America and in Britain, the women's movement has
organised campaigns to 'reclaim the night' (see Lederer, 1980;
Spare Rib, January 1981). The public space of 'advanced
liberal democracies' has been closed off to women, and even
in the private spaces of family life, the evidence is of an
increasing use of physical violence towards women, as the
privileges of the man are increasingly undermined by demands
by women for shared domestic work, as women themselves
come increasingly under pressure in both the waged and
domestic labour markets.

I have already spoken of the need for a socialist conception
of policing which is responsive to the demands of the women's
movement. The objectives of the 'reclaim the night' movement do demand the re-introduction of beat police in the
central areas of cities and in other areas where the sexual
harassment of women is known to be common. The effectiveness of such policing would clearly have to be monitored by
democratically representative bodies which would include
representatives of women's organisations.

But reclaiming the night and women's rights to full and
equal citizenship generally (even in a socialist society, but
particularly in a capitalist society in crisis) will also involve
legal struggles. These struggles will entail the attempt to

repeal some legislation which is essentially patriarchal in character and function, demands for the effective enforcement of other legislation (which is practically useful to women and also politically useful as a base for further advances) and also, I shall argue, the struggle to create new legislation. These struggles should begin with current awareness of the need for a public law which will defend women's ability to walk in streets, parks and public space generally without harassment, and extended into areas traditionally designated as private law, in the defence of women's rights in the family and also *vis-à-vis* the state (for example, in respect of social security and taxation laws). We can only give some sense here of the kinds of demands which must be raised and which must become a part of a transitional socialist strategy: the precise character of these demands must arise, in part, out of particular struggles of the women's movement and the experience women have of the state's response. It is apparent that the conventional social democratic tradition has very little to offer women in the struggle against patriarchy as such.

In the three areas of prostitution, domestic violence and rape, specific strategies have already begun to be clarified and formulated by women themselves as a result of campaigns and official state responses over the last decade.

Legislation against prostitution in Britain is centred around the Street Offences Act of 1959, which was inspired by widespread official concern, shared by male Conservative and Labour MPs alike and voiced by the Wolfenden Report, to clear the streets of the 'unsavoury' and allegedly increasing public nuisance of women soliciting for sex, especially in London. In the lengthy reorganisation of official opinion attempted in the Wolfenden Report, a clear distinction was to be made between the spheres of public and private morality.

Firm measures were to be taken to defend the sensibilities of 'the common man' towards the open sale or display of sexuality in public, whilst a more permissive official response was to be recommended against behaviours that people engaged in privately.

The 1959 Act therefore increased the maximum penalty for women found guilty of soliciting from fourteen days' to three months' imprisonment, and an intensive police campaign was mounted in the months before the Act came into force to remind 'girls loitering on the regular beats . . . to expect no leniency in the future' ('The New Style Tart', *New Statesman*, 7 November 1959). In 1960, the number of convictions for 'offences by prostitutes' in England and Wales declined drastically from 19,663 to 2,726.

What had happened, of course, was that prostitutes had turned to alternative means of contacting their clients (moving into clubs, hotels, saunas or other commercial outlets, or making use of contact magazines). But many girls continued to do business 'from windows' or simply by frequenting urban areas with established reputations for prostitution. Throughout the 1970s (coincident with the rapid decline in employment opportunities, especially for women), the numbers of soliciting offences steadily increased, and by 1978 there were 3,764 offences (of which 1,500 were offences by girls under twenty-one). Of these offences, 178 resulted in an immediate prison sentence, 244 in suspended sentence, 1,293 in fines, and the others in a variety of different outcomes.

Two years earlier, the accustomed silence of social democracy and public discussion on the prevalence and the penal treatment of prostitution had been broken by the formation by prostitutes and social workers of the Programme for Reform of the Law on Soliciting (or PROS). Claiming several hundred members and with organised groups in five major cities, PROS campaigns around four demands:

1. In the short term, the abolition of all prison sentences for the offences of loitering and soliciting for the purpose of prostitution.
2. The abolition of the term 'common prostitute' in legal proceedings.[33]
3. The abolition of the offence of loitering for the purpose of prostitution.
4. The abolition of the offence of soliciting for the purpose of prostitution.

(*PROS Bulletin*, 3, 1979, p. 3)

The English Collective of Prostitutes (ECP) and the organisation Prostitution Laws are Nonsense (PLAN) have gone further and demanded the 'total abolition of all laws concerning prostitution'. Their arguments for abolition are in part specific to the increasing problems involved in prostitution (resulting from police harassment, interference of professional social workers and exploitation by pimps and landlords), which they argue are due to the prostitute's weakness before existing law. Prostitutes are unable to protest against unjust arrest, unjust removal of their children into care, or unjust rental charges or physical violence from pimps because they are liable to arrest as 'common prostitutes' on the basis of a policeman's decision to charge. So the illegal status of soliciting and loitering for prostitution actually prevents the regularisation of prostitution under other legislation (for example, under laws governing wage rates, public hygiene or public nuisance).

But the ECP's and PLAN's call for the abolition of prostitution laws is also premissed on the repressive effects of these laws on all women. The harassment of prostitutes by police under existing law often carries over into the harassment of women generally by police, especially at night, and especially if women are not accompanied by men. The enforcement of existing law is one of the contributory factors in the prohibition to women of certain urban spaces (in coffee bars, or just walking home), and certain periods of the night: it is law enforcement which deters women from exercising the right to freedom of movement, by suspicion. Women and girls who live in or near red-light districts are also likely to be harassed by 'kerb-crawlers', who have to search for prostitutes in this way because existing prostitution laws do not allow for a more regularised and commercial form of soliciting.[34] But the fundamental objection raised by the ECP and PLAN to the laws is that they are a 'trespass on the rights of all women' as to how to control their own bodies. They are therefore patriarchal laws, in that in order to try to penalise women for marketing their sexuality for gain outside of marriage, they try also to coerce all women into the confines of the conventional nuclear family.

This is not to deny that the main victims of existing laws on prostitution are prostitutes. The responses of the police, the press and (eventually) the courts to the murders of the

Yorkshire Ripper have made clear the continuing importance
to conventional morality of the distinction between respectable women and others. Prostitutes are officially and conventionally seen as a 'pariah class', whose unsavoury occupation
necessarily and inevitably puts them at risk of violence and
even murder. It is allegedly a part of the way of life they
have 'chosen'. What makes the harassment or murder of
women who are not prostitutes so heinous is the fact that
they have allegedly 'chosen' to live a life of 'respectability'.
The functions of the routine treatments of prostitutes, as a
more or less sub-human species, for the reproduction of
ideologies celebrating the rewards of nuclear family existence,
in all its patriarchal splendour, should be self-evident. Women
who have chosen to find independence (both from the nuclear
family and from low-paid jobs that are normally available to
women) and drifted into prostitution pay the heaviest price
of all women for their troubles. Other women pay the continuing price of dependency and domination.

The arguments of the three prostitutes' organisations are
currently posed in terms of a liberal and humanitarian objection to the use of prison sentences for prostitutes coupled
with a revolutionary feminist appeal to the interests of all
women in being able to control their own bodies, and to sell
their labour to men, in whatever form, at a market price.
These arguments are not socialist arguments in themselves,
for a socialist programme on sexuality would clearly involve,
minimally, the freeing of sexual exchanges from the cash
nexus. Engels' vision of a society of spontaneous sexual love
is currently unimaginable outside of certain subcultures.[35]
But the dismantling of patriarchal domination over women is
an active area of current political struggle, so far as the regulation of sexuality itself is concerned, and also with respect to
both the domestic and wage labour markets. A 'transitional'
socialist criminology must demand the abolition of laws
criminalising prostitution, whilst also prioritising a freeing of
sexual relations from puritanical and repressive moralities and
the fetishism of commercialised pornographic sexuality.

Historically, as I indicated in Chapter 3, the institution of
the family has been a major source for the repression of

women's and men's sexual needs alike, whilst also being apparently an institution for the partial fulfilment of other human needs (for company, emotional contact, etc.). The future of the family in a socialist society is a matter for constant debate and reflection, and I made some remarks on this in the last chapter. What is clear in the present period, however, is that the sanctity of the family in both the major ideological formations (of Conservatism and social democracy), and also in legal and police ideologies, has worked to the general advantage of men and to the detriment of women and children. Statistics indicate that there have been very substantial increases in recent years both of wife battering and of baby battering. But the police continue to be reluctant to intervene in the essential privacy and integrity of the family. They are convinced that domestic matters are essentially private matters, and, more justifiably, they are convinced that domestic disputes are better dealt with by social workers than by the police. In their unwillingness to involve themselves in family disputes, except where they suspect serious physical assaults, the police do thereby help to reproduce the control exercised by the male over the family (through his relative monopoly of violence), and also they ensure the continuing privatisation of the injuries done to women within the family. This privatisation may also, of course, have dire consequences for the children of troubled families.

Studies in the United States of police response to wife battering suggest that many women despair of receiving help from these (or other) quarters and finish up drinking, existing on drugs prescribed for 'depression', attempting suicide, and/ or battering their babies (see Klein, 1979, p. 27). It is only when women turn to refuges or shelters established by other women that they receive any significant attention and support.

A critical observation is in order here. The call made by Dobash and Dobash, Klein and others for more intensive police intervention in domestic violence cases is clearly intended to deal with situations in which violence is continuous and the woman cannot leave the home to search for help or for a lawyer, for fear of leaving her children, or for financial reasons:

> The police alone provide 24-hour service to individuals in
> distress, but given their training and policies, it is likely
> that they will provide little or no assistance to a woman
> being assaulted by her husband.
>
> (Dobash and Dobash, 1979, p. 211)

This formulation does seem to confuse and conflate women's
need for protection from a violent husband/man with her
need for personal support from sympathetic women and social
agencies. Only 2 per cent of the women studied by Dobash
and Dobash did made contact with the police. As currently
established, the police (for all that they are a twenty-four-hour
service) *are* unlikely to provide the latter; the call for more
vigorous police intervention in immediately dangerous and
repressive domestic violence situations has surely to be
coupled with the demand for *twenty-four-hour social services*
that are able to act in support of battered women, frightened
children and even disturbed and isolated men alike.

The continual privatisation of the problem of women's
subordination within the family has, however, been under
significant challenge in the last year. The sentences of three
years' imprisonment which were passed on the Maw sisters at
Leeds Crown Court in November 1980 for the manslaughter
of their drunken, battering father provoked such protests as
to result in the hasty convening of an Appeal Court in December, which reduced the younger sister's sentence to six months
(*The Guardian*, 4 December 1980). A feminist demonstration
outside the court demanded that both girls be freed on the
grounds of acting in self-defence. Similar demonstrations of
sorority with women accused of acts of violence against brutal
men within the family have also occurred in North America
in recent years (see Klein, 1979, p. 28); and feminist lawyers
have increasingly articulated trial strategies based on concepts
of self-defence rather than on pleas of mental impairment.
Similar developments are to be expected and encouraged here.
But the development of feminist legal strategy must be
accompanied by new relationships with the police to ensure
that women who are experiencing violence within a family,
either directly or through the children, or within some other
kind of relationship with men, *can* turn to the police for help

when necessary. To think of the enforcement of existing law by the police, however, clearly involves the kinds of reforms in police accountability and recruitment which I discussed earlier in this chapter.

The existing laws governing rape and other sexual offences mirror the patriarchal assumptions of both official Conservatism and conventional social democracy,[36] and, like these ideologies themselves, have been put under challenge by the vigorous growth and arguments of the women's movement, as well as by horrific events.

Any legal or political response to rape and to sexual attack in Britain in the 1980s will obviously have to be formulated in part by reference to the questions of the Yorkshire Ripper. Between October 1975 and December 1979, twenty women and girls living in the North of England were attacked in a similar and brutal fashion (by Peter Sutcliffe, arrested in January 1980 and convicted in April 1981): thirteen of them died (see, among other books, Nicholson, 1979). As in the famous case of the original Jack the Ripper, who killed five women in 1888, most (but not all) the targets of the Yorkshire Ripper are thought to have been identified by him as prostitutes. But much more important is the fact that in the Ripper murders, as in most multiple murders, the targets were women and girls.[37] The most notorious of these cases in the United States involved Richard Speck, who murdered eight student nurses in a Chicago boarding-house in 1966, and Albert DeSalvo, the Boston Strangler, who murdered thirteen single women aged between nineteen and eighty-five, in 1962–3 (see Frank, 1966); and in Britain, apart from the original Ripper and Yorkshire Ripper cases, particular notoriety has attached to the case of John Reginald Christie, who murdered eight women and interred them in the walls of his house at No. 10, Rillington Place, Notting Hill over a thirteen-year period in the late 1940s and 1950s (Kennedy, 1971).

The overwhelming (but often taken for granted) feature of sexual murders, then, is the fact they are usually committed by men against women. This is also a key feature of the 'aetiology' of rape and of domestic violence. We should add that instances of sexual murder of women (like the Jack the Ripper killings) and of rape (especially in war-time conditions) have become the object of attention in literature and in film ('The Virgin Soldiers', 'Soldier Blue', and, in 1980, a whole series of films depicting violence against women), in which the injuries done to women (if actually treated seriously) are secondary to the eroticisation of the events that is constructed for the purposes of 'entertainment'. Sexual assaults on women are patently not seen to be an abnormal form of entertainment in patriarchal culture.

The real incidence of rape and sexual assault is notoriously difficult to estimate, because of the unwillingness of victims to report the assault to the police,[38] and also because of the legal definition of the offence.

In English law, for an offence of rape to be recorded, the police must ascertain that the assailant was not the complainant's husband, and also that he was not under fourteen. They must also discover that penetration of the woman's vagina occurred by the penis (since the definition of rape does not cover penetration of anus or mouth, or the use of bottles, broom handles, or other objects). Since the passing of the Sexual Offences (Amendment) Act in 1976, the legal definition of rape has been that

> A man commits rape if (a) he has unlawful sexual inter-
> course with a woman who at the time of the intercourse
> did not consent to it and (b) at that time he knows that
> she does not consent to the intercourse or is reckless as to
> whether she consents to it.

In 1978, in England and Wales, 1,243 offences were recorded by the police as rape (as against 422 in 1963). But there were also in 1978 11,814 cases of indecent assaults on females and 3,491 cases of unlawful sexual intercourse with girls under thirteen. Some of these cases of unlawful sexual intercourse may have been freely entered into, but the general picture presented by most analyses of sexual offences dealt with by the police is of an ongoing, continuous use of force to assault the body and psyche of women by men, with the reported numbers of rapes in particular being, by everyone's account, a vast underrepresentation of the total of violent sexual assaults actually occurring. The FBI in the United States has asserted that only about one-tenth of violent sexual assaults occurring in that country are reported to the police, and this has been supported in a number of victim surveys there. There is little direct evidence on the real prevalence of sexual assault in Britain, but it seems clear that it is one of the most under-reported of the serious crimes against the person, and it is also clear that, when totalled together with molestation and other sexual attacks, sexual crimes committed against women and children are on the most common (and least publicised) of 'mundane' everyday crimes in this country.

The massive amount of research which has been undertaken recently by feminists and others into rape has also consistently revealed the operation of partriarchy in the practices of the police and the courts. Among other things the research has shown that the police in Europe and North America are more likely to drop cases of rape before trial on the grounds of insufficient evidence than they are in other types of court case. Of the 1,243 cases reported in 1978, only 592 resulted in criminal proceedings (two of these involved women being charged with rape) (*Criminal Statistics*, England and Wales, 1978, tables 1(a), (b) and (c)). Courtroom trials of rape cases are also relatively unlikely to result in guilty findings (in 1978, only 318 cases of the 592 cases taken to court and of the initial 1,243 cases known to the police resulted in guilty findings, a conviction rate of 25 per cent). 'Even if the rate of reporting was as high as 25% of all rapes', it has been pointed out, 'this would mean that 90% of rapists got off' (Rape Crisis Centre, 1977, p. 18).

In the discretionary decision of the police as to whether to proceed with a rape complaint, and in the deliberations of magistrates, judges and juries as to the guilt of the male accused, the primary criterion in operation appears to be the character of the victim. Considerable attention is given by police interrogators and by courts as to the general character, the 'sexual history' and the specific behaviours at the time of the alleged rape of the woman complainant. No equivalent amount of attention is given to the male who stands accused of the physical rape of the woman.

The purpose of this questioning appears to be to establish whether the woman was the kind of woman 'who can't "officially" be raped' (Clark and Lewis, 1977). The women 'who can't be raped' are those who display in their history, demeanour or behaviour those characteristics which police say make for (what they call) 'bad' rape cases (those which are not worth taking to court). In Clark and Lewis' thorough empirical analysis of rape cases in Toronto, these characteristics included being a single parent and/or divorced, being on welfare, having had psychiatric care in the past, 'having a reputation' for drinking or for unacceptable sexual behaviour, having had some experience of drugs, living in certain disreputable (dilapidated or bohemian) parts of town, etc. Women with reports of this kind on their police file are relatively unlikely to have their complaints taken up by the police and also relatively unlikely to be successful with their case in the courtroom, *if* they were able to reach the courts. These women are what Clark and Lewis call 'open territory victims' of rape, in effect judged by the police and the courts to be of dubious moral character, untrustworthy in the accusations they might make of men, and therefore to be unable to complain of sexual assault by men. In effect, say Clark and Lewis, women of this character are thought to be common sexual property. This is because it is women who are not in 'open territory', but who are respectably married, in a conventional nuclear family, preferably with children and living in reputable parts of the town — in other words, women who are the private property of individual men, women who are privately valuable — who are nearly always designated as serious complainants in rape cases. These are the women who are officially believed when they speak of being raped. These are what Clark and Lewis call the 'authorised rape victims', and what other writers have called the 'legitimate victims of rape'. And, as Clark and Lewis (1977, p. 92) point out, 'this process of selection may have nothing to do with whether or not the complainant was actually raped'.

Other feminist writers have shown how rape trials in the United States, Britain, Italy and elsewhere put the victim on trial rather than the man accused of the crime, who is virtually immunised from having his character and person subjected to close examination.[39] Certainly it is unheard of for men who are brought into police stations on a woman's complaint of rape to be subjected to a medical examination on their sexual parts. But an examination of this kind does take place routinely when *women* report a recent rape to police stations, or are brought into police stations or a hospital subsequent to a rape (Coote and Gill, 1975, p. 9), this being done in order to establish evidence of the attack.[40]

The *overt* rationale for the various humiliations to which women complaining of rape are subjected to in the police station and in court is often repeated in judicial reminders to juries in rape trials to the effect that 'rape is a charge which is easy to make and hard to prove'. The source of this view is Matthew Hale, a lawyer writing in 1736, who continued by speaking of 'the confident testimony of malicious and fake witnesses'. The likelihood that is alleged of women being malicious and false witnesses in such cases has resulted in the statutory requirement that a woman's evidence in sexual offences generally must be independently corroborated (Sexual Offences Act 1956, sections 2, 3 and 4). This demand for corroboration of evidence has no other parallel in statute law in Britain, and does not extend to sexual offences where the victim is male.

The overall effect of existing laws of rape and sexual assault, and the way they are enforced and applied by police and courts, has clearly been one of deterring women from making complaints to the police, and also of encouraging a sense of powerlessness among women who might otherwise use the law to erect some defence for themselves, other women and their children. And because most women also have come to 'understand', subconsciously, the coded messages about lifestyle and behaviour that are contained in existing rape law, and the dangers of being a woman in 'open territory', rape laws have until recently been quite successful in controlling women's behaviour. Many women feel that they *have* lost the freedom to walk out at night, except in male company, in many Western countries,[41] and they have developed a cautious, repressed view of urban space as being divided up into safe areas and other, open (and dangerous) territories. They are therefore subjected to the patriarchal control of the male as a chivalrous protector in unsafe territory, as well as being further encouraged in their view of the family structure as a place of solace and protection.

The restrictive character of existing rape law works to express and to reproduce these facts and effects of patriarchy, and must be challenged. I want to argue that the primary requirements are a rape law of much broader scope, for the abolition of the need for corroboration of women's evidence, for the abolition of courtroom references to women's previous sexual history, for the abolition of legal references to consent (rather than will), and for the legal recognition of rape in marriage.

A new rape offence (to be called 'sexual assault') is required which, amongst other criteria, does not require the penetration of the woman by a penis. If such an offence existed, charges could be successfully brought against men in cases which are at the moment reported initially as cases of rape, but which fail because of lack of material evidence (of penetration). The existence of a broader offence, of 'sexual assault', might also encourage greater numbers of women to report domestic violence to the police. Its two main effects would be to challenge the restrictiveness of existing rape law, while retaining the sexual character of violence against women in the charge, and also signalling to women that law could be used against men who attempt to enforce their patriarchal position *by violence and physical coercion*.

The formulation of a demand for a new criminal offence might upset some civil libertarians, and it would also run counter to the reasoning adopted by some feminist criminologists and socialist lawyers. Civil libertarians would see the attempt to use state law as a form of social defence and social justice for women as a dangerous exercise in state authoritarianism: to this, the response must be that the struggle against male violence must be continued on all fronts, including state law itself and also including all the various arenas of ideological struggle (including the media). State law will be no more coercive than it is currently for being asked to take on the defence of women from patriarchs.

Some feminist criminologists, including Lorenne Clark and Debra Lewis (writing on Canada), have reacted to the urgent need felt by women for legal protection, calling in particular for the deletion of the charge of rape, in all its specificity,

from the Canadian criminal code, and the replacement of the
rape charge by 'new assault charges', which, while being
based on principles acknowledging the full equality of men
and women, would none the less make it easier for women
to take men to court, and also would encourage women to
report men to the police for criminal violence (Clark and
Lewis, 1977, ch. 2). But these arguments appear to have been
accepted in part by the Federal Government in Canada. In
December 1980, the Canadian Minister for Justice, Mr Jean
Chrétien, announced that a long-awaited Bill revising the
criminal law on sexual offences would replace the terms 'rape'
and 'indecent assault' with the offences *'sexual* assault' and
'aggravated *sexual* assault'. In this way, the sexist character of
particular assaults on women could be highlighted and subjected to particular prosecution. The law would also ensure
that a victim of rape

> would no longer . . . be forced to reveal his or her sexual
> history. (Questions about a victim's past sexual activity
> may still be asked at an *in camera* hearing, but the victim
> would be under no compulsion to answer.) The law would
> make it clear that a victim of sexual assault could not be
> assumed to have given complaint merely because he or she
> failed to file a complaint right away or failed to offer what
> the court judged to be sufficient resistance, and it would
> remove all references to penetration as a necessary condi-
> tion for a sexual assault to have occurred. The law would
> spell out that a spouse can be victim of a sexual assault by
> his or her marriage partner, thus clearing the way for
> charges of rape against a partner.
> (*Liaison*, Monthly Newsletter of the Criminal Justice
> System, 8(1), Ottawa, Ministry of the Solicitor
> General, p. 22)

Clark and Lewis' arguments are different from those advanced
for Britain by the radical lawyer, Geoffrey Robertson QC. Robertson (1975) believes that it is the emotional character of the
rape label which causes women to hesitate in reporting an offence to the police, and that it is also this emotional element
which causes judges to sentence to long terms of imprisonment
(on a tariff, in the middle 1970s, of three to six years). Both

these problems could be solved by integrating rape into the existing offence of assault. So Robertson's concerns are significantly different to those of Clark and Lewis: he wants to encourage more women to report being raped to the police, while simultaneously wanting the courts to be less punitive towards convicted male rapists. This is an essentially sexist position, under current conditions, since it fails to deal with the specific character of rape (which is a direct attempt to control and humiliate women by the use of fundamental physical and psychic violence). Robertson is also silent on the question of women's attempts to 'reclaim the night', and on the pressing need for women to be able to turn to the law in their own defence against sexual assault.[42]

I would argue, with Anna Coote and Tess Gill and the Canadian Minister of Justice, and against Geoffrey Robertson, for the retention of the sexual character of a rape charge, precisely because rape is a *sexual* crime committed by men against *women's bodies*, and therefore a crime involving particular kinds of psychic as well as physical damage. It does also exclude most women from 'open territory' (as Clark and Lewis call spaces outside the family, work and other 'respectable' areas) and it is therefore a major control on women's freedom. The problem with existing rape law is that it is still too restrictive in scope and application,[43] and also that the procedures for following through a complaint involve further trials and physical and psychic humiliations primarily for the woman victim rather than the man.

In arguments around the need for a new law of 'sexual assault', other transitional advances can be made. In particular, following the precedent established by the Canadian government, the 1976 Sexual Offences (Amendment) Act should be amended to disallow any reference in rape trials to a woman's past sexual history (which the 1976 Act continued to allow when the judge considered it relevant). Also all references in the Act to the woman giving 'consent' should be replaced (as the Rape Crisis Centre in Britain has argued) by the phrase 'reasonable grounds for believing that she willed it'. A formulation of this kind avoids reproduction of the idea of passive-subordinate female sexuality, of the notion that sex is more important for men than for women, and that it is a 'woman's duty' to provide sexual enjoyment for the man, which are current in existing law and which are present even in the proposed revision of the relevant law in Canada.

The effect of these two amendments would be to undermine the defences that are used by men in the majority of rape trials. They would in fact prioritise the woman's statement that she had been raped as the primary evidence in such cases. As the second report of the Rape Crisis Centre observes: 'The burden of proving that the woman consented to intercourse should be placed on the man whenever his defence is one of consent' (p. 11).

In constructing the proposals it submitted to the Criminal Law Revision Committee, the Rape Crisis Centre in London was heavily influenced by its intense recent experience of the courtroom processing of rape cases. The project workers were clearly impressed by the enormous burden of proof that still rested on women in such cases, even in the aftermath of the 'amending' legislation passed in 1976, and they were appalled at the ease with which men accused of rape were being acquitted, often on minor legal technicalities. So in contrast to other critics of rape law, who have concentrated on removing the requirement in existing law, dating from 1736, that women's evidence in sexual matters must receive independent corroboration, the Rape Crisis Centre want women's evidence to be at the very centre of rape trials. The demand may appear revolutionary, but of course the effect of this reform of the law would merely bring the practice in rape cases into line with the rest of criminal law. Subsequent to such reform, it would become the task of prosecution counsel to prove the man guilty of rape 'beyond reasonable doubt', just as it is the taks of prosecutors to prove guilt in such terms in other criminal cases.

In the short term, further pressure must be put on giving legal recognition to rape in marriage, which is to be the subject of the new Canadian laws on sexual offences. This is crucially important in registering the changing significance of legal and common law marriage for many men and women: marriage should no longer be allowed to transform a woman's body into the property of her husband. It is also important to define rape as an offence against all women, thus preventing police and lawyers acting for men continuing to imply that there are women of virtue and women of vice, with the latter legitimate targets for sexual violence (by reason of being unmarried or independent of any one man). The law must be required to offer a defence of marriage as a conditional contract only between a free woman and a free man that confers no special rights and no particular disadvantages on either partner, whether these are financial *or* sexual; and the law must also protect all women (and men) from sexual interference committed *against their will*, whatever the social standing or occupation of the victims of such attacks might be.

I have spoken of the need for socialists to give support in solidarity and sorority with the women's movement to the liberalisation or the abolition of some law and also to the strengthening of other law, and the creation of at least one new criminal offence, 'sexual assault'. There is at least one other important area of legal struggle.

It is not at all clear that the recent demands for 'the closure of porn shops, the suppression of films and advertisements depicting women as targets of male sexual violence, the intensification of police action against rapists, wife-beaters, etc.' (B. Taylor, 1981) can be met within the framework of existing legislation. An offence may have to be created, for example, which specifically criminalise the depiction of women as legitimate targets of sexual violence. There are obviously great problems in justifying such a law. I would not argue that the films, videotapes and magazines which depict such sexual violence against women should be outlawed on the ground of their 'effects', i.e. that they might encourage imitative behaviour on the part of the men who view them. There is no sound evidence for such a view. But as Beverley Brown (1981) and others have shown, this liberal behaviourist criterion is irrelevant. What is crucial about pornography is what it legitimates ideologically. 'Soft' pornography legitimates (patriarchally) male sexuality by portraying the naked or half-clothed female body in heavily sexually scripted postures or scenes. In recent years, some soft pornography has tried to legitimate a 'liberated' women's sexuality with pictures of naked men, and with the elaboration of different sexual scenes in which women's sexual needs are more prominent. Although most soft pornographic magazines and films are patriarchal, the terrain is now contested, and some celebration of women's sexuality is allowed. The only grounds on which this kind of pornography could be outlawed would be on the basis of some new moral puritanism which attempted, like its Victorian precursor, to deny the joys of male and female sexuality. For socialist feminists and their allies to move in this direction would be to threaten one of the most important women's gains in recent years: the recognition of their sexuality outside of the activity of reproduction. It certainly would make no sense to propose the outlawing of this kind of pornography on the grounds that it helps to reproduce patriarchy, since in this respect it is no different, and probably less insidious in its effects, than the average romantic comedy on television. Both depict women in patriarchal terms, but both do so relatively 'consensually'. So the patriarchal character of soft pornography and romantic comedies, whilst still fundamental and still objectionable, is qualified by new scripts and images, and therefore acceptable to many.

'Hard' pornography is altogether different, and our present concern is that some of the themes of hard pornography are now playing into cinema films on the mass circuit. Films which depict the mutilation of women in sexual contexts, or which set up woman as a legitimate target for violence because of her sex (or a behaviour allegedly associated with her sex but actually associated with her enforced role, like nagging) have an ideological factor in common: they work to celebrate a patriarchy that is enforced by coercion and indeed by terror. They make sense only as a reactionary, male, 'redneck', populist response to the advance of the women's movements over recent years. They legitimate the violent responses of some husbands to the stirrings of women's consciousness in their wives, and they also legitimate the use of violence for instrumental purposes. Women have to respond to what is a direct ideological attack on the movement towards greater independence within the family (this in itself does not necessarily involve the law), but they also have to gain the power to prosecute men who produce and promote the films, videotapes and magazines that celebrate a coercive form of patriarchy. To fail to do so would be analogous to black groups failing to press for the outlawing of films celebrating racist attacks by the British Movement.

Transitional legal demands can also be raised, and are likely to be raised in coming years, across a broad range of other feminist and socialist terrains. We have already identified the importance of the demand for 'disaggregation' of women from the aggregated family income in the area of taxation and social security law (Bennett *et al.*, 1980). It is to be hoped that feminists may also begin to pose challenges to the use of apparently permissive criminal law, like the care proceedings of the Children and Young Persons Act of 1969, to put young girls into care for their own protection, because of the precocious exercise of their sexuality. It is in the interface between different areas of law that the scope and functions of social policy and social control *vis-à-vis* women are regulated, with fundamental consequences for all women clients of the state welfare and legal apparatus. Socialist feminists and their allies have a heavy burden of analytic and practical work to do in identifying the crucial areas in which the patriarchal relation is reproduced by 'law' and 'public policy', in making these areas publically problematic, and in developing demands from them as a part of the more general struggle for social transformation.

*　　　　*　　　　*

The discussion of transitional demands presented here has focused on the question of prison (prioritising prisoners as the main political agency), the police (with police critics and new local police authorities the significant agency), law (to be combatted on all fronts by socialists outside and within the legal profession) and the question of patriarchy and legal reforms (prioritising the women's movement). The examination is obviously not exhaustive of all the crime topics that could be included within a transitional or prefigurative socialist criminology, and there are also other, possible agencies which could be discussed in such an analysis.

As suggested earlier, however, the role of academic social theorists is less important in prefigurative struggles than the theorists themselves would like to believe, because the theories are not directed sufficiently to specific and practical problems. In particular, we can see that 'critical' theorists (like the deviance theorists of the late 1960s and early 1970s) who continue to theorise abstractly and unhistorically about the evils of 'social control', or, following Foucault, the insidious character of a 'disciplinary society', seem particularly irrelevant to the struggles that have now to go into the construction of 'practical' demands (for example, in the area of prison reform) or policy construction (in various areas of law). The heritage of this critical tradition will live on as a way of reminding socialists of the dangers of 'labelling' in the process of social control and also, as suggested earlier, as a critique of the claims of 'experts' or 'professionals', *in any form of state*, to provide the services their rhetorics proclaim. But, in themselves, these essentially academic traditions of social policy thinking and criminology have not been able to reach a firm agreement on the character of the social order their critical reflexions anticipate (or prefigure): and it is into that space that specifically socialist and feminist politics and transitional strategies have to be inserted.

This point can be put in another way. Identifying the failures of post-war social democracy, for example in providing the sense of social order its 1940s rhetorics anticipated, is not to identify the impossibility of social democracy as such. I tried in Chapters 2 and 3 to identify the limitations of social democratic criminology and social policy. I have begun to suggest ways of reformulating socialist responses to them. This task will not be solved or advanced by indicting existing social democratic responses to crime and to social problems generally as illegitimate exercises in social control, unwarranted because of their unseen, unintended or mischievous effects on their clients. Increasingly, as my analysis of particular questions (like prison or policing) has proceeded, it has become increasingly clear that there are two key questions in the examination of social control: the question of the relationship of social control to a democratic state formation and the

practical effectivity of different systems of social control as
a guarantor of social order.

Democratisation and socialist reconstruction

In *Arguments for Socialism*, Tony Benn advances an argument
for a thoroughgoing democratisation in Britain which concentrates on the need to make 'government . . . more accountable
to Parliament and to the people' (Benn, 1980, p. 108). He
sees the alienation of people from parliament and government
as deriving in particular from parliament's inability to deal
with 'the bigger and more centralised units of production or
bureaucracy' which have resulted, primarily, from 'technological change'. Benn then proceeds to make a series of practical demands for making governments and the civil service
accountable to parliament, and also for making both government and parliament less private and indeed less secretive in
their proceedings.

The arguments for democratisation presented here extend
Benn's analysis in the sense of demanding the democratisation
of the existing institutions of the state, like the prison or the
police force, in order to transform their character. Democratisation of policing is not simply advanced as a means of
observing existing police practice and making it more accountable. Democratic control of the police is demanded in order
to subordinate police practices, especially in so-called community policing, to the demands of a wider range of social
interests for effective policing than the current 'professional'
and state definition of policing allows. Democratisation of
the prison is demanded as being the most effective means of
challenging the massive rate of imprisonment in this country,
of 'problematising' prison's alleged contribution to social
order and of displaying the real character of prison as an
instrument of 'expulsion'. Democratisation of the law and
the legal system is demanded in the attempt to put an end to
the astonishingly class-bound and patriarchal character of the
British judiciary, courtroom procedure and legal rules themselves.

So the call for democratisation here is forwarded as a way

of opening existing state institutions to the influences and
demands of organised social interests that currently relate to
the state only as clients, employees, or, in the case of police
and courts, as accuseds.

It is a way of 'enfranchising' women,
prisoners, blacks, tenants, welfare recipients and other interest
groups that are currently handled by the state in different
capacities, and who experience the state primarily as a bureaucratic and impersonal agency (a part of a disciplinary apparatus, run by an unidentified 'them', rather than as a part of
'our' community). Such an enfranchising, for example of
women's organisations in relation to local police committees,
would significantly transform the character and function of
particular aspects of the police and the *local* state. In this
respect it would prefigure, by making possible, the construction of other demands by women on the local state apparatus
generally (for example, in relation to the provision of housing
for single women, battered wives, etc.) or the police specifically (in relation, for example, to the way in which rape and
domestic violence are handled in particular forces).

Such a view of the need for democratisation does not derive
simply from a generalised view of the alienation that citizens
feel from the bigger and more centralised units of production
or bureaucracy. It depends instead on the recognition that
the institutional apparatuses of the British state, built up over
centuries and predicated on deep traditions of deference
towards aristocratic rule and of an assumed continuity of
patriarchal family life as the foundation of social order, are
increasingly irrelevant to particular, identifiable social interests. In particular, I have tried to reactivate another tradition
in socialism which identifies these institutions and apparatuses
as class institutions (working by coercion or in ideology to
reproduce the class relations of a capitalist society). But I
have simultaneously tried to show the inadequacy of conventional social democratic understanding of class: unexplicated
references to the 'interests of working people' are no substitute for recognising that the working class is now fractured
into a variety of different specific interest groups and class
fragments. The unification as a class of men and women, of
blacks and whites, of skilled and unskilled workers, of employed and unemployed, and of the variety of interest groups

contained within the penal system, cannot be accomplished at a merely rhetorical level: it is a project that requires that these fragments can first have their real interests recognised as an important element in socialist politics. And such a project of recognition — the opening out of the Labour Party to these different class fragments and interest groups — is made all the more urgent by the economic collapse of the traditional basis of Labour politics (the blue-collar working class) under the logic of monetarism, and by the ideological advances of right-wing populism.

The recognition of the particular needs of these different interest groups in reconstructed socialist perspectives must be achieved by a fundamental modification of the conventional commitment of the Labour Party on the question of the state. To call for the democratisation of the state is *not* to surrender to right-wing individualism or to economic interests who see chances of gain in the privatisation of some forms of state activity (for example, in health care or even in child care). Indeed, given the current sorry situation of the National Health Service and local authority nursery and child care provision, a *renewed* commitment is obviously necessary to the defence of the state as the only institution that can ensure proper health care for all and the only institution that can provide child care on behalf of working fathers and working mothers, single parents and others on low incomes. It is often only through state provision of such facilities, indeed, that young children can encounter children from other social classes, races and general background. The state is also the only apparatus that is capable of organising income redistribution in a capitalist society, as well as being the only centralised apparatus that can collect taxation and provide services (like energy) for the population as a whole (see E. Wilson, 1980). It is indeed the only institution that can *universalise* the availability of health, education and welfare. Finally, the state is, of course, the only apparatus through which the economic future of the mass of the people can be underwritten. The left's current rejection of corporatism of the Wilson and Callaghan government, and its increasing commitment to an alternative economic strategy, still involves a central role for the state, especially in organising the use of public expenditure in investment into industry and in the economy generally. As Tony Benn observes in his *Arguments for Socialism*, 'only public expenditure can convert human needs into economic demands able to command resources and help restore full employment' (Benn, 1980, p. 149).

What is crucial in carrying out socialist economic and social policies through the state is that the identification and evaluation of 'human needs' occurs in the most democratic and public fashion, at both local and national level.

This recommitment to the state as an economic apparatus and as the sole institutional apparatus concerned with the provision of universal health, education and welfare cannot however be an excuse for an unreflexive recycling of Labour's familiar bureaucratic and authoritarian statism. The problems that confront socialists in Britain in 1982 (and also now in North America) are increasingly ideological, in the sense that socialist alternatives to right-wing populism are already impugned ideologically, by the popular press, the Thatcherite leadership and also in popular common sense as forms of authoritarianism and inefficient bureaucratic statism. Cold war analogies are often introduced as a way of implying that the ideas of democratic socialism are of a piece with the ideas used to legitimate the rule of the state bureaucracy in Soviet Russia. It is only by showing that the real interests of the many different subordinate interest groups in the British class structure lie with a reconstructed socialism that such a socialist future can indeed be prefigured. So the thoroughgoing democratisation of state activity has to be at the centre of socialist demands, not only in relationship to the industrial workplace but also in relationship to every aspect of state social provision and to state policing and social control generally.

Right-wing criminology: class rhetoric and social disorder

There is no doubt that socialists have been put on to the defensive in Britain by the result of the 1979 general election and by the speed and vigour of the Thatcher government's attack on the welfare state and the social democratic consensus, as well as by the cancerous effect that the threat of unemployment has had on trade union militancy. Internation-

ally, the advancing recession has signalled the end of Keynesianism and thereby has also undermined the social democratic
and liberal descriptions of capitalism as a healthy mixed
economy, more or less always able to reproduce itself without
a fundamental collapse into recession. Social policies which
have assumed the continuing existence of a surplus with which
the state has financed its social expenditure have nearly all
been put under threat. The threat posed to the economic
wage by unemployment and the threat to the 'social wage'
(the welfare state) have put 'working people' and the 'fragments' alike on the defensive, as each individual has looked,
first, to the defence of his or her individual job.

In such circumstances, it is perhaps inevitable that the
individualistic themes of radical Right thinking should have
started to find an echo in some academic and intellectual
circles (especially in the United States, but also in Britain), as
well as to have what appears to be a massive and unchallenged
effect amongst working people as a whole. The fact that
right-wing populism appears to speak to the reality of many
working people's lives (and in particular their experience of
the state) has caused considerable pessimism and despondency.

This despondency is unjustified, especially in the medium
term. In particular, the widespread preoccupation on the Left
with the apparently successful use by the Right of the ideologies of 'authoritarian populism' does sometimes forget the
highly contingent and unstable character of a confused and
fragmented public opinion, especially in the working class.
The authoritarian populist rhetorics of Thatcherism prospered
in the very specific conjuncture of the public sector workers'
struggles of the winter of 1978—9, which presented the Tory
leadership and the popular press with a heaven-sent opportunity for massive ideological work on the anti-social, irresponsible and subversive character of trade unions. A small
Labour lead of some 2 per cent in the public opinion polls in
November 1978 was turned into a Conservative lead, in one
public opinion poll at the start of the 1979 election, of over
25 per cent. At the most apposite moment, a 'winter of dis-
content' was transformed by ideological work into an immediate threat to authority, law and social order, resulting
from the fact that organised labour and criminals, in Mrs

Thatcher's words, had both got 'the same message'. They were both intent on 'mugging' the rest of society and defying the Rule of Law. The Tory Party won an election victory for desperate measures for economic reconstruction on the basis of a *momentarily* quite unambiguous rhetoric about social order and law.

Working people's experiences of Thatcherism have certainly not led them to embrace this populism in its economic and political forms. The success of the Conservative Party in 1979 of cutting into traditional Labour voters' affiliations is unlikely to be repeated again. To say this is not, of course, to deny that Thatcherism has worked with enormous effect in unsettling popular support for the welfare state and for 'liberal' social policy generally. Nor is it to say that the apparent inability of Thatcherism to break the hold of popular social democratic or Keynesian beliefs *vis-à-vis* the national economy could result in large numbers of electors returning to traditional Labour voting patterns or even to turn to the Left. It is obvious that the mass of working people are on the defensive and very confused, and that this confusion has been compounded by the creation of the new Social Democratic Party. But it is important to realise that forthcoming elections, and other extra-parliamentary struggles, will be fought on ground that is much less advantageous to the Thatcherite Right than that of 1979. Not only will populist ideologies and policies lack the newsworthiness and the appeal of being different from the post-war social consensus generally and the Callaghan government's authoritarian statism in particular, but they will also be seen to be ideologies that have allowed, and indeed made legitimate, a fundamental weakening of the industrial economy and also contributed to the reintroduction of the human waste of long-term unemployment as a feature of life for three million people.

Crucially, it is the responsibility of the various socialist fragments to show also that right-wing populism cannot work as a form of social policy. So, for example, socialists working in the health service have to show how the growth of private medicine is parasitical on society as a whole, and that the residual public health service cannot provide fundamental health care for the rest. And in the area which we have been discussing here, crime and social order, socialists have to show that authoritarian populism cannot provide for the human need (for *social order*) which Thatcherite rhetoric appeared to prefigure.

Two years into the Thatcher government, there is little sign of the national economic regeneration that was promised in 1979, nor is there any real evidence of the 'social peace' which was implicit in the law and order rhetoric of the election. As we showed in Chapter 1, the slight declines in the official crime rate of 1978 and 1979 now look to have stopped, and the crime rates reported by the police to the Home Office are once again on the increase. To the usual desperate outbreaks of hooliganism and vandalism among the rejected working-class youthful population have been added massive increases in racist attacks on the homes and persons of blacks and Asians, continuing increases in predatory crimes in public inner-city and city-centre areas and on public transport (especially at night) and significant increases in reported cases of domestic violence and sexual assault and rape.

Continuing increases in the rate of crime and in particular in the desperate forms of interpersonal violence (either for gain or as an expression of forms of nihilism) are entirely to be expected. If reformist welfare state policies adopted during the post-war period were unsuccessful in producing material conditions and the social relations within a capitalist mode of production which could significantly reduce interpersonal violence, property thefts and 'anti-social' activities as such, then it is even more difficult to see how a withdrawal from welfare and an accelerated commitment to coercion could produce the appropriate conditions for a 'crime-free' society. Increasing the police presence in society may or may not deter individuals from acts of predatory crime or interpersonal violence in public places observed by the police (there are different research results reported on this) but they cannot influence the conditions that produce inequality in access to material goods and life chances or which produce interpersonal, racial or sexual competition, envy, mistrust and violence.

We can expect that the Right will attempt to portray increases in crime rate in forthcoming years as evidence of the need for further increases in social discipline and also as evidence of the need for further increases in police power and in state expenditure on law and order. The Left must clearly challenge this interpretation, by identifying Thatcherism and right-wing populism as *ineffective as social and penal policy*. In so doing, socialists will increasingly be able to reassert older and more fundamental connections than was allowed within the liberalism and social democracy I have discussed in this book: it will be possible to show how the social relations of capitalist societies as such, whether in health or in decay, must divide human beings from human beings, and therefore produce a variety of acts of crime and violence, in the very nature of the form that social organisation must assume. The freeing of 'the market' (that is, of capitalists) from the regulation of the state cannot usher in a new era of interpersonal responsibility and self-discipline, as the New Right believes, and neither can the economics of the market-place repair the dislocation of fractured urban communities. Human beings' responsibility to each other and their cultivation of social and interpersonal 'discipline' depend not on the anarchy of the struggle for survival or profit, but on the creation of a genuine community of interest of all citizens. It is no accident that homicide and crimes of violence are commonest of all in societies like the United States, Hong Kong and many South East Asian countries, with the least degree of community control over 'free enterprise' capital. It is no accident that it is in societies like the United States that New Right criminologists like James Q. Wilson and Ernest van den Haag are most vocal in proclaiming the loss of community, but also in being most desperate in their recommendations for remoralisation and 'incapacitation'.

So the increasing dislocation of civil society through crime and violence under Thatcherism does create a political space for socialist advance. The Left must enter this space, not in the manner of the social democrats of the post-war period — as experts working primarily within and through the state, on behalf of the people — but increasingly through community and special interest organisations at local level, struggling to make popular demands (for example, for policing), and articulating popular fears and anxieties. A public and popular socialist criminology has to be constructed in practice, through the different fragments that are working towards explicitly socialist goals and also within established institutions of the class. In so doing, the socialist Left may finally put an end to the 'truth' on which the contemporary New Right has relied: that the crime question is one which works, by its nature, to the advantage of the Right. It should also be able to make obvious another rather different old truth, by reference to the character and prevalence of crime under late capitalism — that the obverse of solicalism is barbarism.

Notes to Chapter 4

1. This particular calculation is that of Bottoms, in Bottoms and Preston (1980, p. 5).
2. *The Report of the Committee of Inquiry into the UK Prison Services* (The May Report), February 1980. This report was pre-occupied with the question of the qualifications and pay structure of prison officers, with overcrowding and, to a lesser extent, the revision of the prison rules. Its discussion of living and working conditions in prisons was quite abbreviated and, by contrast with reports produced on the prison system in other countries, very guarded in its descriptions.
3. The increase in the length of sentences being served is to some extent a result of the passage of the Homicide Act in 1957, which substituted 'life imprisonment' for capital punishment in the vast majority of homicide cases. But it is also 'undoubtedly related to the idea that especially long sentences are required for the "dangerous" or "exceptional" offender who, it is often believed, represents a growing threat to society' (Cohen and Taylor, 1980).
4. Between 1955 and 1964, the number of escapes from British prisons rose from 35.8 per 1,000 prisoners to 72.0. Sometimes, indeed, the escapes involved 'outsiders' breaking into prison to aid the escape, as happened in the freeing of Charles Wilson from Winson Green Prison in Birmingham in 1964 and again in July 1965 when Ronald Biggs, another of the Great Train Robbers, escaped from Wandsworth Prison. But the escape which precipitated the establishment of the Mountbatten Inquiry was that of George Blake, sentenced to 42 years for spying for the Soviet Union, from Wormwood Scrubs in October 1966.

5. The two control units were established at some time in 1972, but then closed 'temporarily' in March 1975 and again in October 1975, in response to campaigns against the inhumane conditions existing within them (see Fitzgerald and Sim, 1979, p. 105). The current position is that the control units still exist and are 'available for use if the need arises' (Merlyn Rees, *Hansard*, 24 October 1975).

6. The treatment by the popular press of the prison demonstrations of 1972 was more of a comment on its own ideological preoccupations than on the seriousness of the events taking place in the prisons. The first prize was won by *The Sun* (5 August 1972) with the headline 'Love Strike Hits Jails'. The report continued:

> The biggest ever protest hit Britain's jails yesterday as 5,000 prisoners went on strike for love.
> Prison grapevines hummed as the eight-week-old convicts' union PROP — the Preservation of the Rights of Prisoners — got the sit-in under way. The right of prisoners to make love to their wives is PROP's number one aim.

In the statement sent by PROP just prior to the strike to the Home Office and to the press containing specific proposals requiring 'urgent consideration', there was *no mention* of conjugal visits. This statement concentrated on the right to belong to PROP, on the right to strike, and the establishment of trade union committees by prisoners inside prisons (Fitzgerald, 1977, pp. 152–3).

7. The Minimal Use of Force for Tactical Intervention (MUFTI) squads are units of prison officers in particular regions of the Prison Service who have been specially trained in riot control. On being called to a particular prison, they are armed with staves, riot shields, visors and helmets, and then allowed to use 'minimal force' to end actions of protest being taken by prisoners. The first use of such a squad was at Wormwood Scrubs in August 1979, when 300 officers put an end to a peaceful sit-in of 200 prisoners. After some earlier denials, the Home Office later admitted that five prisoners had been 'hurt' and that another 53 received 'minor injuries' (Anna Cotte, ' "Tinderbox" Tensions at the Scrubs', *New Statesman*, 12 October 1979, pp. 536–7).

8. King and Morgan (1979) calculate that the prison system will comprise 147 separate 'functional units' by 1984 and that 94 (or 64 per cent) of these units will have been brought into use since the war (para. 23). They also observe that the prison system has in this respect '[fared] better than either psychiatric or general hospitals and only a little worse than schools in the public sector' (para. 30).

9. The exception here is the attendance centre sentence. Attendance centres are intended for use as a short, brisk form of punishment 'in the community'. They are held every Saturday afternoon and *run by the police*. Their clientele obviously includes many young people arrested for offences at soccer games.

10. Guns were issued to the Metropolitan Police on 6,649 occasions during 1979, and to police elsewhere in the country on 1,732 occasions. In 1970, the comparative figure was 1,072 occasions nationally. These figures do not reveal how many guns were issued on each occasion and they do not include what the police call 'protection arming' (during visits of royalty, etc., but also in moments of crisis, as after the murder of Airey Neave MP in 1979) (*State Research*, 19, 1980, p. 162).

11. This programme, 'The Public and the Public', was produced by and for Granada, but in a late programme change, was screened on the ITV national network, a decision clearly influenced by the recent riot in St Paul's, Bristol. Prominence was given to a survey undertaken in the North West by Opinion Research Centre and MAPS (of 2,000 residents) in Huyton and Wavertree in Liverpool and Moss Side and Blakeney in Manchester. The data from this survey showed that 63 per cent of young people generally and 58 per cent of blacks of all ages had little or no confidence in the police. Whilst 48 per cent of people living in the region saw police as their friends, only 18 per cent of young people agreed. 49 per cent of blacks thought the police force 'anti-immigrant'.

12. The Police National Computer, designed and put into operation between 1965 and 1973, now handles something between 40 and 60 million transactions annually, drawing on files held on over 2.5 million people (Duguid, 1980). The less well known computer of 'C' Department of the Metropolitan Police, operational from January 1977, has taken over and massively expanded the records of Special Branch, the Central Drugs Intelligence Unit, the Immigration Intelligence Unit, Fraud Squad and C11 (Criminal Intelligence). According to the tender document issued to manufacturers, the police requirement was for the capacity of this computer to increase to nearly 3 million individual records by 1985. Of these, by far the largest holding will be of Special Branch files, which will total 1,414,000, with 'immigration intelligence' the second most significant group (287,000) (Campbell, 1980, pp. 98—100). Public acquaintance with these computers is restricted to the random police checks on car ownership which have been occurring throughout the country in recent years. These constitute an occasion for collating the simple information on identification stored in the computers.

13. In May 1978 the Home Secretary revealed that there was a total of 1,259 police officers in the Special Branch in England and Wales. This compares with a figure of about 200 officers in Special Branch in the early 1960s, all of whom were based at Scotland Yard. All Britain's police forces now have a permanent Special Branch (*State Research*, 13, 1979, pp. 121–4).

14. Following the Police Act of 1964, the number of police forces in England and Wales was reduced from 117 to 49. Subsequent reorganisation has reduced this further to 43. The new forces, by virtue of their size and geographical coverage, are consequently that much less amenable to very localised forms of control. Their responsibilities do however coincide closely with the local authority areas constructed by the Local Government Act of 1970, and it is at the level of the new local authorities, therefore, that formal accountability is supposed to operate.

15. The opposition of solid working-class areas to the police in an earlier period is documented in Cohen, P. (1979). The traditional self-discipline of the community worked not only to control and punish misdemeanours within the community, but also to prevent police from penetrating into the community. It was in the dislocation of the economic changes and the rehousing movement of the early post-war years that the police were able to establish a presence, for the first time, in these areas.

16. Keith Waterhouse, Writing for *The Daily Mirror*, cast some doubt on the judge's claims: 'not many classes of person get letters by the hundred. Pop stars do, disc jockeys do . . . but I would have thought it unique for mail to arrive by the sackful at the chambers of a circuit judge of the Central Criminal Court' (quoted in Taylor, L., 1976, p. 260).

17. There is even some evidence to suggest that the intensified presence of police in an area, even over a short period, may result in a decrease in street crime and burglary *in that area*. What is not clear is whether this is a function of young 'burglars' and 'muggers' turning to other areas, where the police presence is less visible or effective (see Dean, 'The Other Side of the Tracks', *The Guardian*, 19 November 1980).

18. The police raids were a product of a new agreement worked out between the Home Office and the Association of Chief Constables during the last months of the *Labour* government of 1974–9. Under this agreement, the police personally serve notice of refusals of applications for an extension to stay. In the past, these notices have been sent by registered post, and, in many cases, if MPs intervened, deportation was postponed. The police are now involved in finding *and* detaining overstay immigrants (*The Guardian*, 9 July 1979).

216   *Law and Order*

19. For an account of the treatment given young blacks at a police station in the Metropolitan Police area by a senior research officer at the Home Office, see Bob Forde, 'The Routine Racism of the Met', *New Statesman*, 27 March 1981, p. 13. Forde's observations were anticipated in an official report by Lambeth Council into relations between the police and the public, and especially into the police's relations with young blacks. Published three months before the Brixton riots, this report (based on 257 submissions) argued that police strategy in Lambeth was 'to lay siege to the black population' (see Frances Wheen, 'Living in a State of Siege', *New Statesman*, 30 January 1981, p. 10).

20. In this country, the only socialist to have discussed 'the police task in socialist society' is Robert Reiner (1978). He argues that the achievement of socialism (involving 'changes in the distribution of resources and a less competitive tone in social relations, including sexual ones') would transform the police task from being 'the apparently impossible endeavour of controlling a mass of human misery, degradation and brutality' into one in which the police could at last achieve 'the status of skilled professionals which . . . has eluded them in the past' (p. 79). In particular, preventative police work could be concentrated on the control of violent street crime and routine patrols of public space, established preferably with a degree of routinised citizen involvement. Additionally, police could become highly skilled in the kind of detective work involved in detecting and prosecuting what Reiner calls 'crime in the suites'. Finally, Reiner argues, some police activity would be necessary under strict legislative control in order to forestall 'counter-revolutionary activity and foreign subversions' (p. 80).

21. Operation Countryman was initiated in September 1978 under the Assistant Chief Constable for Dorset, Mr Leonard Burt (the 'countryman'), to investigate allegations that corruption in the 'Met' was continuing, despite Robert Mark's 'purges' of the early 1970s. By June 1979, the Countryman team of 40 officers had assembled allegations against 78 detectives; and the team was reinforced to 90 to enable these allegations to be investigated and clarified. The allegations included the charge that detectives were involved in the planning of big robberies in the City of London, including the robbery at *The Daily Mirror* in 1978, when £200,000 was stolen and a security guard killed. In a series of internal struggles within the police between 1979 and 1981, however, the Operation was put onto the defensive, as the Director of Public Prosecutions rejected the team's recommendations on prosecution. Despite denials from Scotland Yard that the operation has been 'obstructed', the suspicion in Fleet Street was that the 'old firm' had 'nobbled'

Countryman (see *The Leveller*, 50, 20 February—5 March 1981, pp. 8—10).

22. In research (undertaken for the Royal Commission on Criminal Procedure) into interrogation procedures in use by Brighton police, Barry Irving, a psychologist at the Tavistock Institute of Human Relations, concluded that

> the British police are so skilled in interrogation that a 'normal' questioning session can put a suspect under such psychological and social pressure that few could withstand it. Some of those who confess will be guilty; others will be innocent. The problem . . . is that there is no way of telling, merely from the interrogation and confession, which is which ('The Interrogators: How a Policeman Could Make Even you Confess', *The Sunday Times*, 10 August 1980).

Home Office Research into complaints of assault by police on people in custody, completed in 1981 but as yet unpublished, has also attacked police investigation methods, concluding that

> some enquiries are more concerned with establishing the criminal guilt or untrustworthiness of the complainant than with attempting to discover what happened . . . and seem at times calculated to support the police version of events.
>
> (*The Times*, 8 April 1981)

23. For a useful account of the role of the coroner in the Blair Peach case, see National Council for Civil Liberties (1981), and in the Jimmy Kelly case, Scraton and Benn (1981).
24. 'Barrister' was clearly the pseudonym of D. N. Pritt, the communist author of the four-volume *Law, Class and Society* (1971). The almost identical analysis of the magistracy can be seen in Barrister (1938, pp. 43—7) and in Pritt (1971, bk 2, pp. 72—4).
25. Social democratic faith in the provision of full-time professionals as guarantors of impartiality and defenders of the innocent, as well as those whose guilt has not been proven, has been shaken by the experience of stipendiary magistrates since the war. Pritt observes that

> with one or two distinguished exceptions, the stipendiaries have proved to be rather more orthodox and 'prosecution-minded' than lay magistrates, and further from understanding what 'makes the ordinary citizen tick'.
>
> (Pritt, 1971, bk 2, p. 73)

218 Law and Order

26. Social democratic and libertarian opinions have been thrown in a
variety of directions by the debate over the Bill of Rights. For a
polemical critique of the Bill of Rights from the social democratic
Left, see Kilroy-Silk (1977); and for support from the libertarian
wing of law, see Zander (1975). Orthodox civil libertarian opinion
has been a little more cautious over the Bill of Rights than Zander,
and certainly much more worried over its implications for the
Labour and trade union movements (see McBride and Wallington,
1976).
27. This strengthening of the principle of randomness occurred in paradoxical circumstances. In particular, the judiciary were anxious at
the way in which the defence lawyers had cross-examined jurors
selected for the 'Angry Brigade' trial in January 1973, in order to
discover whether the jurors would be biased against the defendants.
Subsequent to the trial, without any consultation with MPs, a
practice direction was issued to all judges affirming that 'it is contrary to established practice for jurors to be excused on more
general grounds such as race, religion, or political beliefs or occupation'. Later in the same year, the removal of jurors' occupations
from jury panels by the then Lord Chancellor, Lord Hailsham, was
thought by some to have been in anticipation of attempts by the
Shrewsbury building workers, due for trial under the Industrial
Relations Act, to discover which potential jurors were trade unionists (Harman and Griffith, 1979, pp. 15—16).
28. The court of appeal arose out of an appeal from the Chief Constable
of South Yorkshire, Mr James Brownlow, against a court order
issued by Judge Pickles in Sheffield Crown Court which required
the Chief Constable to provide defence and prosecution solicitors
who would be involved in a forthcoming trial (of two police officers
charged with assault) with full details of any criminal proceedings
against members of the jury panel. For a full report of the court of
appeal case judgement, see *The Star*, Sheffield, 4 March 1980.
29. In 1978, for example, the evidence of the Association of Chief Police
Officers to the Royal Commission on Criminal Procedure argued
that 'all jurors . . . should be subject to these inquiries' so that
criminal, dishonest or 'irresponsible' elements could be kept off
juries (David Leigh, 'Police Carry On Vetting Juries', *The Guardian*,
21 February 1980). In this way, the ACPO wanted police vetting,
as allowed in exceptional circumstances by the 1975 circular of
Mr Sam Silkin, to be extended to all cases.
30. The discussion which follows on earlier and current debates on
rape, prostitution and so-called 'sexual offences' in general is an
abbreviation of the discussion in Ian Taylor (1981, ch. 4). There

is very little discussion here, in particular, of the reactions of Labour and social democratic opinion to the 'permissive' legislation of the late 1950s and early 1960s.

31. Some women Labour MPs (in particular Lena Jeger and Eirene White) did make major speeches against the Wolfenden Report's (and the resulting Street Offences Bill's) retention of the common law term of 'common prostitute'. This term derived from the vagrancy legislation of 1824, and allowed police to identify a defendant by such a term at the start of a criminal trial, on the grounds that it identified an 'incorrigible rogue', if the woman being charged had received a previous caution from the police for the same offence. Unsurprisingly, many women have since been convicted of soliciting on the basis of police evidence, and in this they have been aided by the removal under the 1959 Street Offences Act of the need for witnesses or police to prove that a woman was a public nuisance.

32. In the winter of 1980–1, my own university put out a series of leaflets on the dangers facing women students at night. Protests by feminists in the students' union to the effect that these leaflets constituted a curfew on women resulted in a pamphlet on 'student safety at night', which made no overt reference to gender, but whose repressive meaning for women was still clear.

33. See footnote 31. Mr Clive Soley MP has recently introduced a Bill into the House of Commons to abolish the use of this term and also to abolish the use of imprisonment for soliciting (*Hansard*, 14 April 1981). The Bill, the Imprisonment of Prostitutes (Abolition) Bill, was, however, 'talked out' in the Commons on 19 June 1981, on the government's insistence that legislation would be unwise until the Criminal Law Revision Committee had concluded its investigation into sexual offences.

34. Some progress was made in 1980 in publicising the harassment of women generally by kerb-crawlers. Police in Birmingham and Wolverhampton began to arrest male kerb-crawlers in red-light districts on charges of loitering (*The Guardian*, 1 October 1980), and on 12 November 1980 in the House of Commons, Mr Tom Cox, Labour MP for Tooting, demanded that the Vagrancy Act be amended to give police powers to arrest kerb-crawlers. He observed that schoolgirls and women in his constituency were continually accosted by men in search of prostitutes (*The Guardian*, 13 November 1980).

35. Zaretsky and others have in any case pointed out that Engels' vision of sexuality under socialism contains 'a bias towards hetero-sexuality': '[He] portrays the sexual division of labour as a natural

or spontaneous phenomenon that derives its oppressive meaning only through the growth of production' (Zaretsky, 1973, p. 34).

36. The patriarchy of Conservative ideologies derives from the general character of these ideologies' celebration of existing property relations, and therefore their concern to preserve a family structure which guarantees the inheritance of wealth. But the actual defence of patriarchy may be expressed in a rather less puritanical fashion than social democratic versions. A version of women's sexuality may be celebrated with the woman portrayed as *temptress* and as a source of entertainment and diversion.

Opposing Mr Jack Ashley's Private Member's Bill on revision of the law on rape in 1977, Mr Nicholas Fairbairn, Conservative MP for Kinross and West Perthshire, now Attorney-General for Scotland, averred that:

> Lest it be suggested that any man or any lawyer has some prejudice against women, may I declare another interest. No-one is fonder of women than I am.
>
> I approach the subject from that basis, and I think it is a fantasy that is in the Hon. Gentleman's mind that there is some outdated hostility to women. A phrase he used seemed to demonstrate all the frightful archaic attitudes to women and of chauvinism that have ever existed. He spoke of a male enthusiasm for sex — as though women hated it, did not want it, wanted to take no part in it, but were compelled to do so in marriage.
>
> (*Hansard*, 19 July 1977, vol. 935–2, cols 1398–9)

So even in discussion of rape itself, the notion of woman as a mysterious and seductive but deceitful object of 'the hunt' must be preserved:

> Hon. Members should remember the words of Ovid — and I translate them into English for those who do not know Latin: 'Whether they say yes or no, they all like to be asked. And, saying she would never consent, she consented.' It is a part of the business of men and women that they hunt and are hunted and say 'Yes' and 'No' and mean the opposite.
>
> (N. Fairbairn MP, *Hansard*, 19 July 1977, col. 1401)

It is characteristic of liberal Conservatism that this 'hunt' is presented as an equal contest, of equal attraction and benefit to all parties, and also that it is described as a fundamental feature of 'the business' of men and women. Mr Fairbairn also seems to think that this particular interpretation of the sexual division of labour can be put, without discussion of the absence of sexual assaults by women on men.

37. There are some exceptions to this rule. Nicholson references the case of Peter Kurten, brought to trial in Germany in 1931, who maimed and killed men, children, horses, sheep and a swan as well as women; and there are some examples of the mass murder of fellow homosexuals by men (the most recent and horrific of which was the case of John Gacy, who was found guilty in Chicago in February 1980 of the murder of 33 young men and boys).

38. The Sexual Offences (Amendment) Act of 1976 provided for victims to remain anonymous in court, and this is thought to have resulted in the 22 per cent increase in the number of rapes reported to the police during 1977–8 (*Criminal Statistics*, 1978, para. 2.16).

39. The relative immunity granted the male in rape cases appeared to be extended in the infamous judgement of the House of Lords in *DPP vs. Morgan* in 1975. In this case, three airmen who had virtually 'gang-raped' the wife of their sergeant (at the sergeant's invitation) appealed a rape conviction because they argued that they had reasonable grounds for believing that the wife had consented. The Law Lords found, by three to two, that a man should be acquitted of rape if he honestly believed that the woman consented, *no matter how unreasonable the belief may have been.* There followed furious condemnations by the women's movement, a Private Member's Bill to reverse this finding, and mass media descriptions of the finding as 'a rapist's charter'. But Professor Glanville Williams on the one hand and Anna Coote and Tess Gill on the other then argued that the Law Lords were merely restating the legal require- ment for the prosecution to prove a guilty mind prior to any conviction (Coote and Gill, 1975, pp. 24–31). The problem with Coote and Gill's libertarian defence of the principle reiterated in *DPP vs. Morgan* is that they may be seen to accommodate to the patriarchal functions of the law in practice, in that the defining element in establishing the fact of rape (an exploitative and violent act committed by definition against women) remains the *word* of the male. The resulting report of the Advisory Group on the Law of Rape, chaired by Mrs Justice Rose Heilbron, attempted to circum- vent this problem to some extent by recommending that a woman complainant's counsel should be able to respond to the attempt to impugn the woman's word (by attacks on her character) as the main defence, by 'letting in' the accused's bad character or previous convictions (Home Office, 1975, Cmnd 6352, para. 142).

40. The conventional assumption, in other words, is that the evidence
    of assault and sexual intercourse will be found on the woman but
    not apparently on her male assailant, and this assumption is carried
    further in police interrogation of women complainants in rape
    cases where evidence of violent resistance is often demanded as
    evidence of the fact of rape itself.
41. In the wake of the Barbara Leach murder by the Yorkshire Ripper
    in 1979, it was women rather than men who were encouraged by
    the police to observe a curfew and stay off the streets at night (see
    Nicholson, 1979, p. 83).
42. Recent feminist campaigns have resulted in the demand, for
    example, for the legalisation of the carrying by women of 'offensive
    weapons' for self-defence. This demand was accompanied by the
    prosecution of a woman in a London magistrates' court for carrying
    an anti-rape spray, of the kind now widely available in the USA.
43. My support for an extension of the law of rape might be read as
    implying that I believe in the existence of dangerous rapists, who
    are likely to commit further offences if they are not apprehended
    and thereby incapacitated institutionally. Existing research on
    sexual offenders, however, has actually tended to challenge the
    popular idea of such offenders being repeaters. In what is thought
    to be the most thorough study of sex offenders' recidivism, a survey
    carried out in Denmark in 1965 (Christiansen *et al.*) found that
    only 10 per cent of sex offenders who were later reconvicted in the
    courts were actually convicted of a sex crime. This finding is con-
    sistent with general surveys of sex offenders in Britain in the 1950s
    (Radzinowicz, 1957), and in the United States (Gebhard *et al.*,
    1965). But an agnostic conclusion on the recidivism of sexual
    offenders generally has to be qualified by the tendency for all
    research to speak of a minority of offenders who do repeat. This
    minority includes 'the indecent exposers . . . those who play sex
    games with small boys . . . and those who make unwanted advances
    to young girls' (West, Roy and Nichols, 1978, p. 141) — which
    some commentators want to call 'misbehaviour' — as well as a small
    number of individuals, usually men, who appear to use 'psycho-
    pathic' violence in performing sexual assaults on their victims
    (Frisbie and Dondis, 1965). Unfortunately no clear factors have
    yet been adduced, by sex researchers, as a distinguishing feature of
    these 'personality types', and thus there is no way of predicting the
    future dangerousness of an apprehended sexual offender (see
    Bottoms, 1977).

    The warrant for my support for a more 'repressive' rape law lies
not in the ability of the new law to identify and incapacitate

dangerous individuals *per se* but rather in its importance in extending the availability of law as a symbolic defence for women, as well as in providing a temporary respite to women caught in sexual relationships involving physical violence from men. The struggle for new laws could also be important in the struggle against the eroticisation of violence against women in film and in other media.

Bibliography

Addison, Paul (1975) *The Road to 1945: British Politics and the Second World War* (London: Jonathan Cape).

Alderson, John (1979) *Policing Freedom: a Commentary on the Dilemmas of Policing in Western Democracies* (London: Macdonald & Evans).

American Friends Service Committee (1971) *Struggle for Justice: A Report on Crime and Justice in America* (New York: Hill & Wang).

Anderson, Perry (1968) 'Components of the National Culture', *New Left Review*, 50 (July) pp. 3–58.

Baldwin, John, Bottoms, A. E. and Walker, Monica (1976) *The Urban Criminal: A Study in Sheffield* (London: Tavistock).

Baldwin, John and McConville, Michael (1979) *Jury Trials* (Oxford University Press).

Bankowski, Zen and Mungham, Geoffrey (1976) *Images of Law* (London: Routledge & Kegan Paul).

'Barrister' (1938) *Justice in England* (London: Victor Gollancz).

Benn, Tony (1980) *Arguments for Socialism* (Harmondsworth: Penguin; first published 1979 Jonathan Cape, ed. C. Mullin).

Bennett, Fran, Heys, Rosa and Coward, Rosalind (1980) 'The Limits to "Financial and Legal Independence": A Socialist Feminist Perspective on Taxation and Social Security', in *Politics and Power 2* (London: Routledge & Kegan Paul).

Bethnal Green Trades Council (1978) *Blood on the Streets: A Report by Bethnal Green and Stepney Trades Council on Racial Attacks in East London* (London: Bethnal Green and Stepney Trades Council).

Bottoms, A. E. (1975) 'On the Decriminalisation of the English Juvenile Courts', in Hood, R. (ed.) *Crime, Criminology and Public Policy* (London: Heinemann).

Bottoms, A. E. (1977) 'Reflections on the Renaissance of Dangerousness' (inaugural lecture as Professor of Criminology in the University of Sheffield, 12 June 1977), *Howard Journal*, 16(2), pp. 70–96.

Bottoms, A. E. and McClean, J. D. (1976) *Defendants in the Criminal Process* (London: Routledge & Kegan Paul).

Bottoms, A. E. and McClintock, F. H. (1973) *Criminals Coming of Age* (London: Heinemann).

Bottoms, A. E. and Preston, A. (1980) *The Coming Penal Crisis* (Edinburgh: Scottish Academic Press).

Bowlby, John (1946) *Forty-four Juvenile Thieves: Their Characters and Home Lives* (London: Baillière, Tyndall & Cox).

Bowlby, John (1947–9) 'The Therapeutic Approach in Sociology', *Sociological Review*, 39–41, pp. 39–49.

Bowlby, John (1951) *Maternal Care and Mental Health* (Geneva: World Health Organisation, Monograph Series No. 2). Popular edition *Child Care and the Growth of Love*, published 1953, Penguin.

Brittan, Leon (1979) 'Penal Policy in the 1980's', Speech to Annual General Meeting of National Association for the Care and Resettlement of Offenders, 1 November.

Brooks, W. N. and Doob, A. N. (1975) 'Justice and the Jury', *Journal of Social Issues*, 33.

Brown, Beverley (1981) 'A Feminist Interest in Pornography: Some Modest Proposals', *m/f*, 5/6, pp. 5–18.

Bunyan, Tony (1976) *The Political Police in Britain* (London: Julian Friedman).

Burlingham, Dorothy and Freud, Anna (1942) *Young People in Wartime* (London: Allen & Unwin).

Burlingham, Dorothy and Freud, Anna (1944) *Infants without Families* (London: Allen & Unwin).

Campbell, Duncan (1980) 'Society under Surveillance', in Hain, P. (ed.) *Policing the Police* (London: John Calder, (Platform Books).

Carpenter, Edward (1905) *Prisons, Police and Punishment:*

An Inquiry into the Causes and Treatment of Crime and Criminals (London: Arthur C. Fifield).

Chibnall, Steve (1977) *Law-and-Order News: An Analysis of Crime Reporting in the British Press* (London: Tavistock).

Christiansen, K. O. *et al.* (1965) 'Recidivism among Sexual Offenders' in Christiansen, K. O. *et al.* (eds) *Scandinavian Studies in Criminology* (Oslo: Universitats Forlaget).

Christie, Nils (1976) 'Conflicts as Property', *British Journal of Criminology*, 17(1) (January) pp. 1–15.

Clark, Lorenne and Lewis, Debra (1977) *Rape: The Price of Coercive Sexuality* (Toronto: The Women's Press).

Clarke, John (1980) 'Social Democratic Delinquents and Fabian Families: A Background to the 1969 Children and Young Persons Act', in National Deviancy Conference (ed.) *Permissiveness and Control: the Fate of the Sixties Legislation* (London: Macmillan).

Cohen, Phil (1979) 'Policing the Working Class City', in National Deviancy Conference/Centre for Socialist Economists (eds) *Capitalism and the Rule of Law* (London: Hutchinson).

Cohen, Stanley (1979) 'The Punitive City: Notes on the Dispersal of Social Control', *Contemporary Crises*, 3(4) (October) pp. 339–64.

Cohen, Stanley and Taylor, Laurie (1980) Preface to Second Edition, *Psychological Survival* (Harmondsworth: Penguin).

Cooper, David (1965) 'Violence in Psychiatry', *Views*, 8 (Summer) pp. 18–25.

Coote, Anna (1981) 'Fixing Up the Family', *New Statesman*, 20 March, pp. 6–7.

Coote, Anna and Gill, Tess (1975) *The Rape Controversy* (London: National Council for Civil Liberties).

Corrigan, Paul (1979) *Schooling the Smash Street Kids* (London: Macmillan).

Cotterrell, Roger (1979) 'Commodity Form and Legal Form: A Review of Pashukanis' Law and Marxism', *Ideology and Consciousness*, 6 (Autumn) pp. 111–120.

Cox, Barry (1975) *Civil Liberties in Britain* (Harmondsworth: Penguin).

Crossman, R. H. S. (1972) *The Politics of Pensions*, Eleanor Rathbone Memorial Lecture at the University of Sheffield (Liverpool University Press).

Cultural History Group (1976) 'Out of the People: the Politics of Containment 1939–1945', *Working Papers in Cultural Studies*, 9, pp. 29–51.

Dashwood, A. (1972) 'Juries in a Multi-Racial Society', *Criminal Law Review*, pp. 85–94.

Deacon, Alan (1980) 'Spivs, Drones and Other Scroungers', *New Society*, 51 (908), 28 February, pp. 446–7.

Deacon, Bob (1981) 'Social Administration, Social Policy and Socialism', *Critical Social Policy*, 1(1) (Summer) pp. 43–66.

Dean, Malcolm (1981) 'The Enemy Within', *The Guardian*, 25 March.

Delphy, Christine (1979) *The Main Enemy: A Materialist Analysis of Women's Oppression* (London: Women's Research and Resources Centre).

Dobash, R. E. and Dobash, R. (1979) *Violence Against Wives: A Case Against the Patriarchy* (New York: Free Press).

Downes, D. M. (1966) *The Delinquent Solution* (London: Routledge & Kegan Paul).

Duguid, G. W. A. (1980) 'The Police National Computer', *Police Research Bulletin*, (34) (Spring) pp. 4–12.

Farrar, J. H. (1974) *Law Reform and the Law Commission* (London: Sweet & Maxwell).

Fitzgerald, Mike (1977) *Prisoners in Revolt* (Harmondsworth: Penguin).

Fitzgerald, Mike and Sim, Joe (1979) *British Prisons* (Oxford: Blackwell).

Frank, Gerald (1966) *The Boston Strangler* (New York: Signet).

Friedenberg, Edgar (1976) *The Disposal of Liberty and other Industrial Wastes* (New York: Anchor Books).

Frisbie, L. V. and Dondis, E. H. (1965) *Recidivism Among Treated Sex Offenders*, California Mental Health Research Monographs No. 5 (California Bureau of Research and Statistics).

Fry, Margery, Grunhut, Max, Mannheim, Hermann, Grabinska, W. and Rackham, C. D. (International Committee of the Howard League) (1947) *Lawless Youth: A Challenge to the New Europe* (London: Allen & Unwin).

Fyvel, T. R. (1961) *The Insecure Offenders: Rebellious Youth in the Welfare State* (Harmondsworth: Penguin).

Gamble, Andrew (1974) *The Conservative Nation* (London: Routledge & Kegan Paul).

Gardiner, Gerald and Martin, Andrew (eds) (1963) *Law Reform Now* (London: Victor Gollancz).

Gebhard, P. H., Gagnon, J. H., Pomeroy, W. B. and Christensen, C. U. (1965) *Sex Offenders: An Analysis of Types* (New York: Harper & Row).

Glover, Edward (1969) *The Psychopathology of Prostitution* (London: Institute for the Study and Treatment of Delinquency).

Godfrey, D. A. (1980) 'The Verge of Despair', *Prison Service Journal*, 40, pp. 10–17.

Gordon, L. and Hunter, A. (1977–8) 'Sex, Family and the New Right: Anti-feminism as a Political Force', *Radical America*, 11(6), pp. 9–25.

Gough, Ian (1979) *The Political Economy of the Welfare State* (London: Macmillan).

Gouldner, Alvin (1970) *The Coming Crisis of Western Sociology* (Boston: Basic Books).

Griffith, John (1977) *The Politics of the Judiciary* (London: Fontana).

Gross, John (1963) 'The Lynskey Tribunal', in Sissons, M. and French, P. (eds) *The Age of Austerity 1945–51* (London: Hodder & Stoughton/Penguin).

Hall, Stuart (1972) 'The Social Eye of the *Picture Post*', *Cultural Studies*, 2, pp. 71–120.

Hall, Stuart (1979) 'The Great Moving Right Show', *Marxism Today*, 23(1) (January).

Hall, Stuart (1980) 'Popular-Democratic vs. Authoritarian Populism: Two Ways of "Taking Democracy Seriously" ', in Hunt, A. (ed.) *Marxism and Democracy* (London: Lawrence & Wishart).

Hall, Stuart (1981) 'The "Little Caesars" of Social Democracy', *Marxism Today*, 25(4) (April), pp. 11–15.

Hall, Stuart, Clarke, John, Crichter, Chas, Jefferson, Tony and Roberts, Brian (1978) *Policing the Crisis: Mugging, the State and Law and Order* (London: Macmillan).

Hardy, Phil and Laing, Dave (1977) 'Who Says the Kids are Alright?', *The Leveller*, 10 (December), pp. 19–20.

Harman, Harriet and Griffith, John (1979) *Justice Deserted: the Subversion of the Jury* (London: National Council for

Civil Liberties).

Hart, J. M. (1951) *The British Police* (London: Allen & Unwin).

Heywood, Jean (1978) *Children in Care: the Development of the Service for the Deprived Child* (London: Routledge & Kegan Paul, revised edition, first published 1959).

Hirst, Paul Q. (1980) 'Law, Socialism and Rights', in Carlen, P. and Collison, M. (eds) *Radical Issues in Criminology* (London: Martin Robertson).

Home Office (1975) *Report of the Advisory Group on the Law of Rape* (Chair: Mrs Justice Rose Heilbron), Cmnd 6352 (London: HMSO).

Hopkins, Harry (1963) *The New Look: A Social History of the Forties and Fifties in Britain* (London: Secker & Warburg).

Jenkin, Patrick (1979) Opening Address to National Conference on Intermediate Treatment, City Hall, Sheffield (July).

Jessop, Bob (1980) 'On Recent Marxist Theories of the Law, the State and Juridico-Political Ideology', *International Journal of the Sociology of Law*, 8, pp. 339–68.

Jones, Howard (1965) *Crime and the Penal System*, 3rd edn (London: University Tutorial Press).

Joseph, Sir Keith (1975) *Freedom Under the Law* (London: Conservative Political Centre).

Kellner, Peter (1979) 'Not a Defeat: A Disaster', *New Statesman*, 18 May, pp. 704–6.

Kennedy, Ludovic (1971) *Ten Rillington Place* (London: Avon Books).

Kettle, Martin (1980) 'The Politics of Policing', in Hain, P. (ed.) *Policing the Police* (London: John Calder, Platform Books).

Kilroy-Silk, R. (1977) 'Wrongs of the Bill of Rights', *The Guardian*, 4 February.

King, Roy and Morgan, Rod (1979) *Crisis in the Prisons: the Way Out*, a paper based on evidence submitted to the Inquiry into the United Kingdom Prison Service under Mr Justice May (Universities of Bath and Southampton).

Klein, Dorie (1979) 'Can This Marriage be Saved? Battery and Sheltering', *Crime and Social Justice*, 12 (Winter) pp. 19–33.

Labour Party (1964) *Crime: A Challenge to Us All* (Report of the Home Affairs Study Group, chaired by Lord Longford) (London: The Labour Party).

Labour Party (1973) *The Deprived Child: A Discussion Document on Policies for Socially Deprived Children* (London: The Labour Party).

Labour Party (1979) *Law, Order and Human Rights* (Labour Party Campaign Handbook) (London: The Labour Party).

Laclau, Ernesto (1977) *Politics and Ideology in Marxist Theory* (London: New Left Books).

Lasch, Christopher (1979) *The Culture of Narcissism: American Life in an Age of Diminishing Expectations* (New York: Warner Books).

Lederer, L. (ed.) (1980) *Take Back the Night* (New York: Morrow).

Leete, Richard (1976) 'Marriage and Divorce', *Population Trends*, 3 (Spring).

Little, Alan (1962) 'Borstal Success and the Quality of Borstal Inmates', *British Journal of Criminology*, 2, pp. 266–72.

Lodge, T. S. (1975) 'The Founding of the Home Office Research Unit', in Hood, R. (ed.) *Crime, Criminology and Public Policy* (London: Heinemann).

London–Edinburgh Weekend Return Group (1979) *In and Against the State: Discussion Notes for Socialists* (London: Publications Distribution Cooperative). Revised and reprinted by Pluto Press, 1980.

McBride, Jeremy and Wallington, Peter (1976) *Civil Liberties and a Bill of Rights* (London: Cobden Trust).

McIntosh, Mary (1981) 'Feminism and Social Policy', *Critical Social Policy*, 1(1), pp. 32–41.

MacLeod, Eileen (1980) 'Manmade Laws for Men: Organising with Street Prostitutes', unpublished MS (Department of Applied Social Studies, University of Warwick).

Mannheim, Hermann (1939) *The Dilemma of Penal Reform* (London: Allen & Unwin).

Mannheim, Hermann (1941, 1942, 1947) 'Three Contributions to the History of Crime in the Second World War and After', unnamed essays reprinted in Mannheim, H., *Group Problems in Crime and Punishment* (London: Routledge & Kegan Paul, 1955) ch. 5.

Mannheim, Hermann (1946) *Criminal Justice and Social*

Reconstruction (London: Routledge & Kegan Paul).
Mannheim, Hermann and Wilkins, Leslie (1955) *Prediction Methods in Relation to Borstal Training* (London: HMSO).
Martienssen, Anthony (1951) *Crime and the Police* (London: Secker & Warburg).
Martin, John P. and Wilson, Gail (1968) *The Police: A Study in Manpower* (London: Heinemann).
Marx, Karl (1842) 'The Proceedings of the Sixth Rhenish Parliament', *Rheinische Zeitung*, 10–14 July, reprinted in McLellan, D. (ed.) *Karl Marx – Early Texts* (Oxford: Blackwell).
Mathiesen, Thomas (1976) *The Politics of Abolition* (London: Martin Robertson).
Meacher, Michael (1980) 'The Case for an Independent Complaints Procedure', *The Guardian*, 21 July.
Miliband, Ralph (1961) *Parliamentary Socialism: A Study in the Politics of Labour* (London: Merlin Press).
Moorhouse, H. F. and Chamberlain, C. W. (1974) 'Lower Class Attitudes to Property: Aspects of the Counter-Culture', *Sociology*, 8, pp. 387–405.
Morgan, Patricia (1978) *Delinquent Fantasies* (London: Maurice Temple Smith).
Mort, Frank (1980) 'The Domain of the Sexual', *Screen Education*, 36 (Autumn), pp. 69–84.
Nairn, Tom (1964) 'The Anatomy of the Labour Party', *New Left Review*, 27, pp. 38–65.
National Council for Civil Liberties (1981) *The Supplementary Report of the Unofficial Committee of Enquiry into Southall* (London: NCCL).
Nicholson, Michael (1979) *The Yorkshire Ripper* (London: W. H. Allen (Star Books)).
Packman, Jean (1975) *The Child's Generation: Child Care Policy from Curtis to Houghton* (Oxford: Blackwell and Martin Robertson).
Pashukanis, Evgeny (1978) *Law and Marxism* (London: Inklinks).
Picciotto, Sol (1979) 'The Theory of the State, Class Struggle and the Rule of Law', in National Deviancy Conference/ Centre for Socialist Economists (eds) *Capitalism and the Rule of Law* (London: Hutchinson).
Pizzey, Erin (1974) *Screem Quietly or the Neighbours Will*

Hear (Harmondsworth: Penguin).

Pratt, John (1981) 'Sexuality and the Appeal of the New Right', *Canadian Criminology Forum*, (Fall).

Preservation of the Rights of Prisoners (PROP) (1979) *Report to the Committee of Inquiry into the United Kingdom Prison Services* (Hammersmith, London: PROP).

Pritt, D. N. (1971) *Law, Class and Society* (four volumes) (London: Lawrence & Wishart).

Radzinowicz, Leon (1957) *Sexual Offences* (London: Macmillan).

Rape Crisis Centre (1977, 1978) *First Annual Report*; *Second Annual Report* (London: Rape Counselling and Research Project).

Rape Crisis Centre (1979) *Rape: Police and Forensic Practice*, Submission by the Rape Counselling and Research Project to the Royal Commission on Criminal Procedure.

Reiman, Jeffrey (1979) *The Rich Get Richer and the Poor Get Prison* (New York: Wiley).

Reiner, Robert (1978) 'The Police, Class and Politics', *Marxism Today*, 22(3) (March), pp. 69—80.

Riley, Denise (1979) 'War in the Nursery', *Feminist Review*, 2, pp. 82—108.

Robertson, Geoff (1975) 'A Slight Case of Rape', *New Statesman*, 89 (2303), 9 May, pp. 614—16.

Rogow, A. A. (1955) *The Labour Government and British Industry 1945—1951* (London: Oxford University Press).

Rolph, C. H. (1955) *Women of the Streets* (London: Secker & Warburg).

Root, Jane and Murray, Pat (1980) 'Hollywood's New Face on Male Violence', *The Leveller*, 43, 29 October, pp. 30—1.

Rowbotham, Sheila, Segal, Lynne and Wainwright, Hilary (1979) *Beyond the Fragments: Feminism and the Making of Socialism* (London: Merlin Press).

Rowthorn, Bob (1980) *Capitalism, Crisis and Inflation* (London: Lawrence & Wishart).

Russell, Ken (1976) 'Police vs. Public: the Rules Change', *The Sunday Times*, 21 March.

Sacks, Albie and Wilson, J. H. (1978) *Sexism and the Law: A Study in Male Beliefs and Judicial Bias* (London: Martin Robertson).

Schur, Edwin, M. (1973) *Radical Non-intervention* (New York: Prentice-Hall).

Scottish Council on Crime (1975) *Crime and the Prevention of Crime* (London: HMSO).

Scraton, Phil and Benn, M. (1981) *In the Arms of the Law* (London: Cobden Trust).

Seabrook, Jeremy (1978) *What Went Wrong? Working People and the Ideals of the Labour Movement* (London: Gollancz).

Silcock, Harold (1949) *The Increase in Crimes of Theft 1938–1947* (University of Liverpool: Department of Social Science (Research), Occasional Papers No. 1).

Smart, Carol (1981a) 'Law and the Control of Women's Sexuality: the Case of the 1950's', in Hutter, B. and Williams, G. (eds) *Controlling Women* (London: Croom Helm).

Smart, Carol (1981b) 'Legitimising Patriarchy? Family Law in Post-War Britain', Paper given to European Critical Legal Studies Conference, University of Kent (March).

Sousa Santos de, Buoventura (1976) 'Law and Revolution in Portugal: the Experiences of Popular Justice after the 25 April 1974', Paper to European Group for the Study of Deviance and Social Control, Vienna (September).

Stedman-Jones, Gareth (1971) *Outcast London* (Oxford University Press).

Stewart, Margaret (1962) 'The Juvenile Court', in Donnison, D., Jay, P. and Stewart, M. *The Ingleby Report: Three Critical Essays* (London: The Fabian Society).

Straw, Jack (1980) 'Wanted: A Firm Hand on the Police', *The Guardian*, 21 April.

Taylor, Barbara (1981) 'Female Vice and Feminine Virtue', *New Statesman*, 23 January, pp. 16–17.

Taylor, Ian (1981) 'Social Democracy and the Crime Question: An Historical and Contemporary Investigation', Unpublished Ph.D dissertation, University of Sheffield.

Taylor, Ian and Young, Jock (1982) *Contemporary Criminology* (London: Routledge & Kegan Paul, forthcoming).

Taylor, Laurie (1976) 'Vigilantes – Why Not?', *New Society*, 38 (735), pp. 259–60.

Thompson, E. P. (1978) 'The State Versus Its "Enemies" ', *New Society*, 19 October, pp. 127–30.

Toffler, Alvin (1973) 'The Future of Law and Order', *Encounter* (July), pp. 13–23.

Van den Haag, Ernest (1975) *Punishing Criminals* (New York: Basic Books).

West, D. J., Roy, C. and Nichols, F. L. (1978) *Understanding Sexual Attacks* (London: Heinemann).

Williams, Glanville (ed.) (1951) *The Reform of the Law* (London: Victor Gollancz).

Wilson, Elizabeth (1977) *Women and the Welfare State* (London: Tavistock).

Wilson, Elizabeth (1980) 'Welfare and the Crisis', *New Left Review*, 122, pp. 79–89.

Wilson, James Q. (1975) *Thinking about Crime* (New York: Basic Books).

Wilson, James Q. (1977) 'Crime and Punishment in England', in Tyrrell Jr, R. E. (ed.) *The Future that Doesn't Work: Social Democracy's Failures in Britain* (New York: Doubleday).

Winship, Janice (1980) 'Sexuality for Sale', in Hall, S., Hobson, D., Lowe, A. and Willis, P. (eds) *Culture, Media, Language* (Working Papers in Cultural Studies 1972–9) (London: Hutchinson).

Winslow, R. W. (1970) *Society in Transition: A Societal Approach to Deviancy* (New York: Free Press).

Wootton, Barbara (1959) *Social Science and Social Pathology* (London: Allen & Unwin).

Worsley, Peter *et al.* (1977) *Introducing Sociology*, 2nd edn (Harmondsworth: Penguin).

Zaretsky, Eli (1973) 'Capitalism, the Family and the Personal Life', *Socialist Revolution* (USA) Part 1 in no. 13–14 January–April, pp. 69–126 and Part 2 in no. 15 May–June, pp. 19–70) (whole text later reprinted by Pluto Press).

Zander, Michael (1975) *A Bill of Rights?* (Chichester: Barry Rose).